# WHAT THE MOON SAW.

## AND OTHER TALES.

WITH ONE HUNDRED AND TWENTY ILLUSTRATIONS BY A. W BAYES,

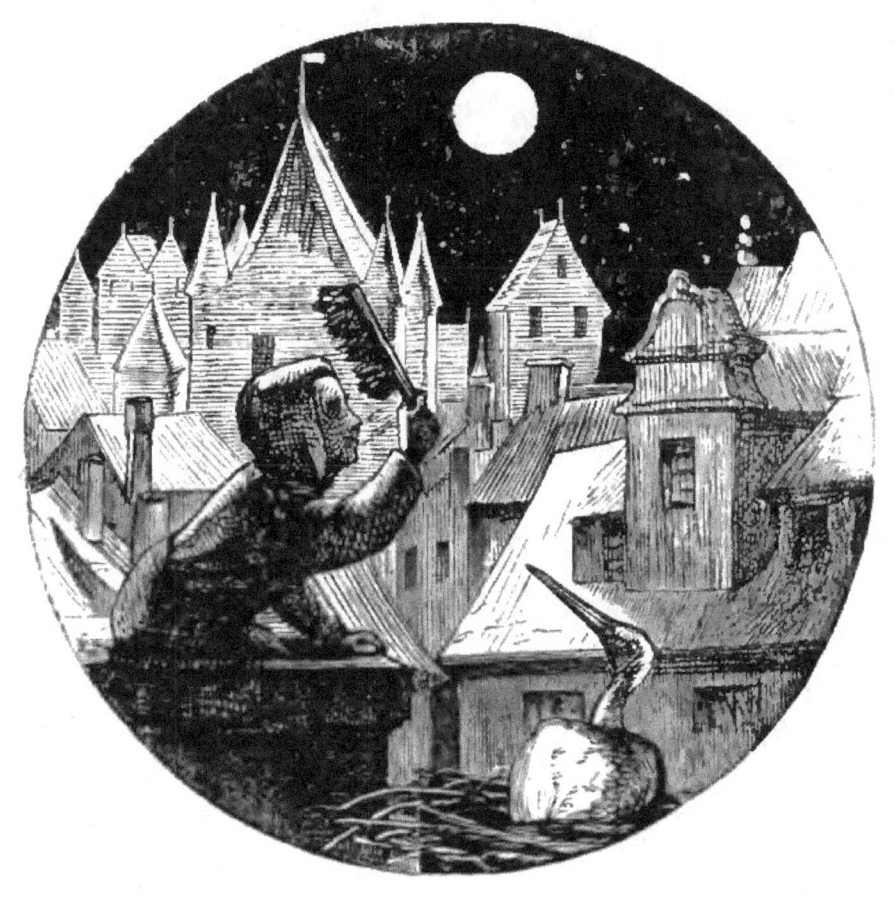

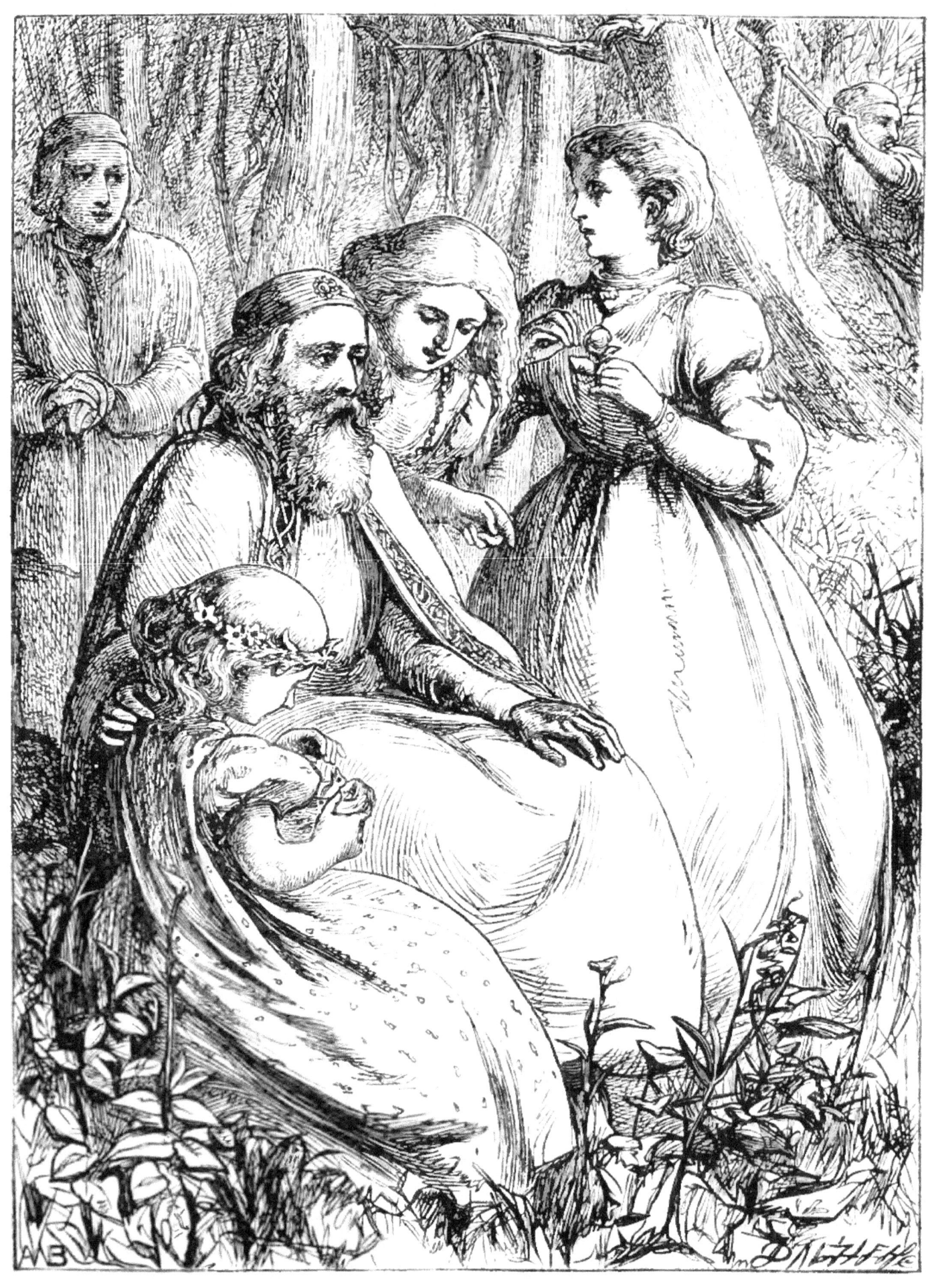

WALDEMAR DAA AND HIS DAUGHTERS.

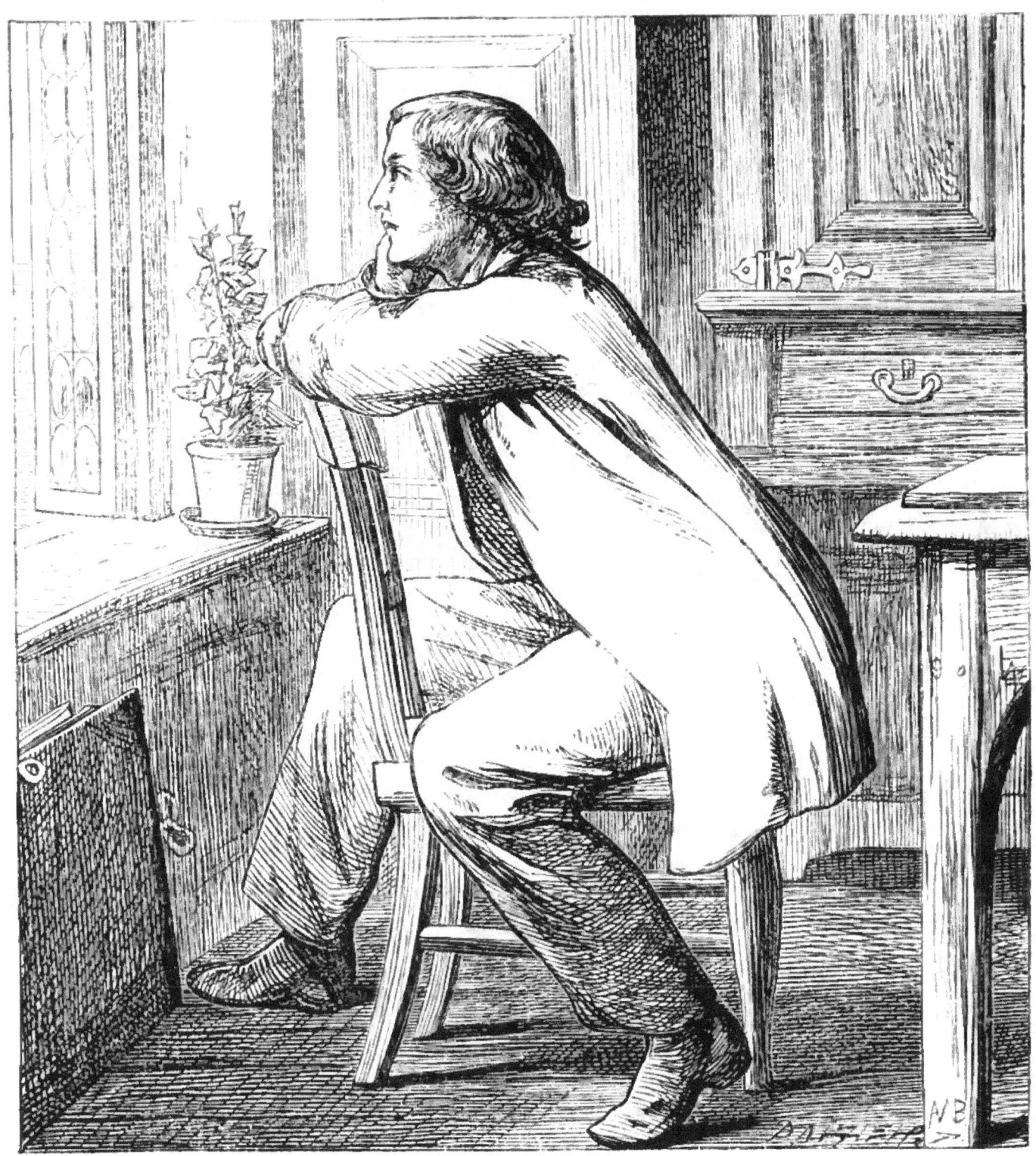

MY POST OF OBSERVATION.

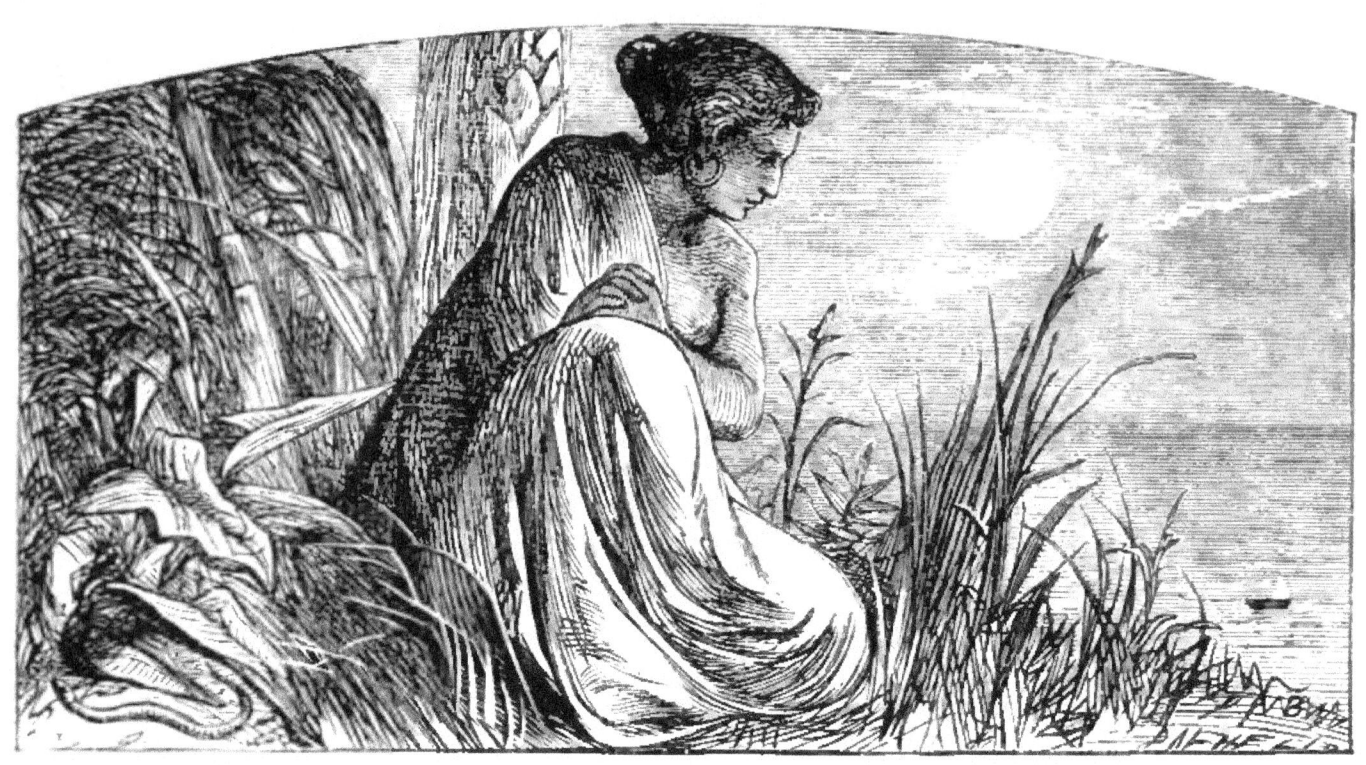

THE INDIAN GIRL.

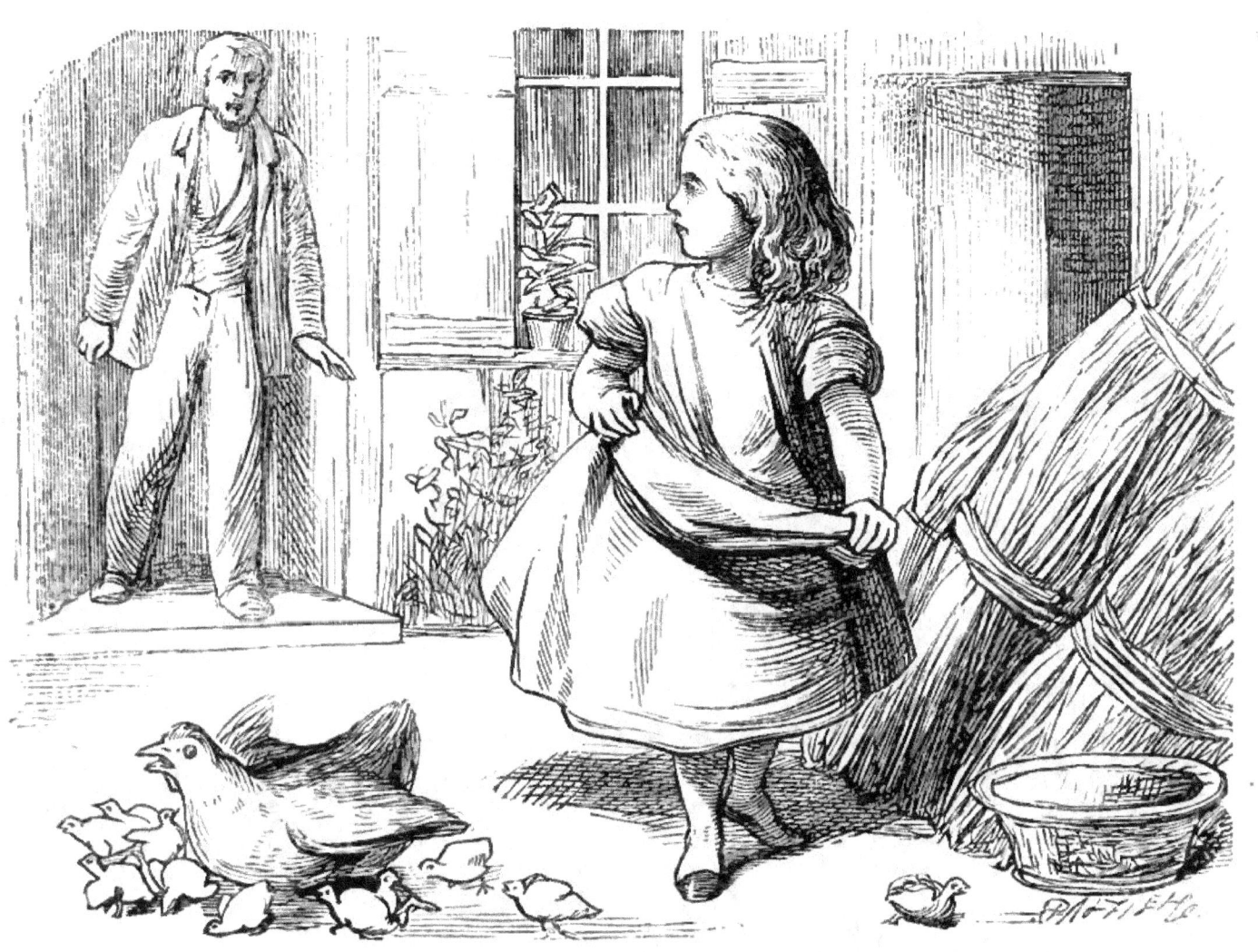

THE LITTLE GIRL AND THE CHICKENS.

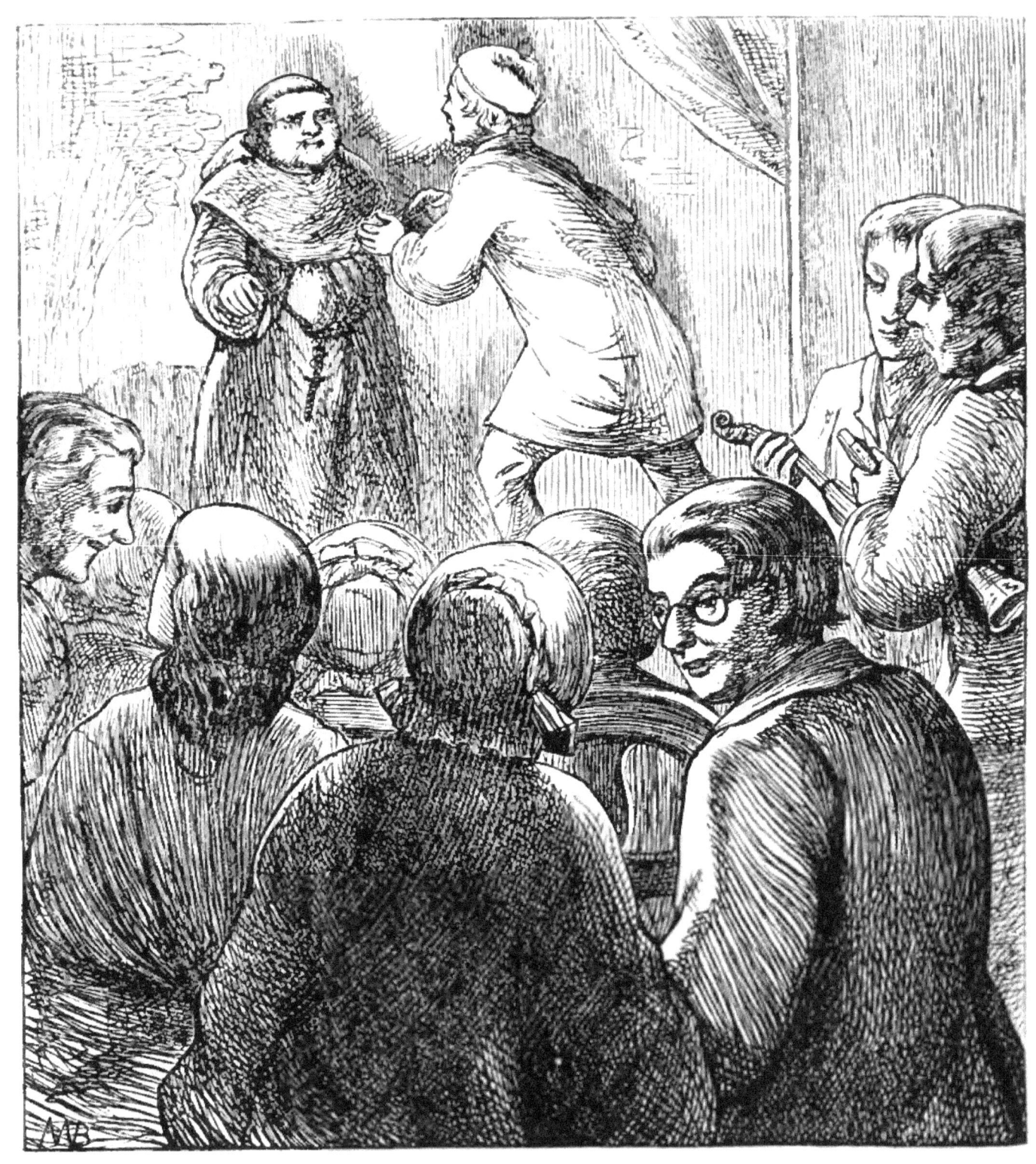

THE PLAY IN A STABLE.

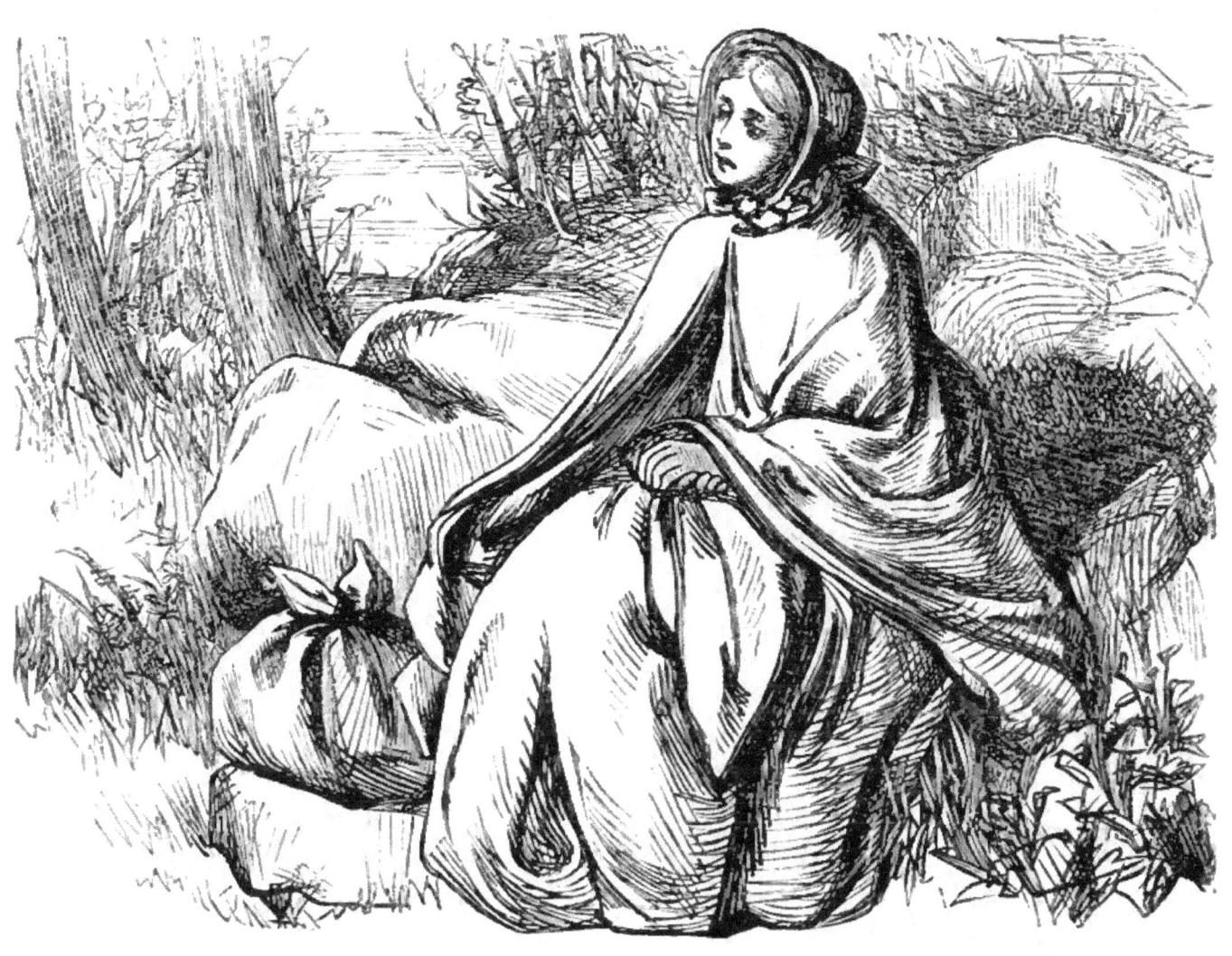

THE POOR GIRL RESTS ON THE HUN'S GRAVE.

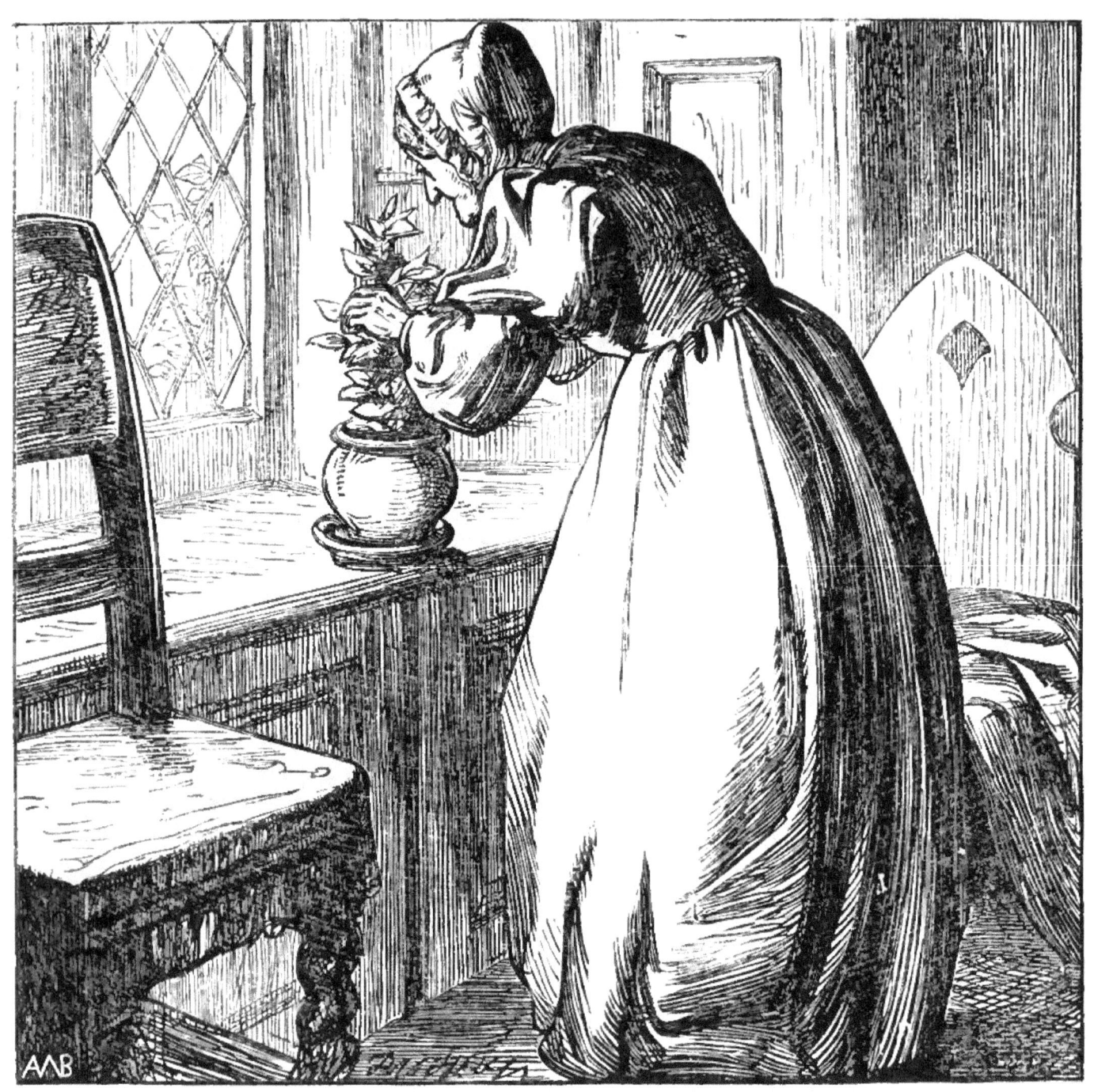

THE OLD MAID.

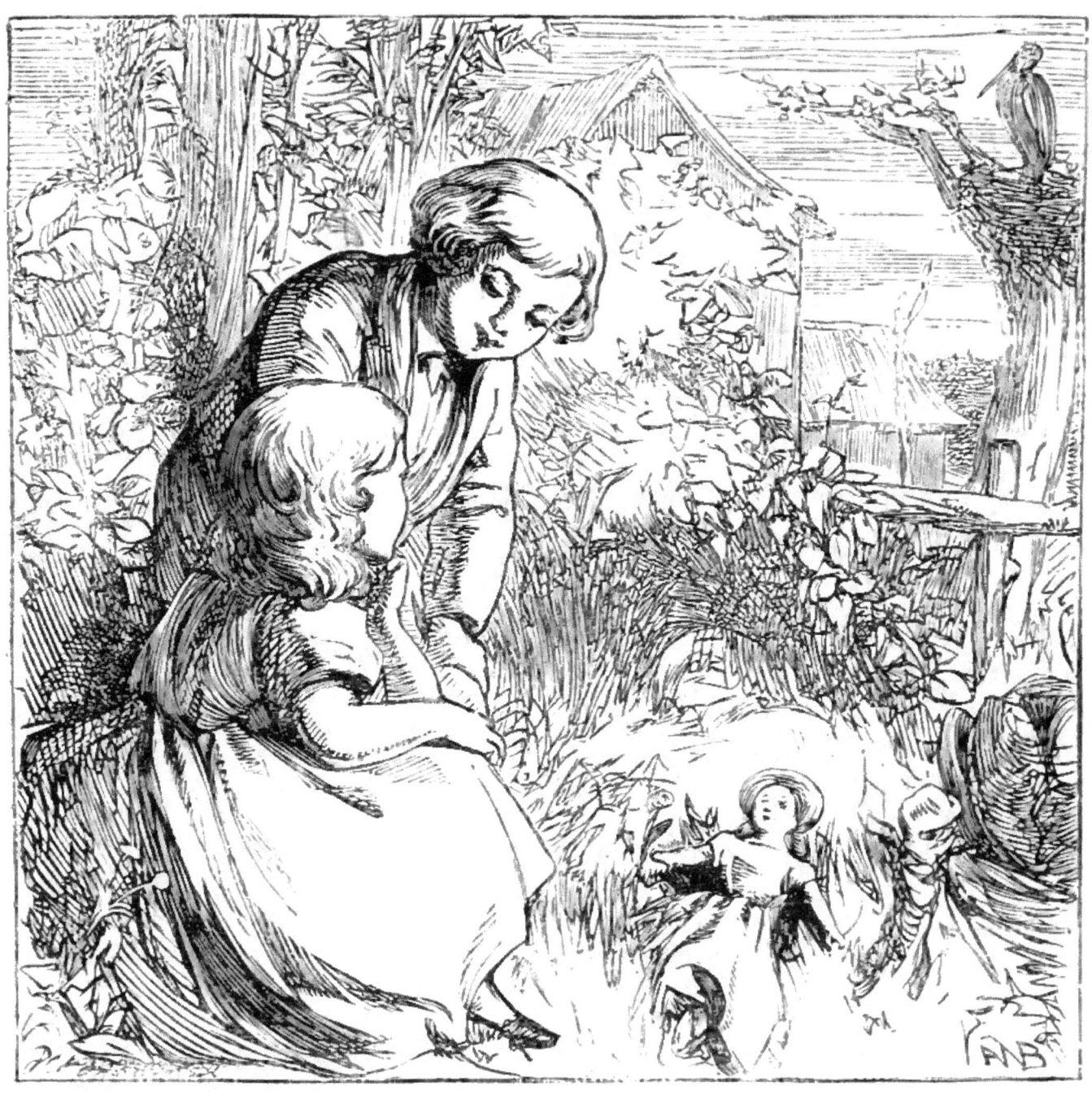

WATCHING THE STORK.

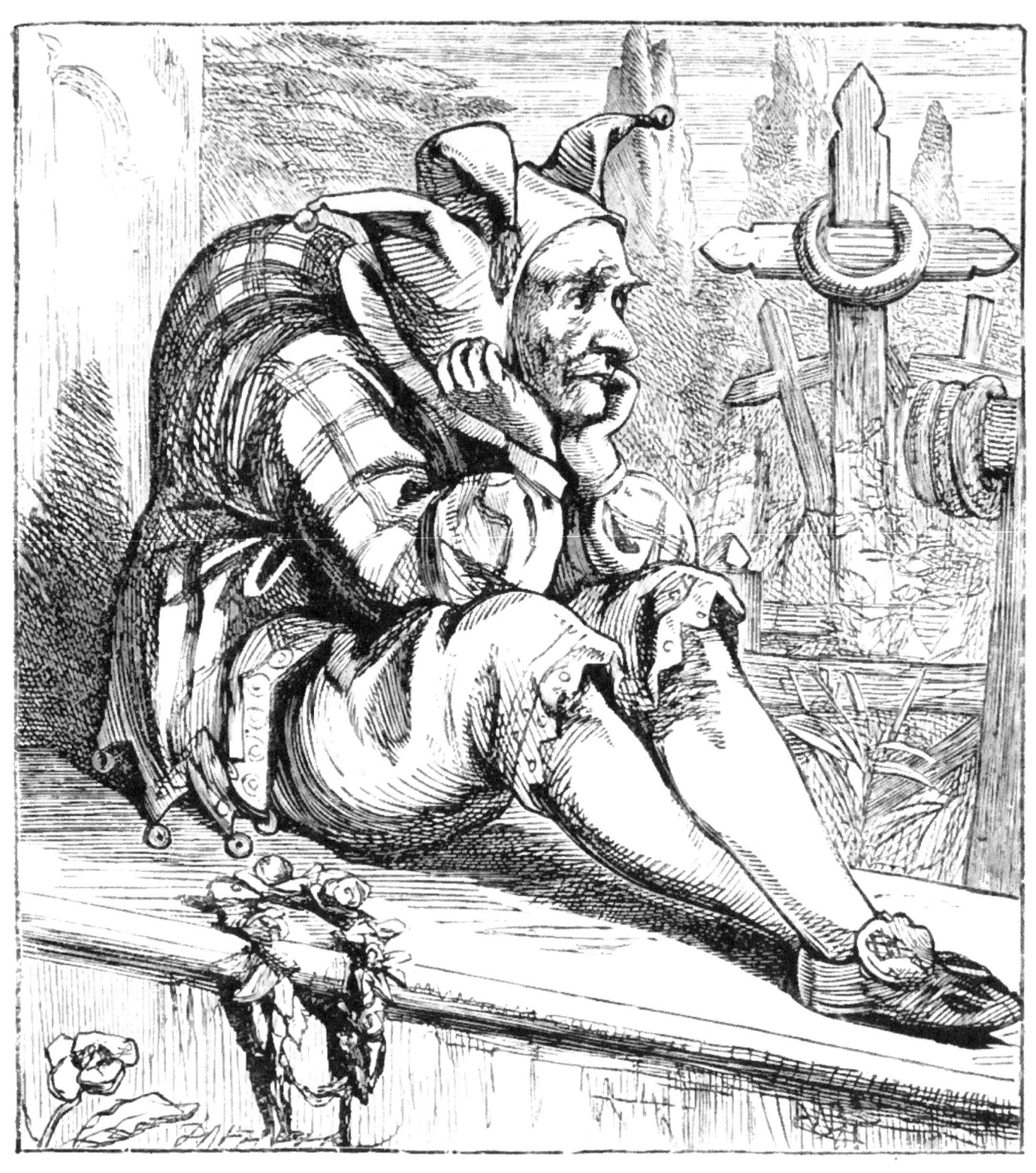

PULCINELLA ON COLUMBINE'S GRAVE.

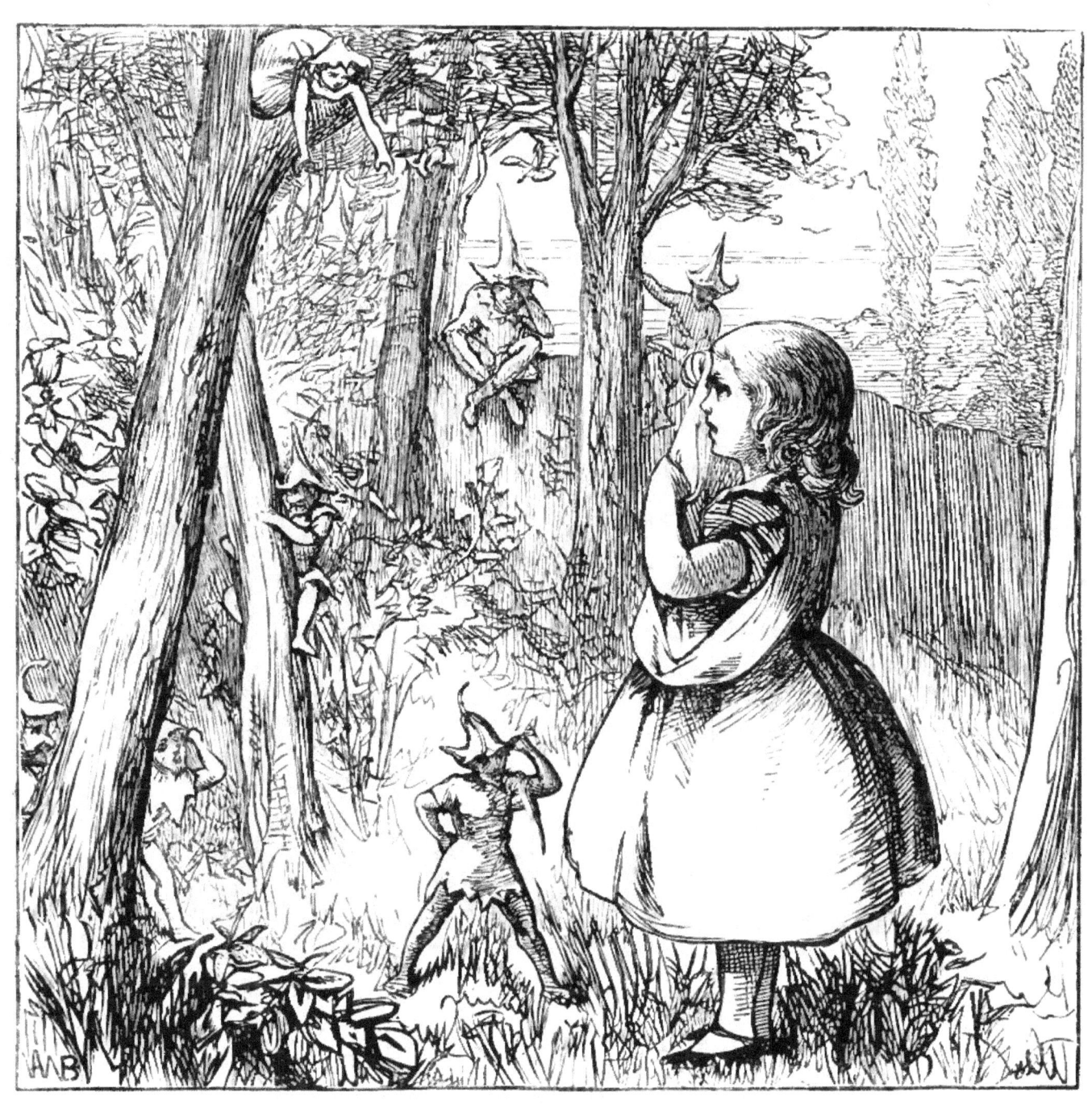

THE LITTLE GIRL'S TROUBLE.

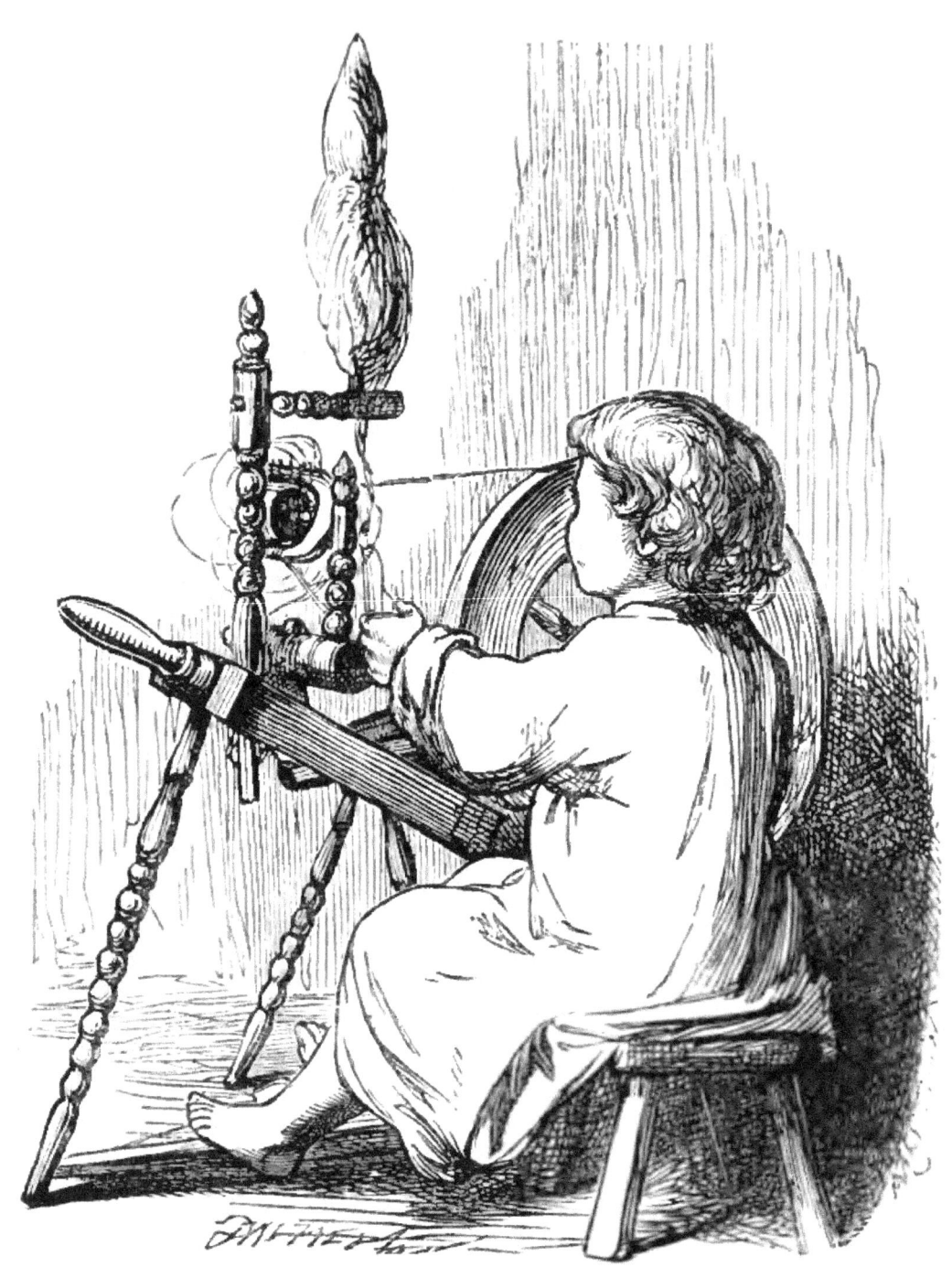

LITTLE BERTEL'S AMBITION.

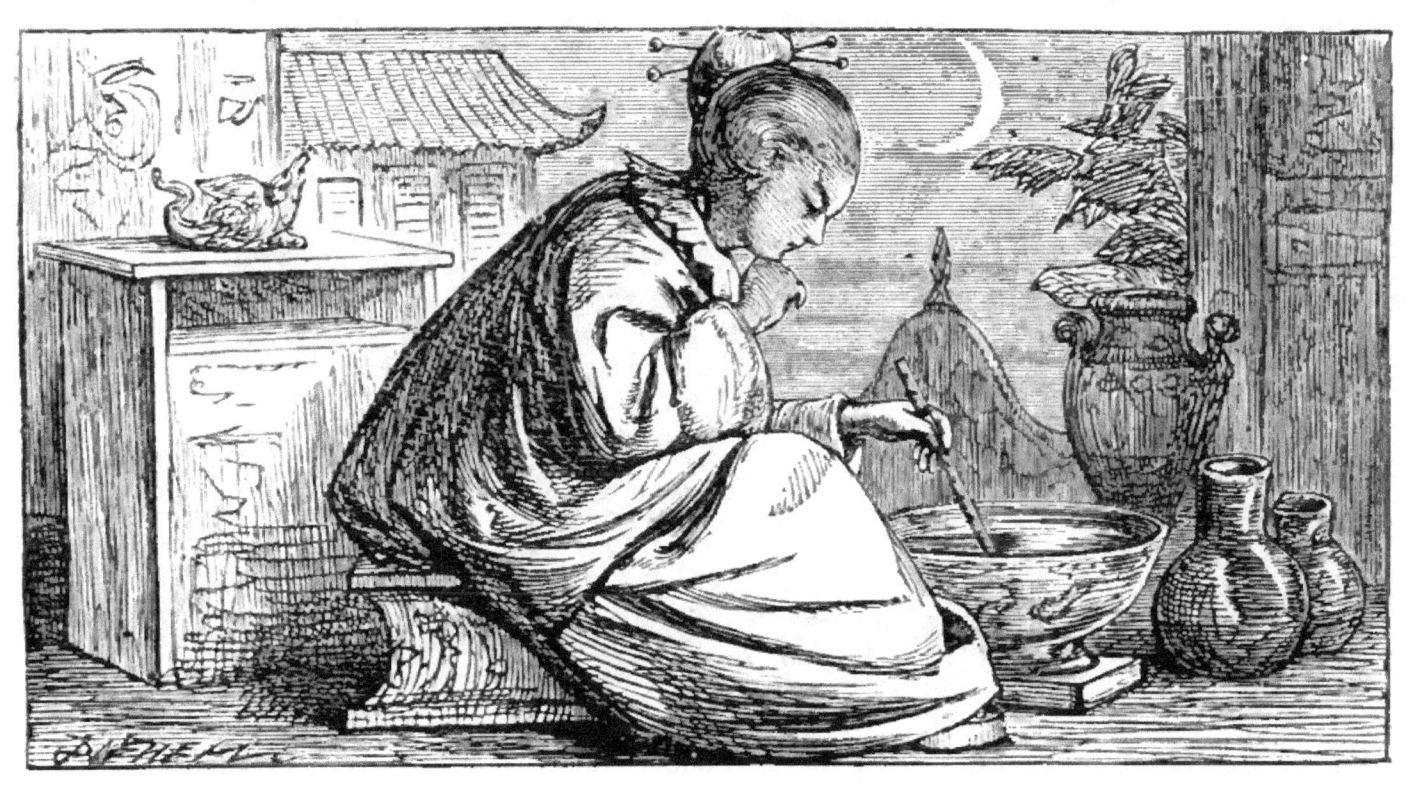

PRETTY PU.

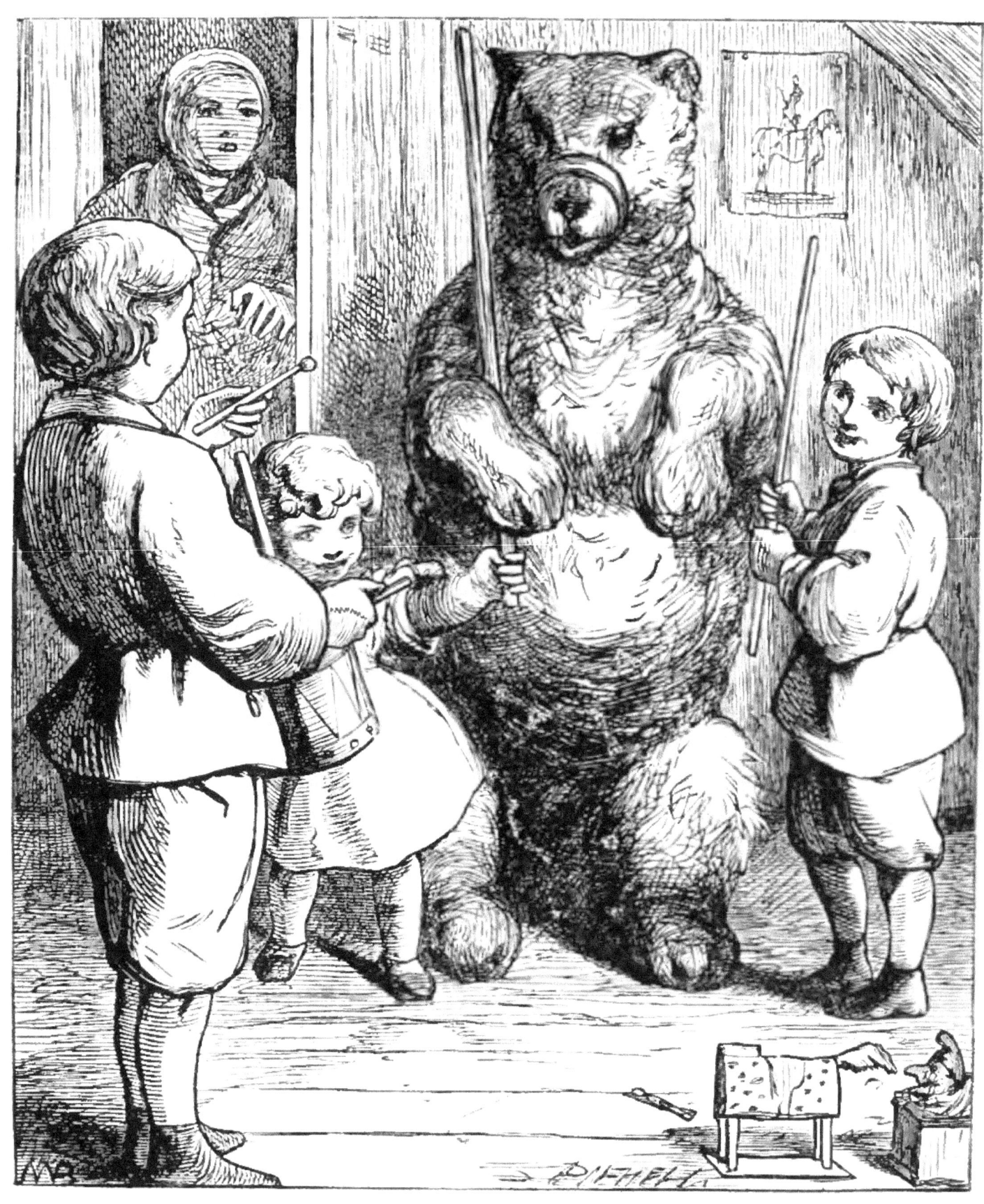

THE BEAR PLAYING AT SOLDIERS WITH THE CHILDREN.

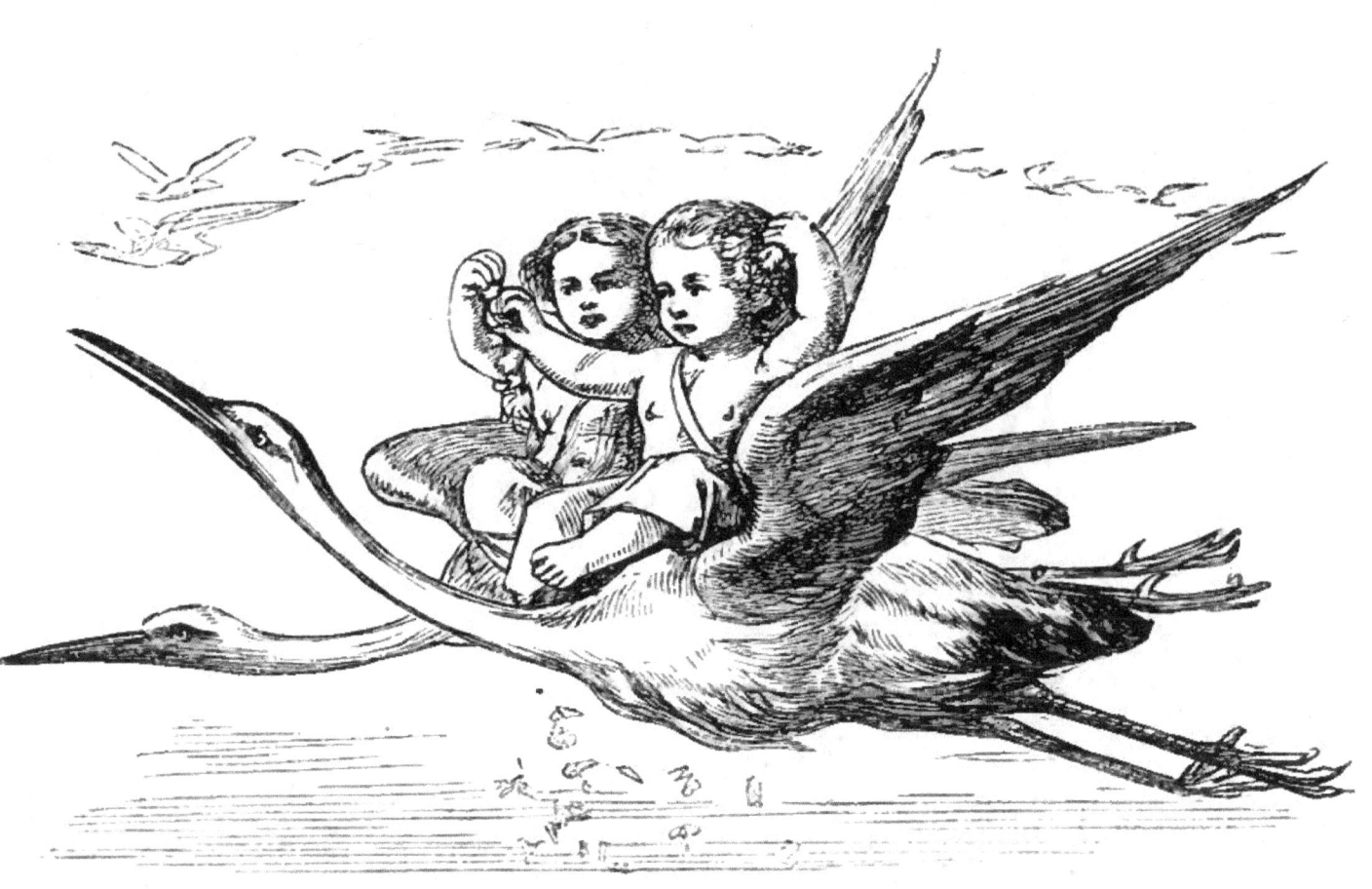

THE STORKS BRINGING BACK THE SPRING.

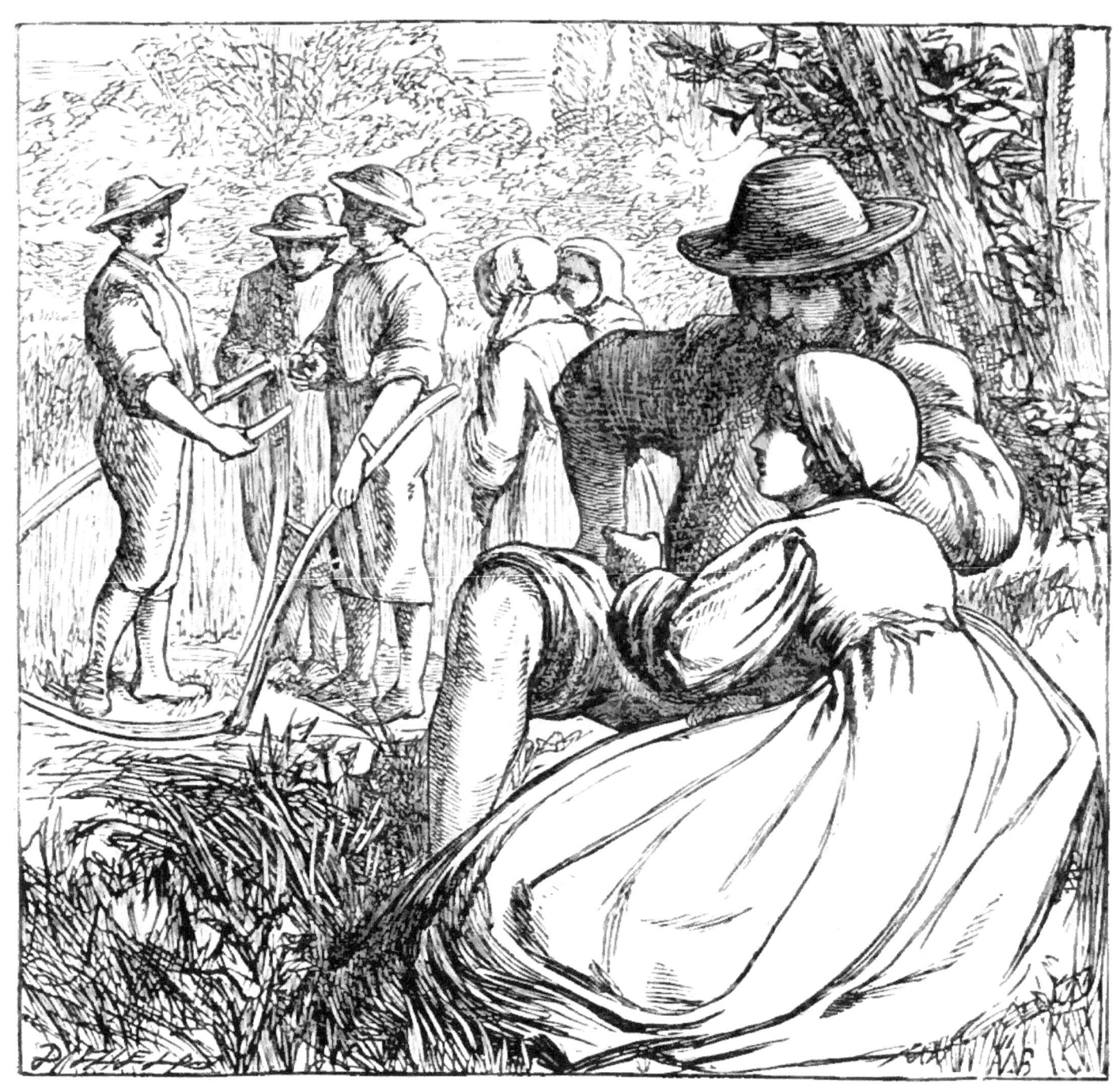

SUMMER TIME.

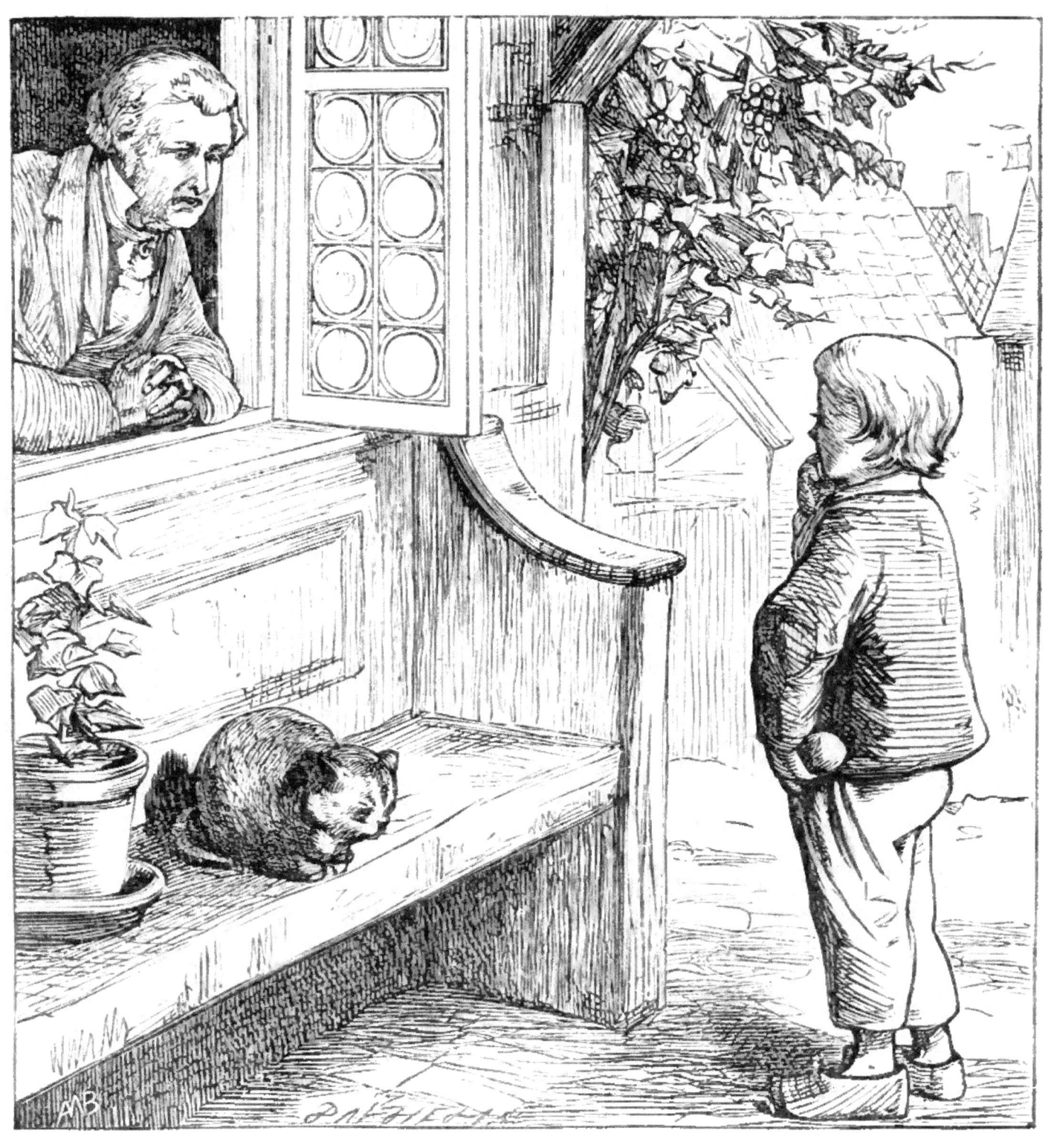

THE MAYOR AND THE WASHERWOMAN'S SON.

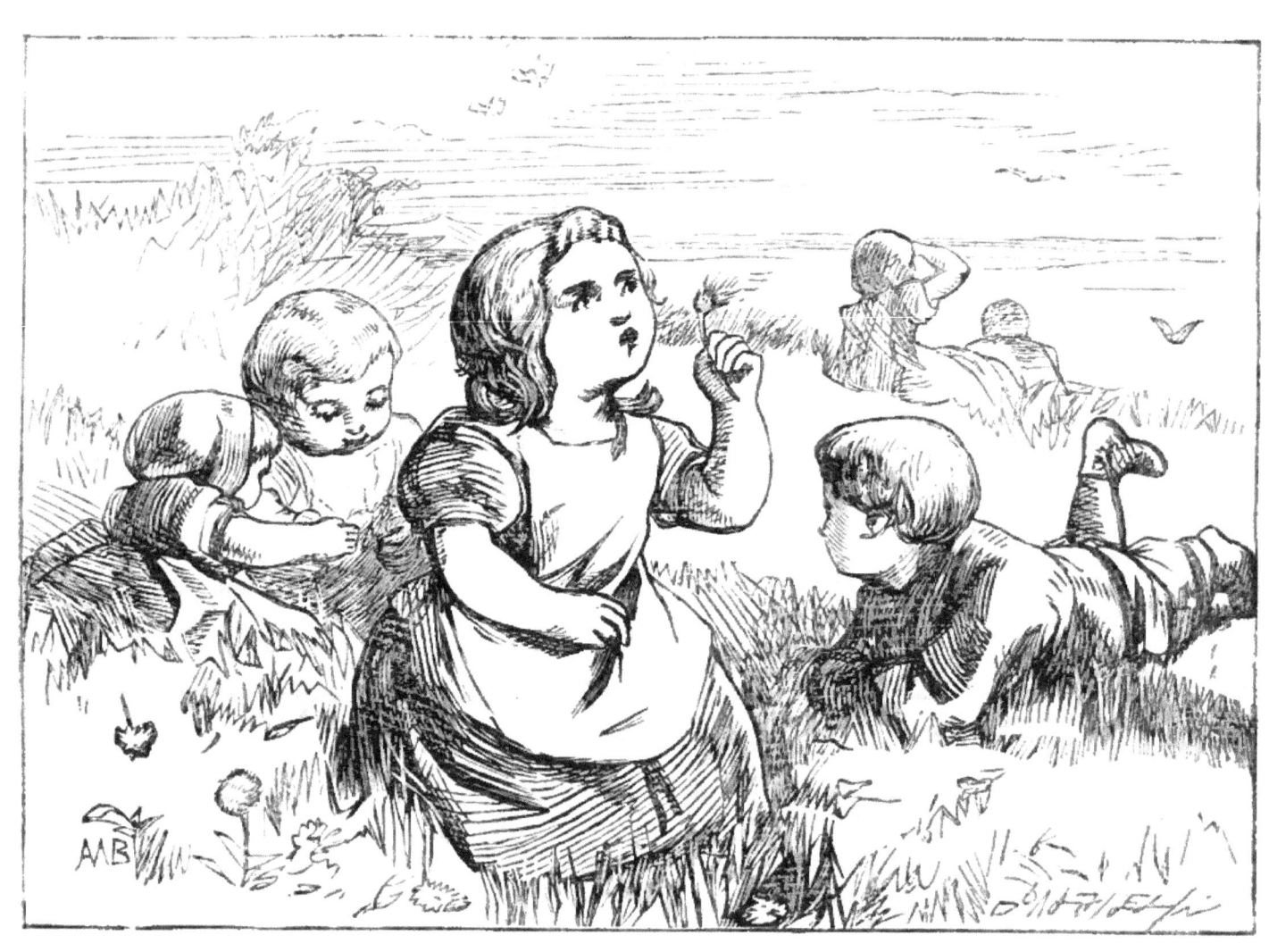

THE CHILDREN AND THE DANDELIONS.

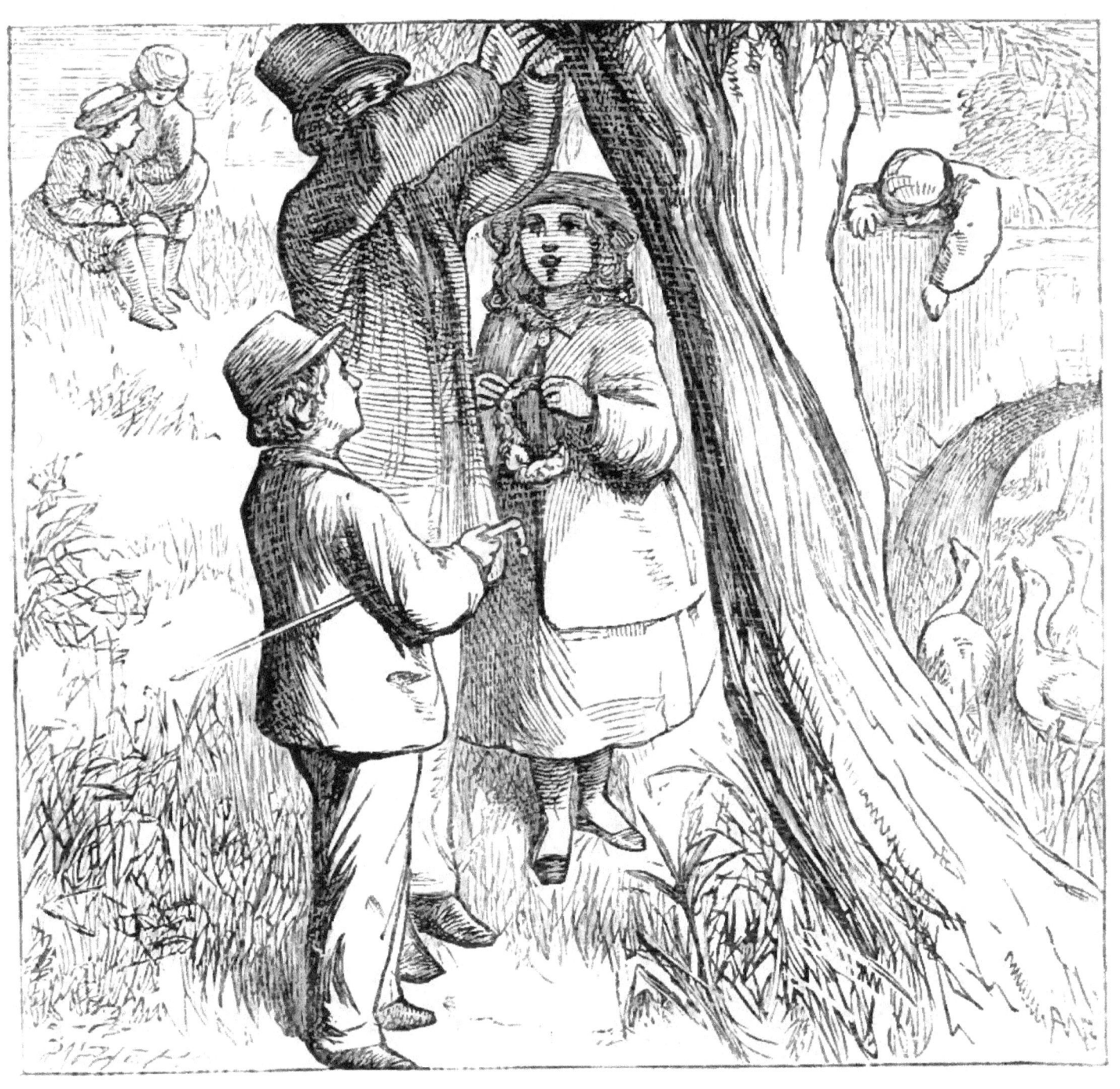

THE OLD WILLOW TREE.

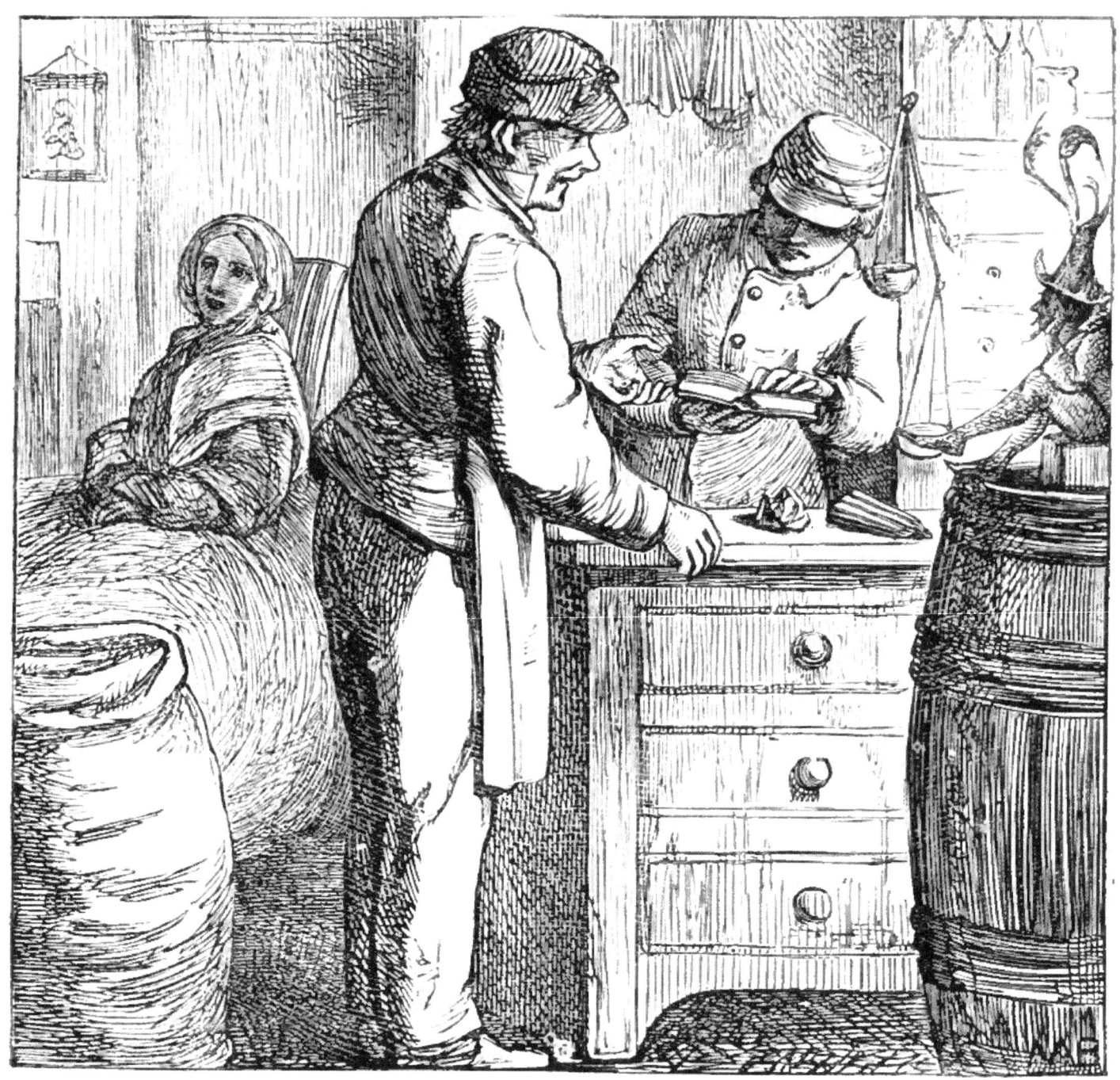

THE STUDENT'S BARGAIN.

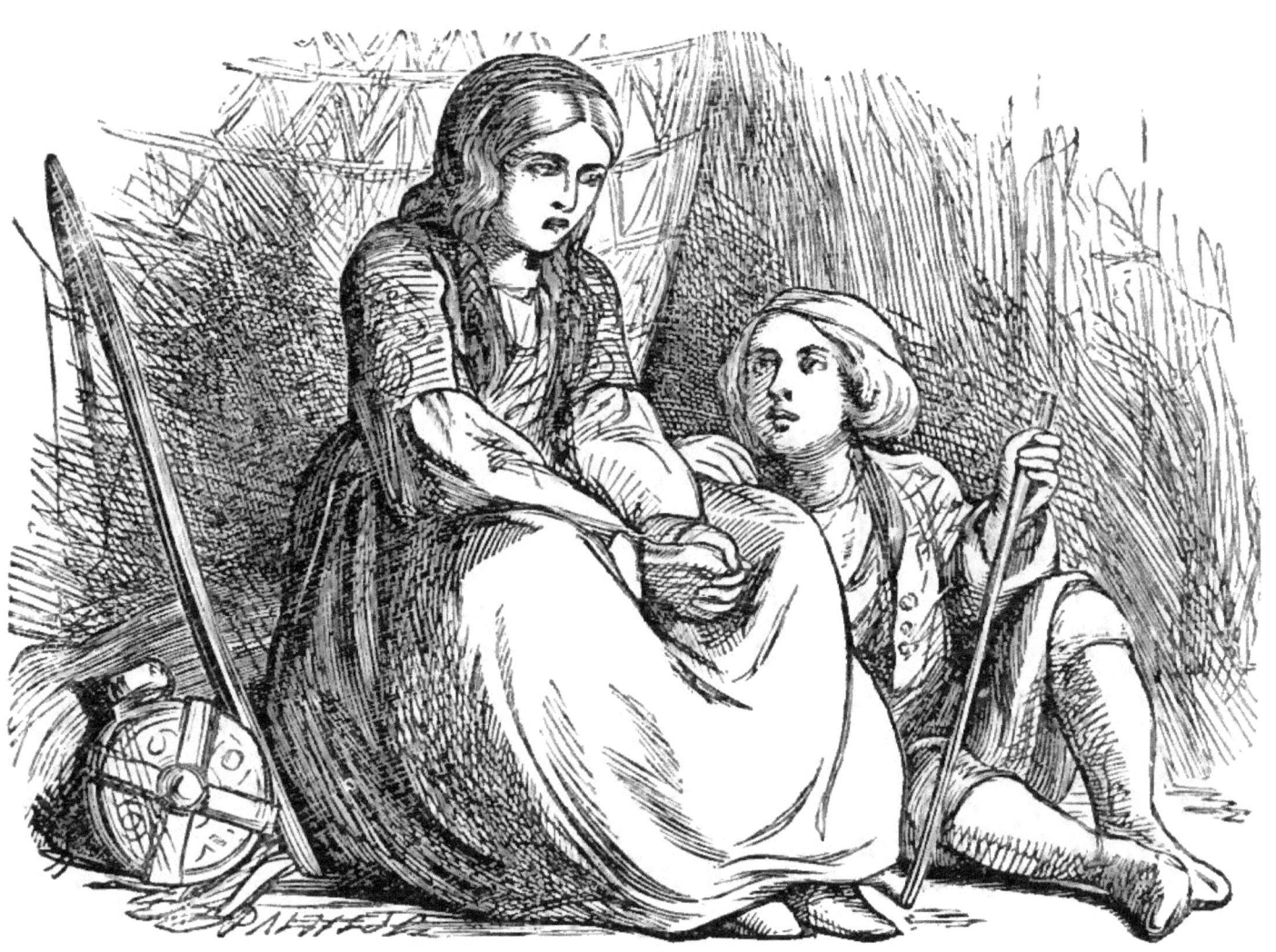

THE GREEK MOTHER'S SONG.

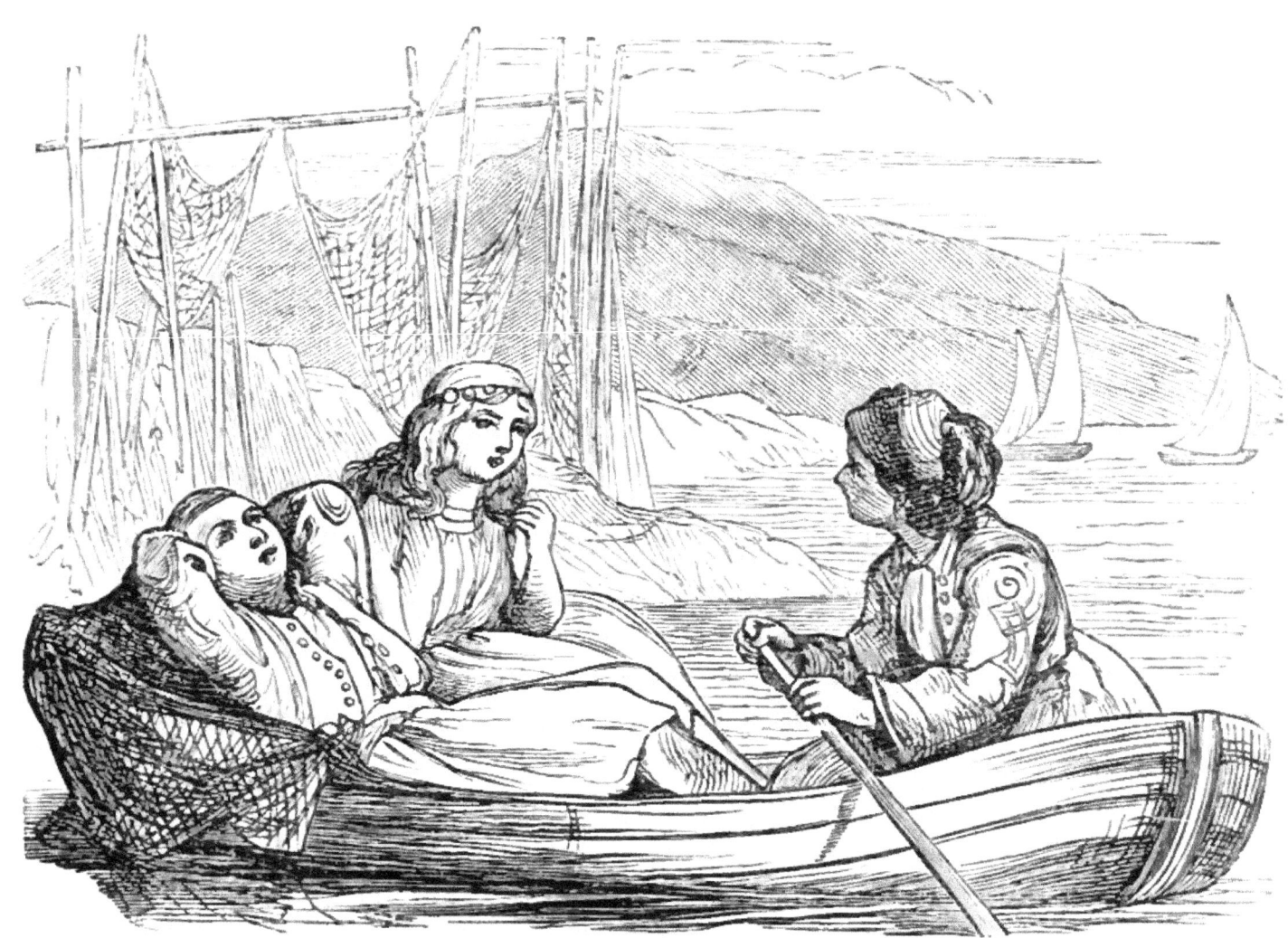

THE FRIENDS AT LEPANTO.

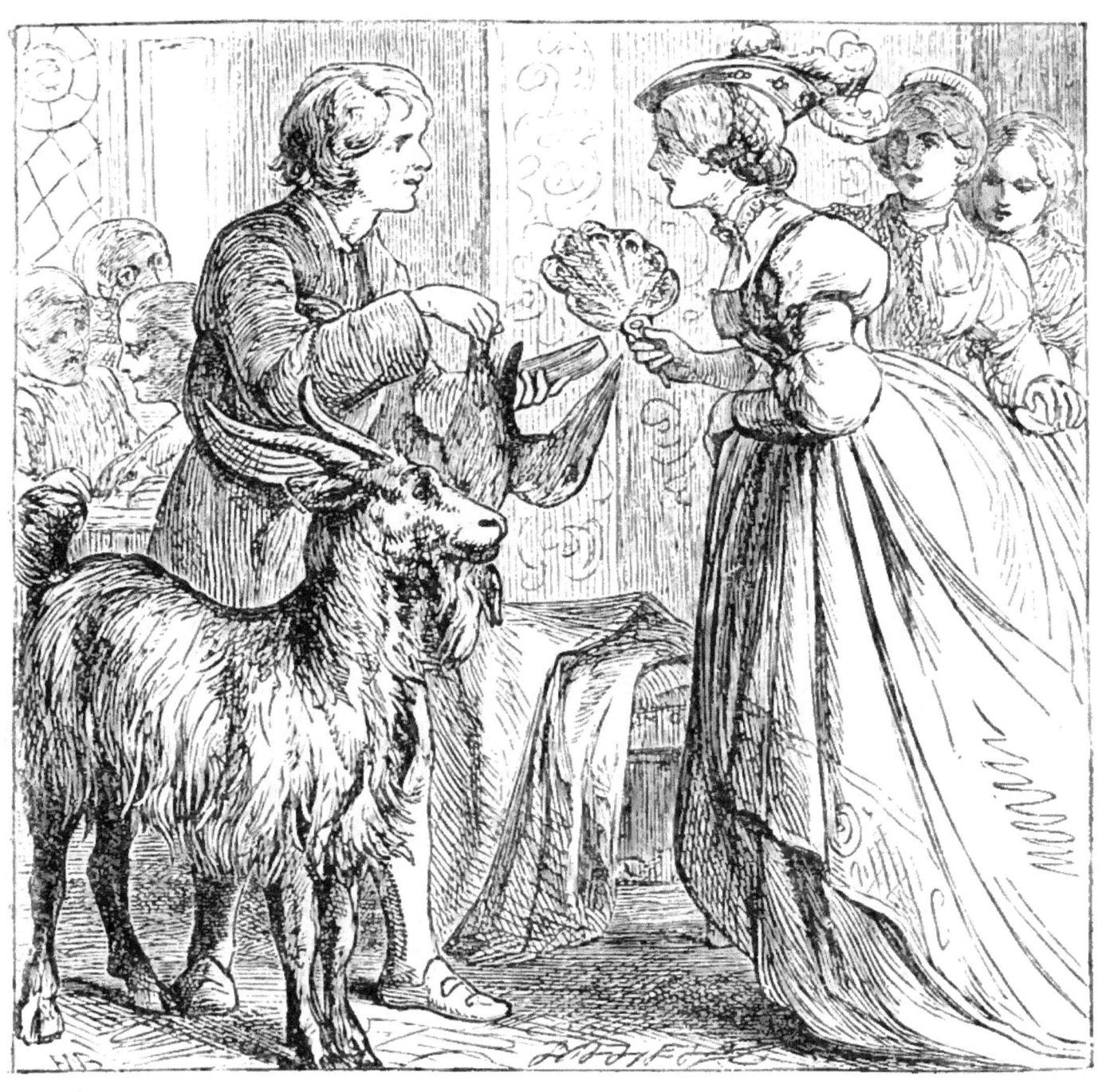

JACK'S INTRODUCTION TO THE PRINCESS.

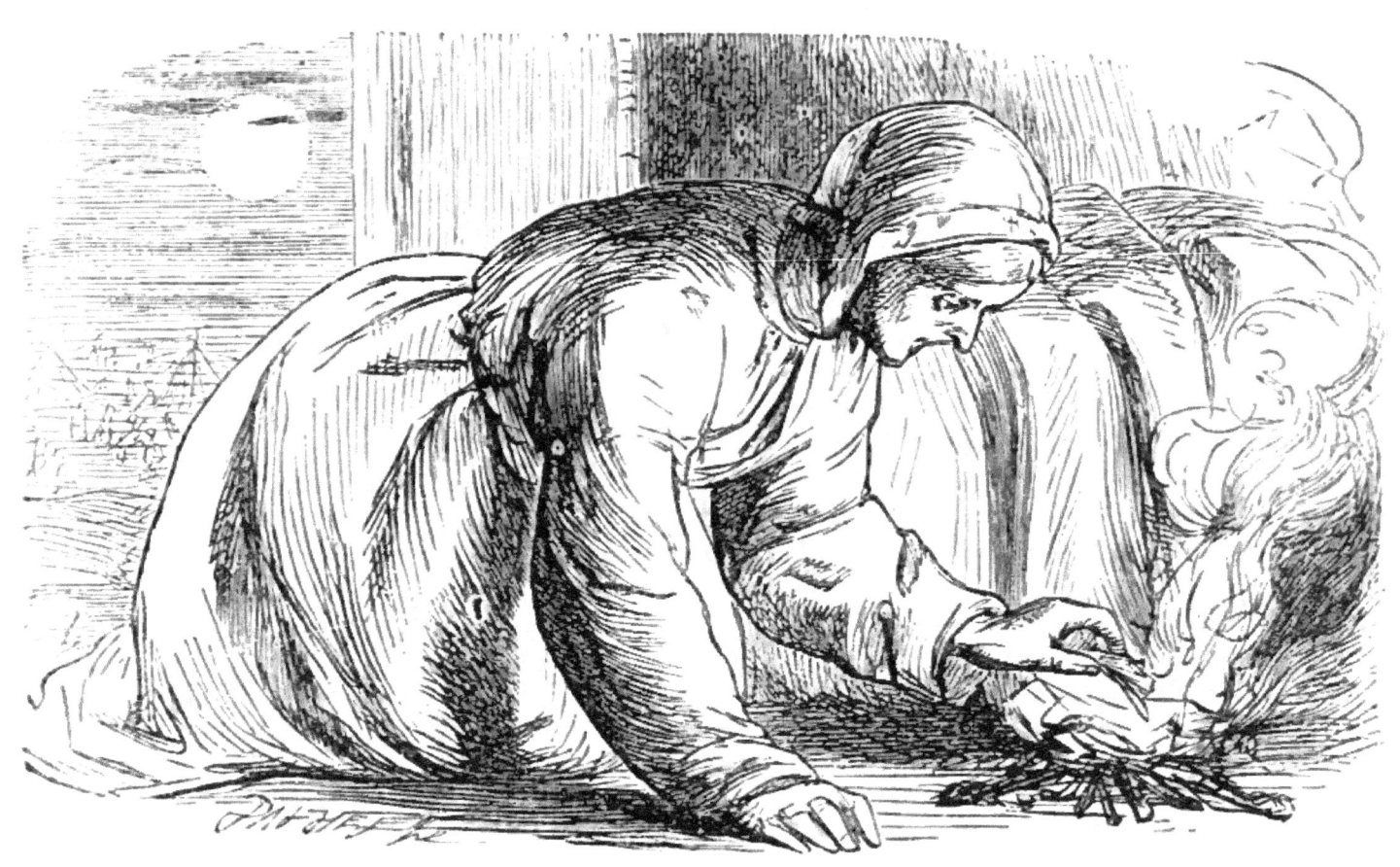

DAME MARGERY FIRES HER BED FOR A BEACON.

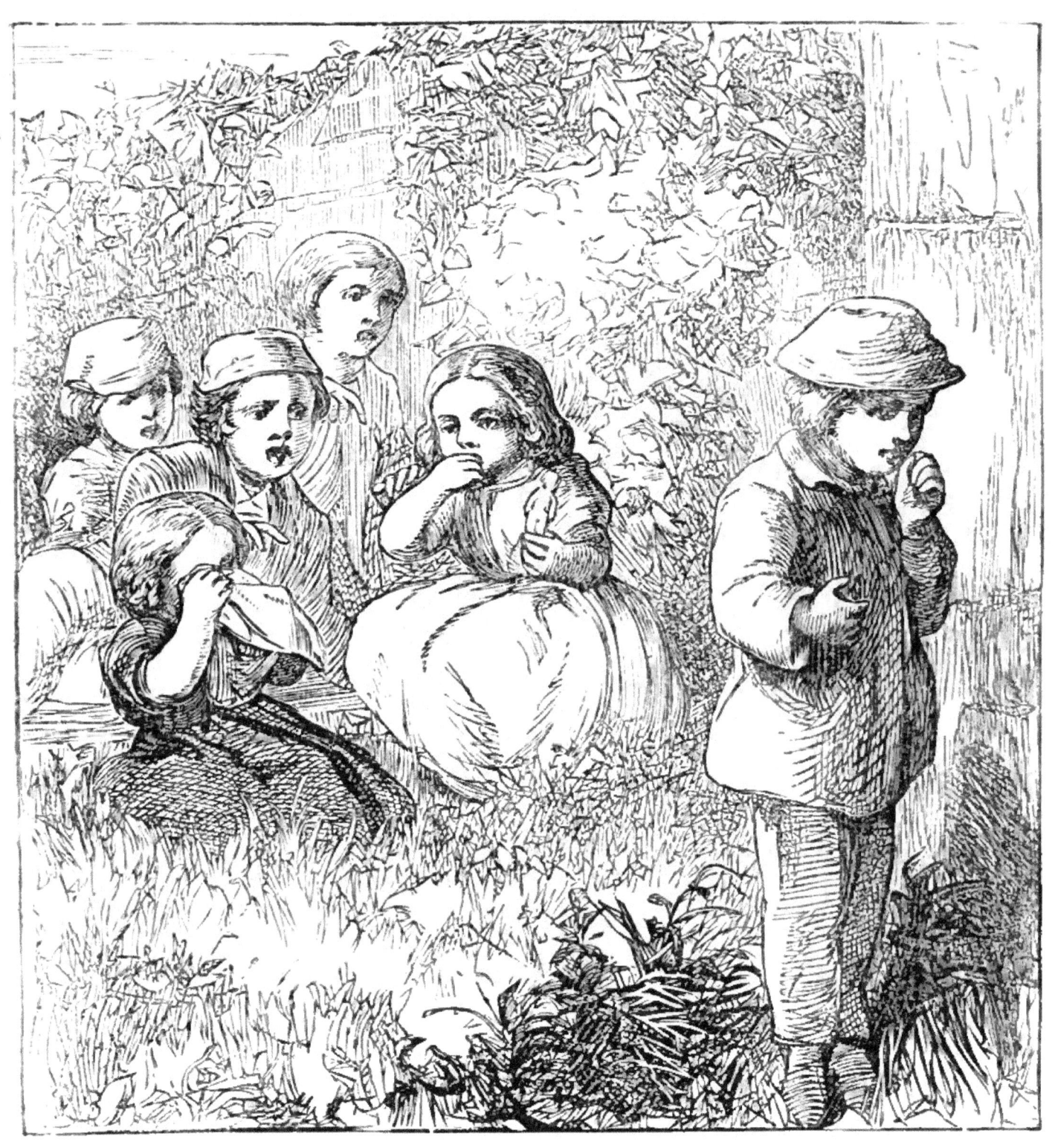

THE NAUGHTY BOY WHO ATE THE GINGERBREAD MAIDEN.

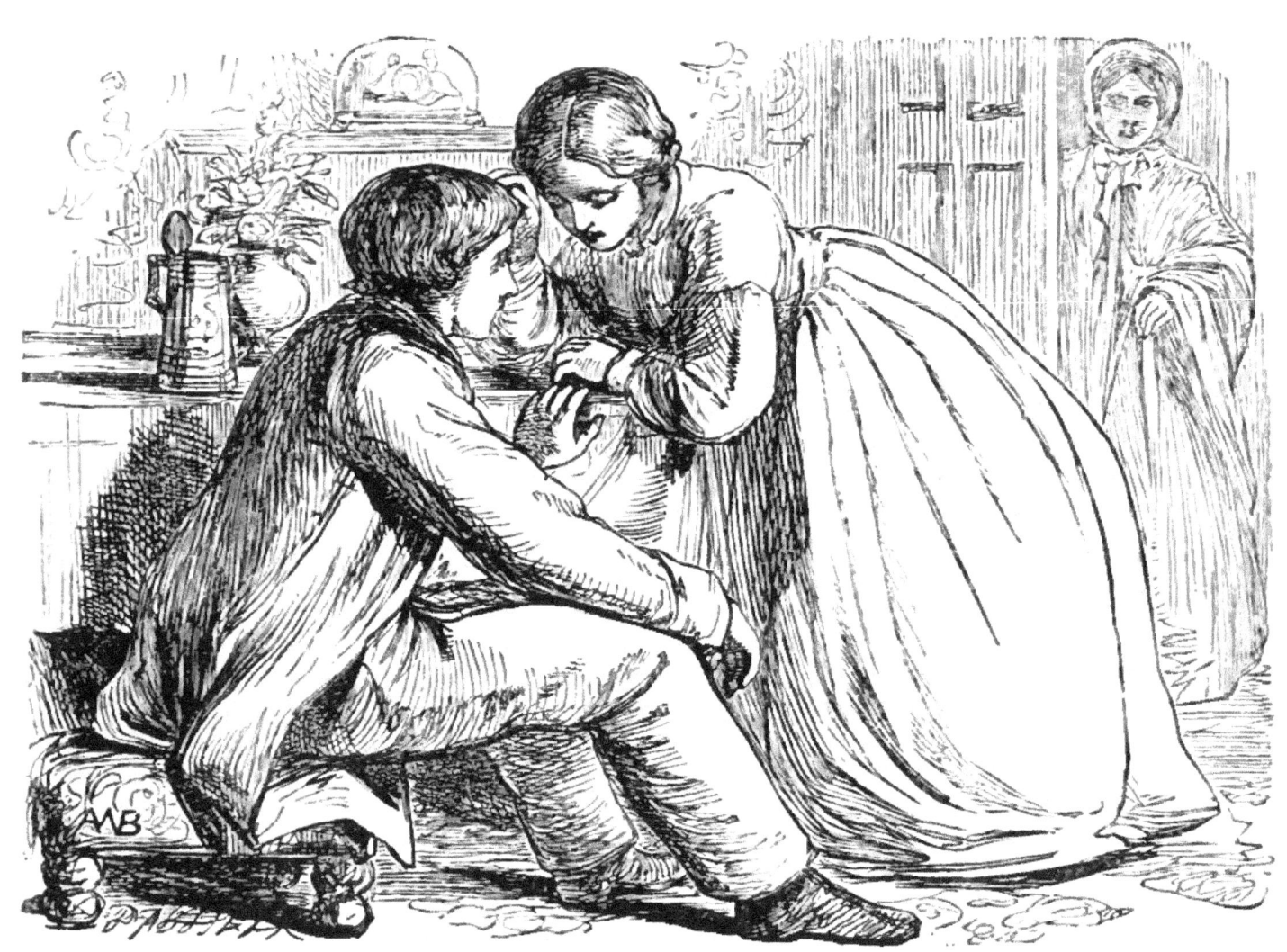

KNUD'S DISAPPOINTMENT.

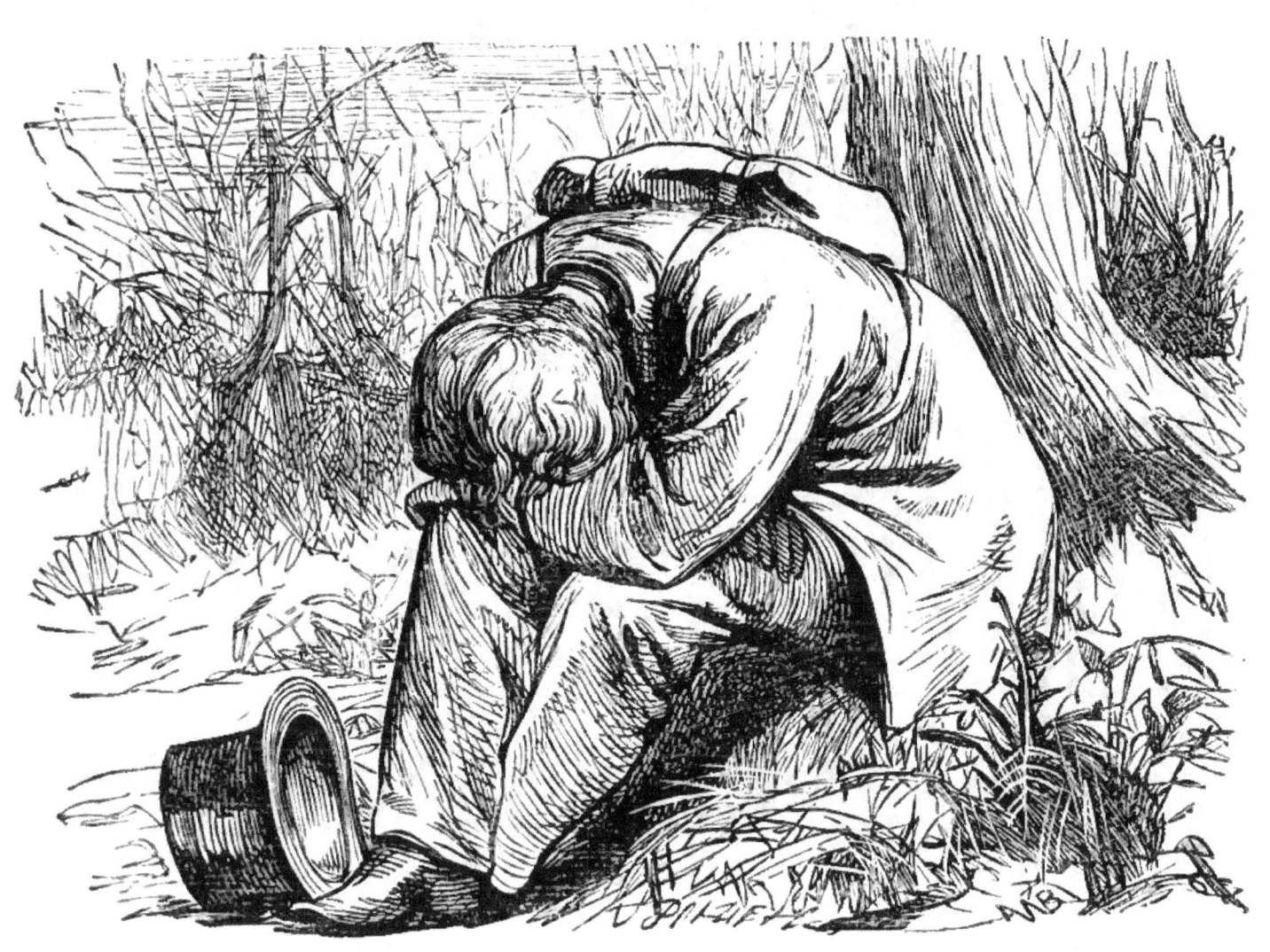

KNUD AT REST—UNDER THE WILLOW TREE.

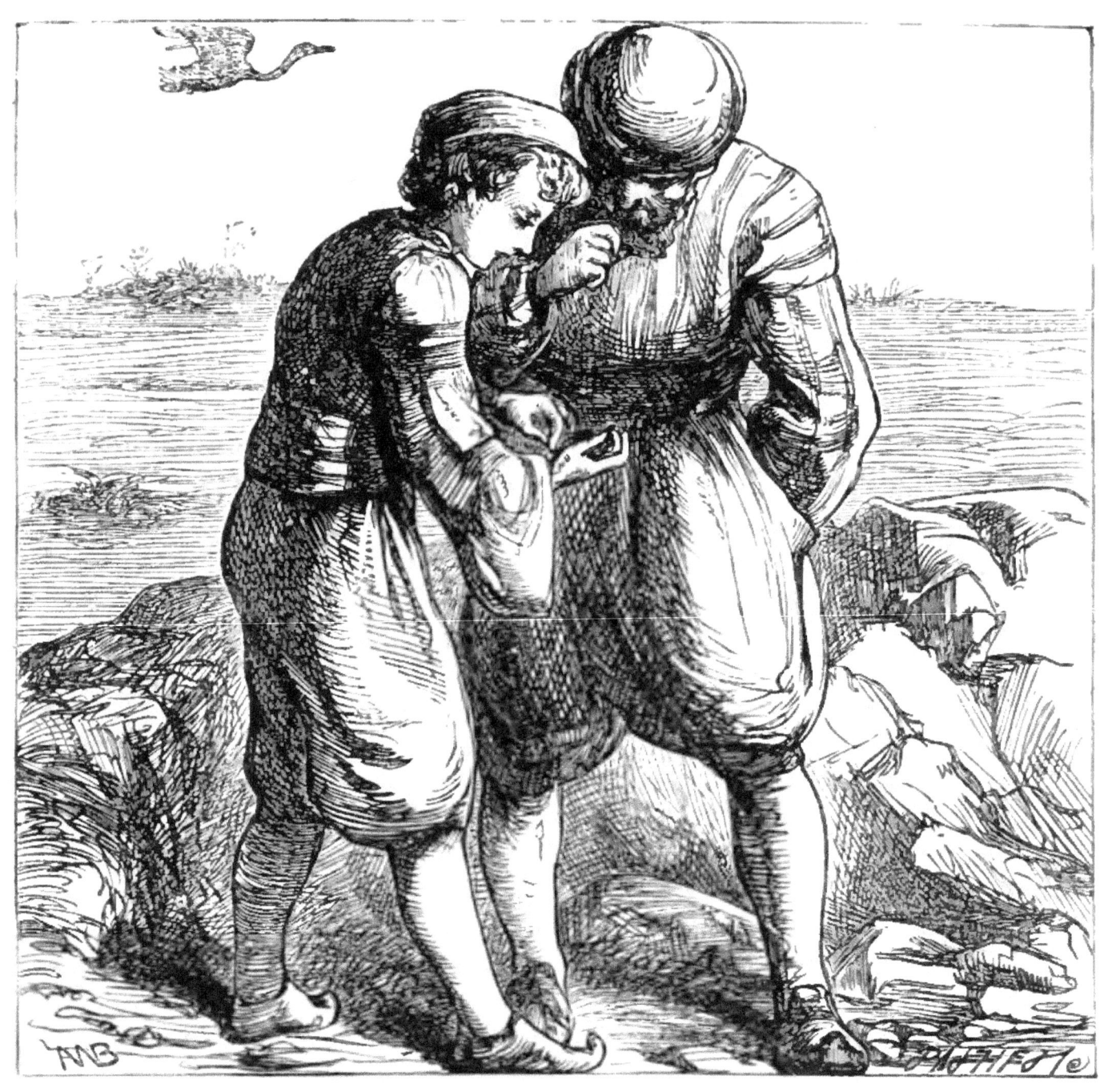

THE SCHOLARS FIND THE BEETLE.

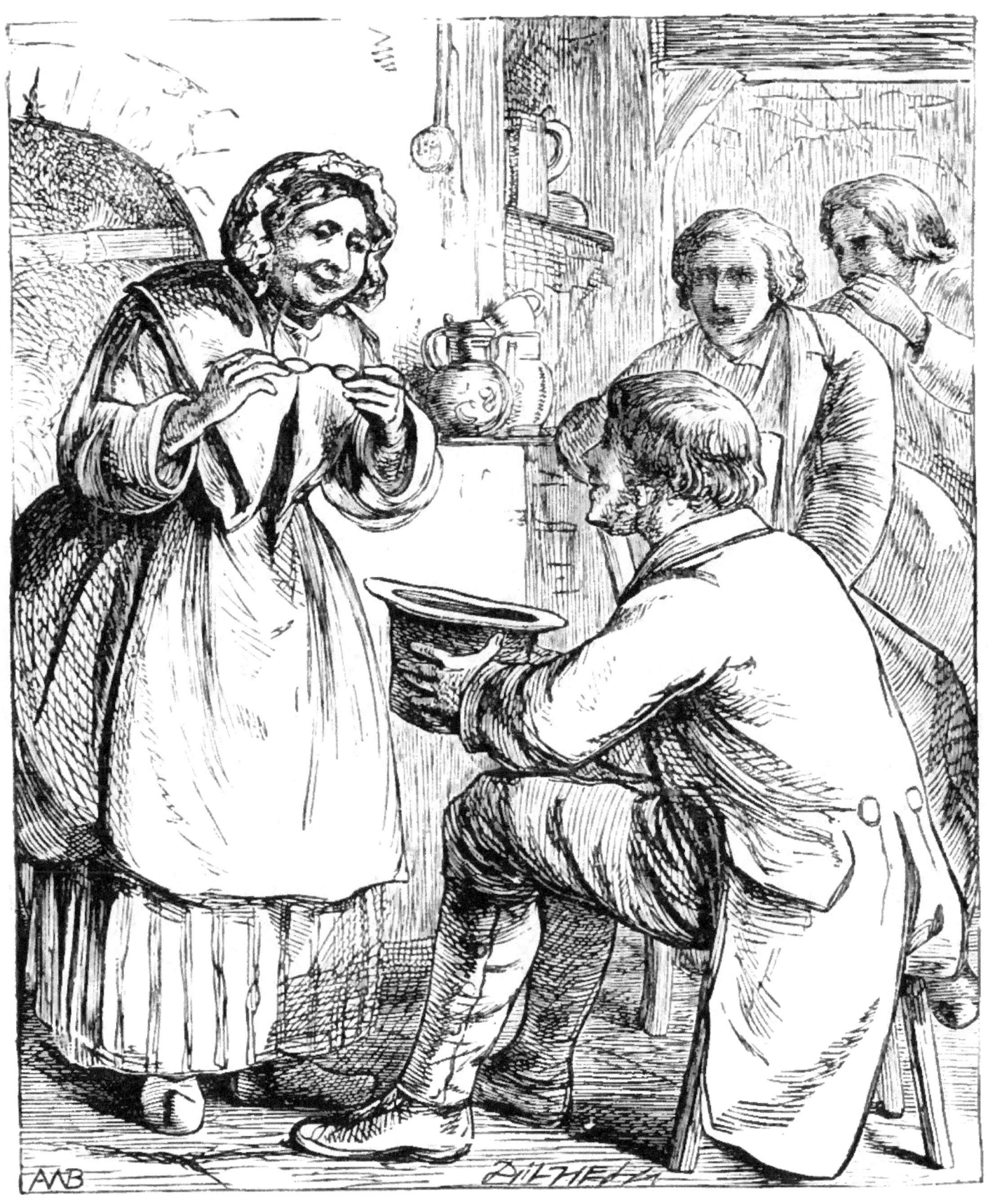

THE OLD MAN RELATES HIS SUCCESS.

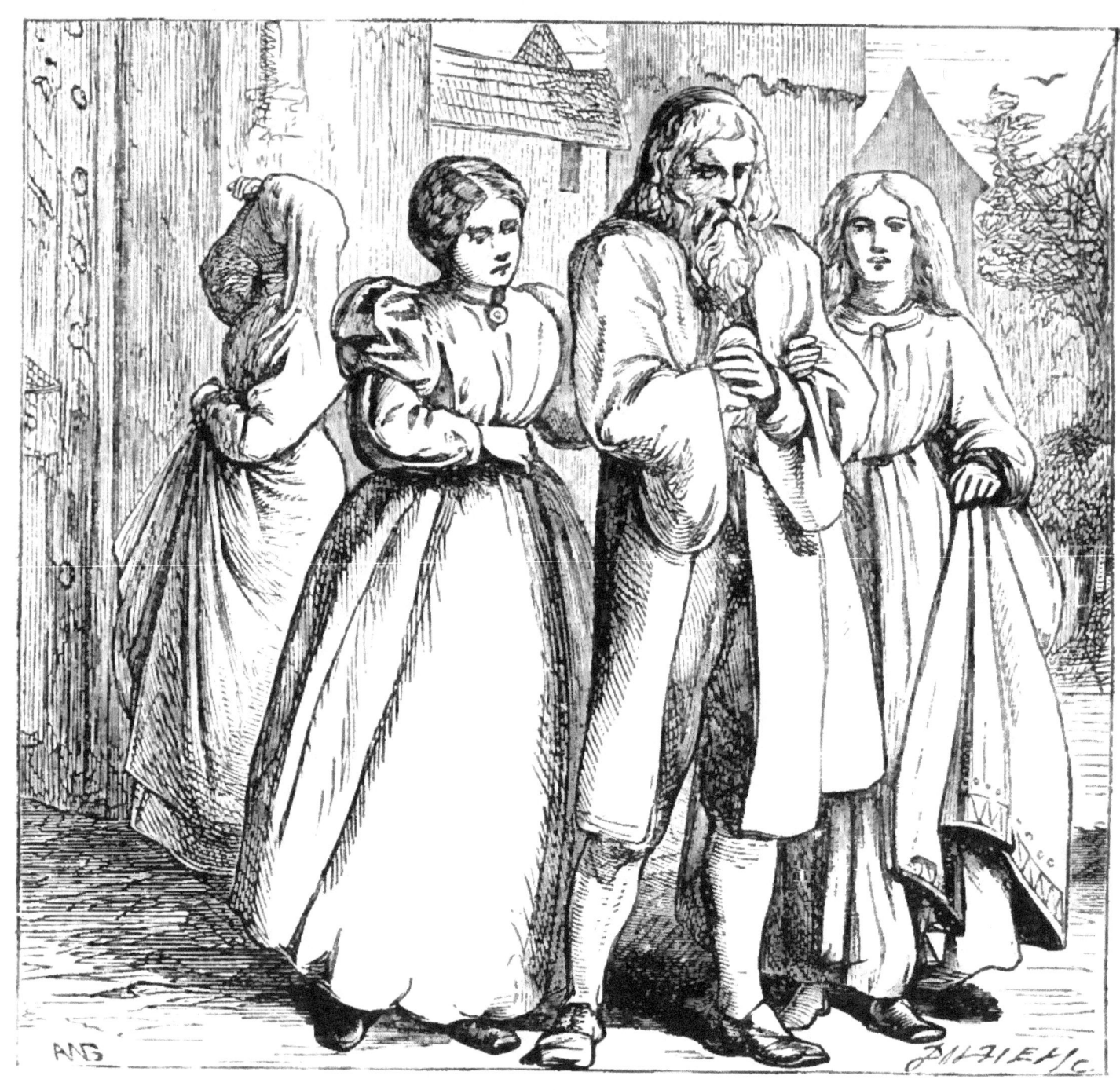

LEAVING THE OLD HOME.

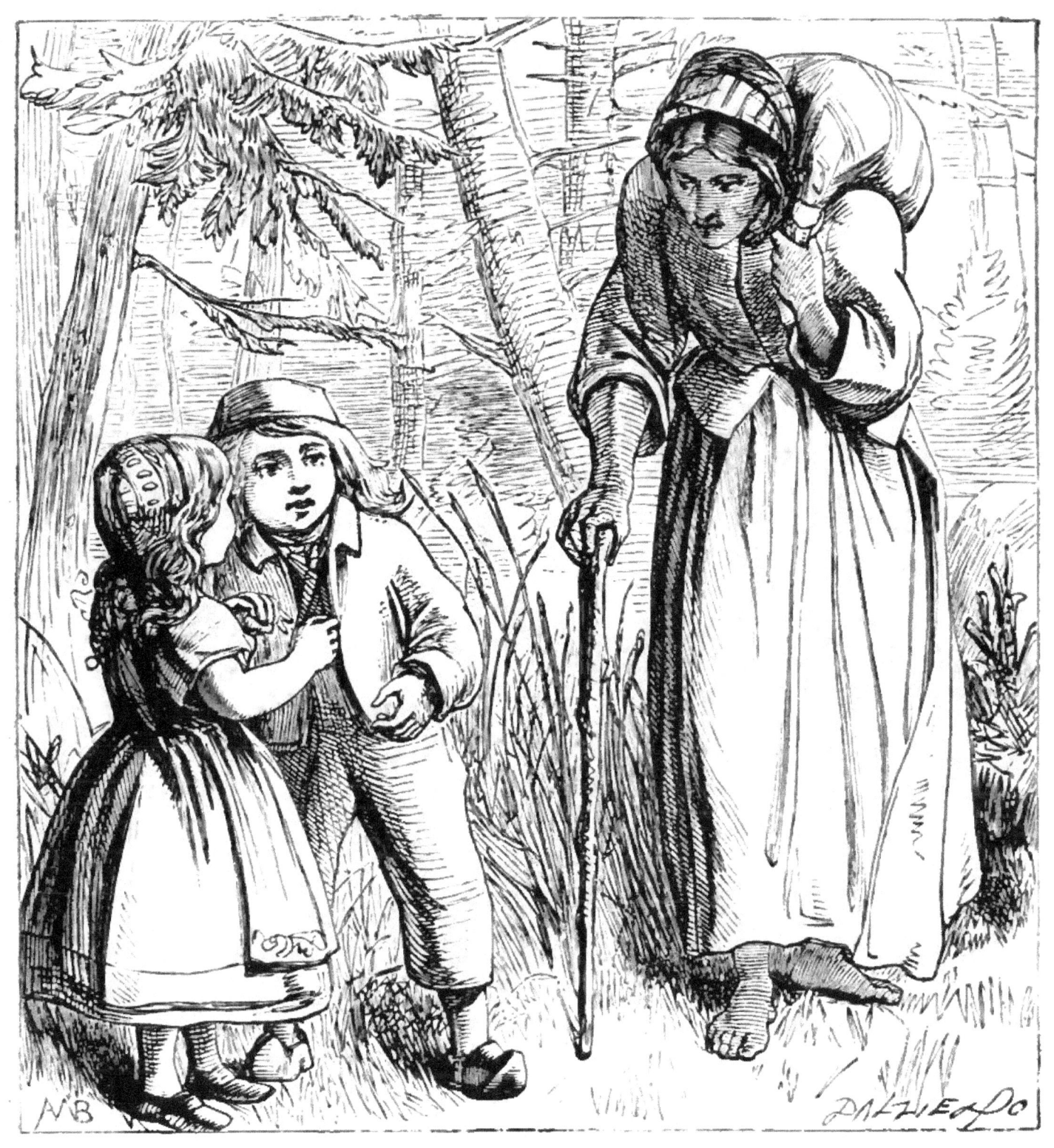

IB AND CHRISTINE MEET THE GIPSY.

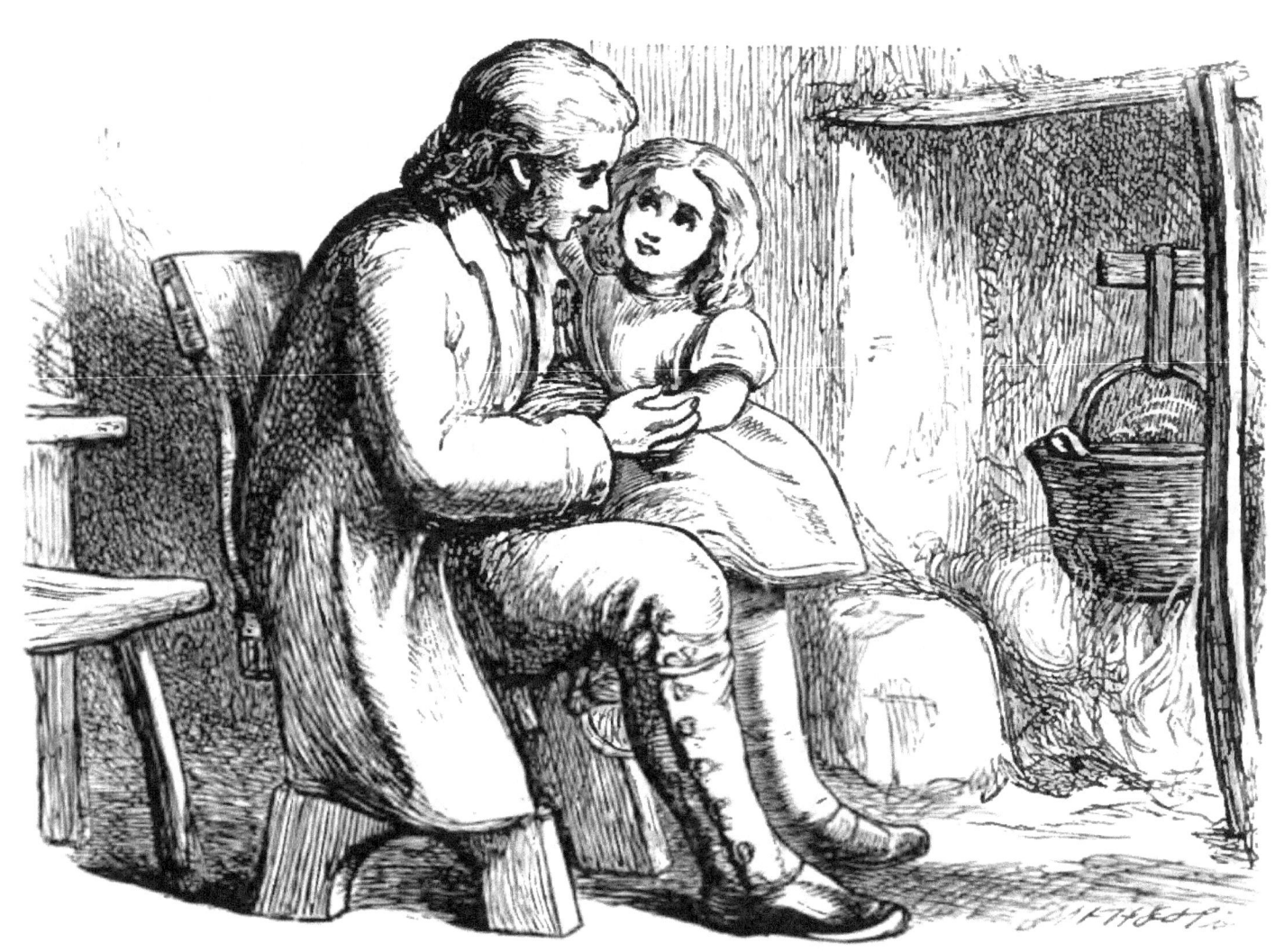

LITTLE CHRISTINE.

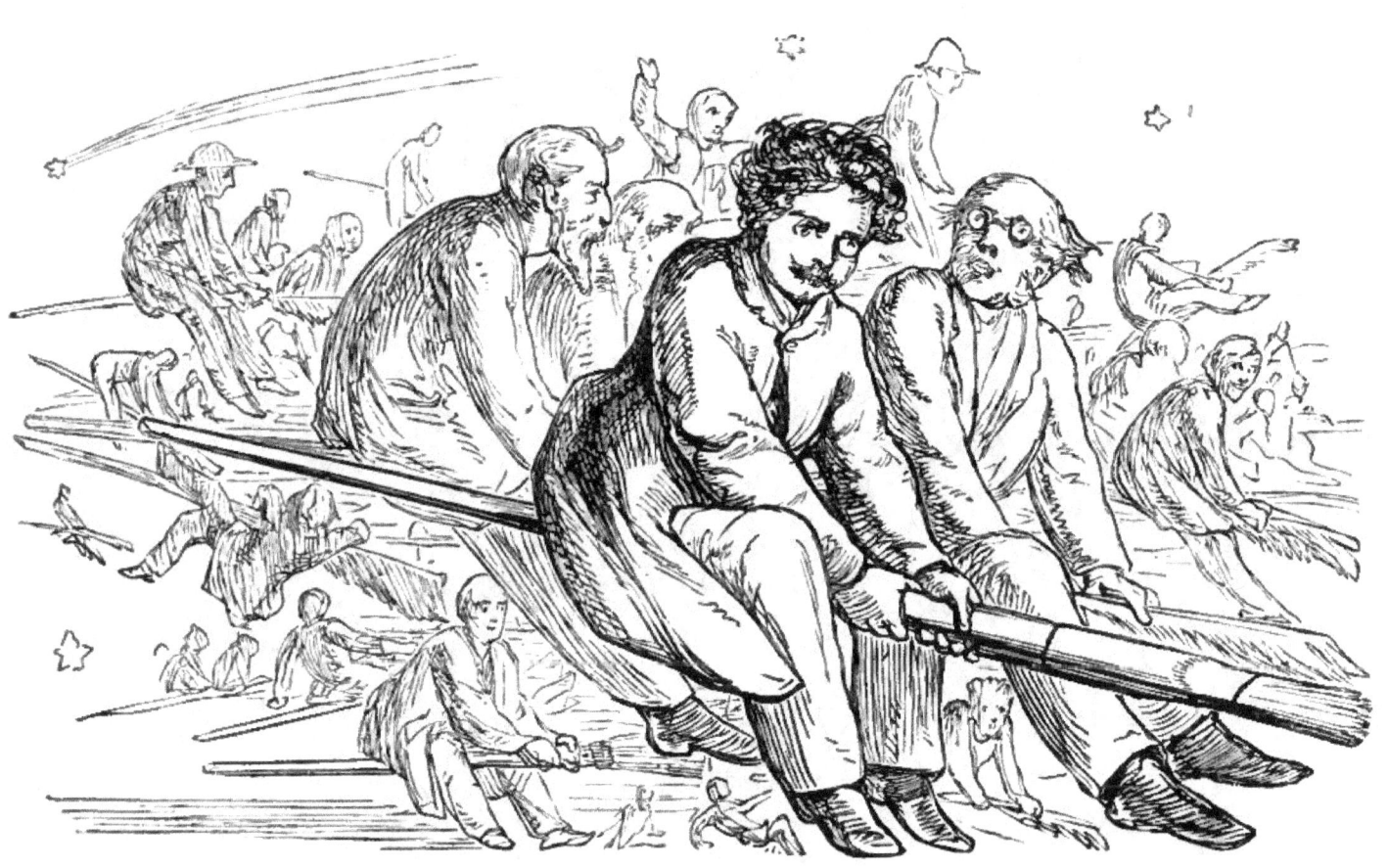

THE RIDE TO AMACK.

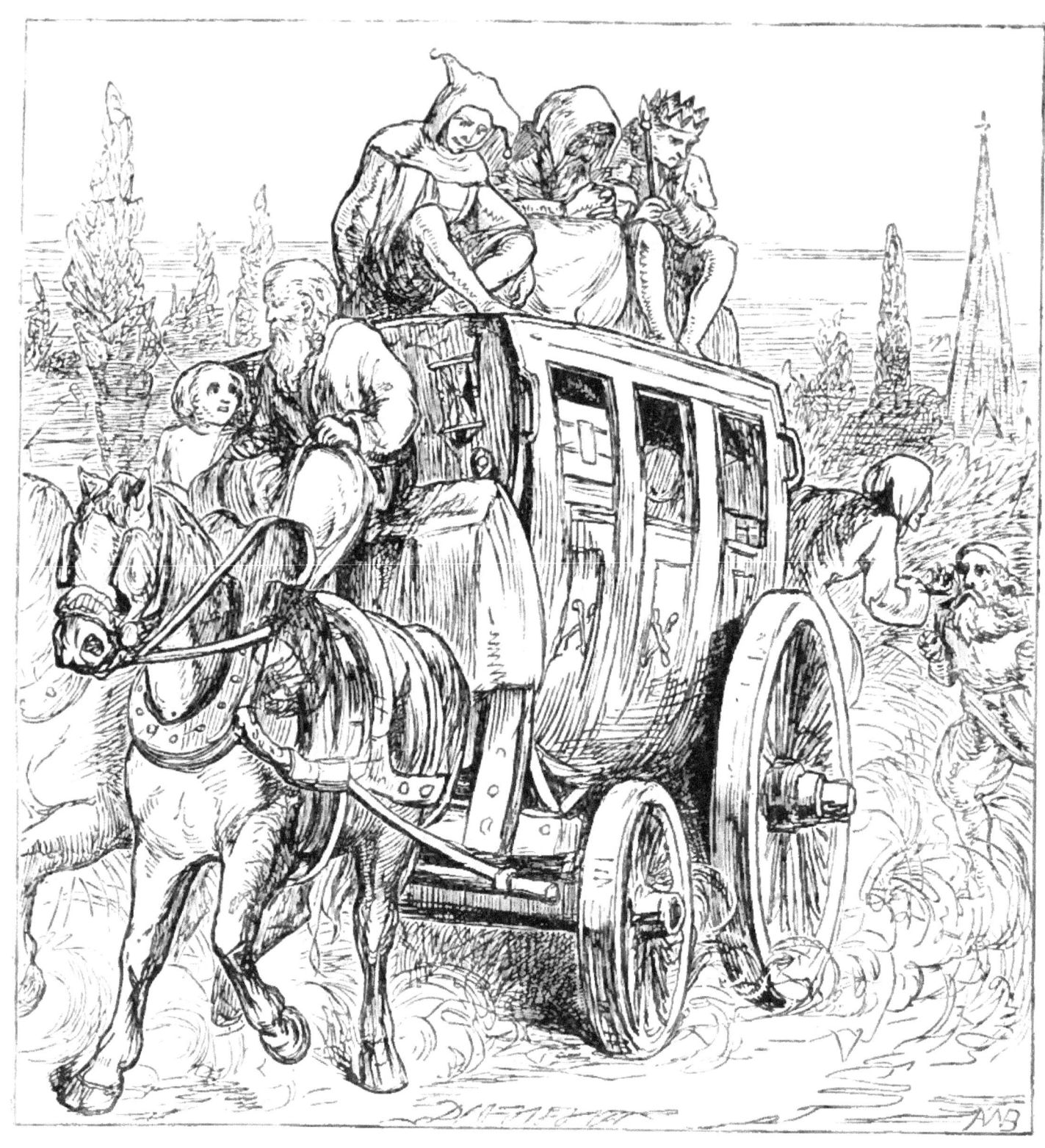

THE REJECTED TRAVELLER.

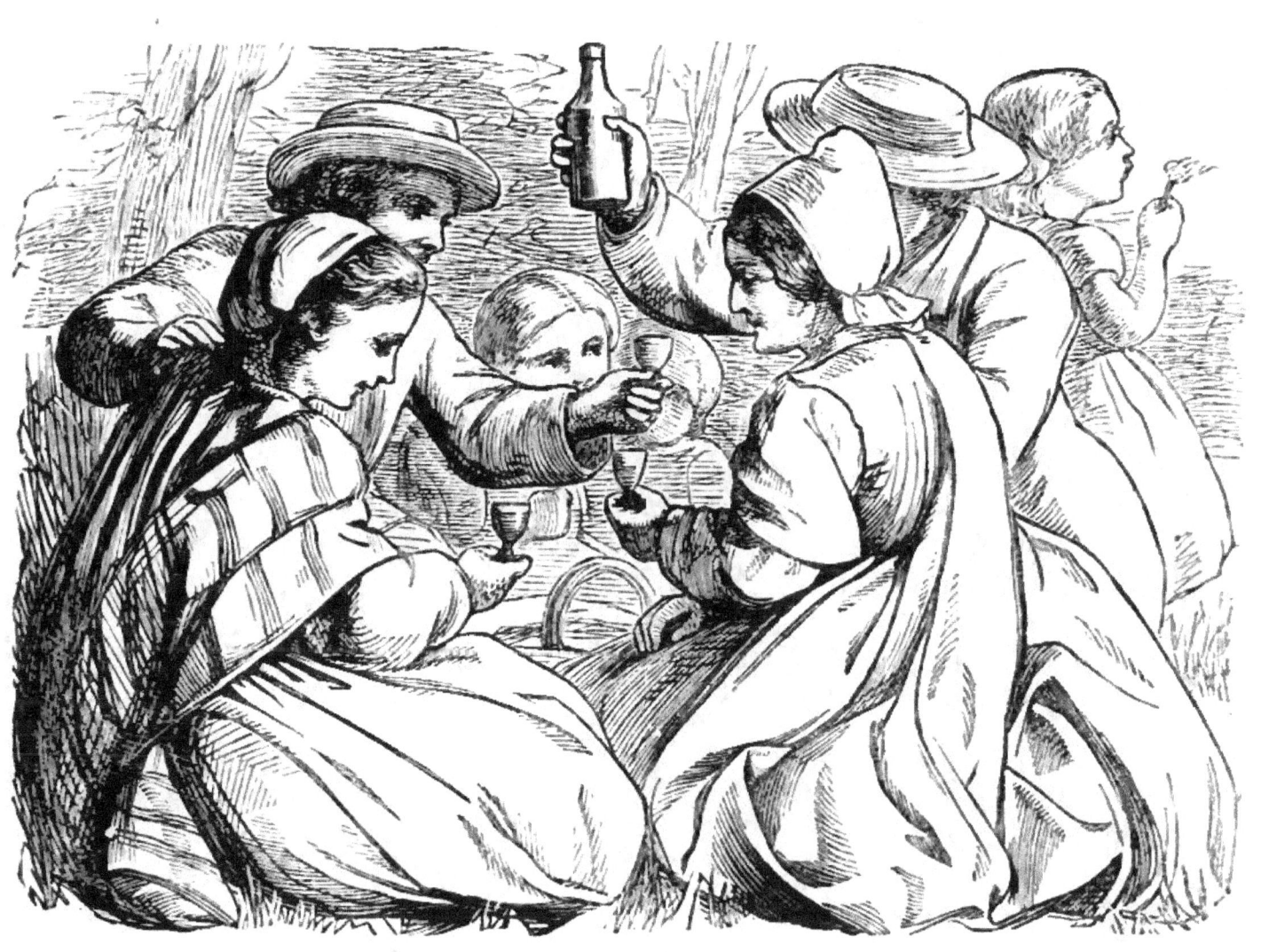

THE BOTTLE IS PRESENT ON A JOYOUS OCCASION.

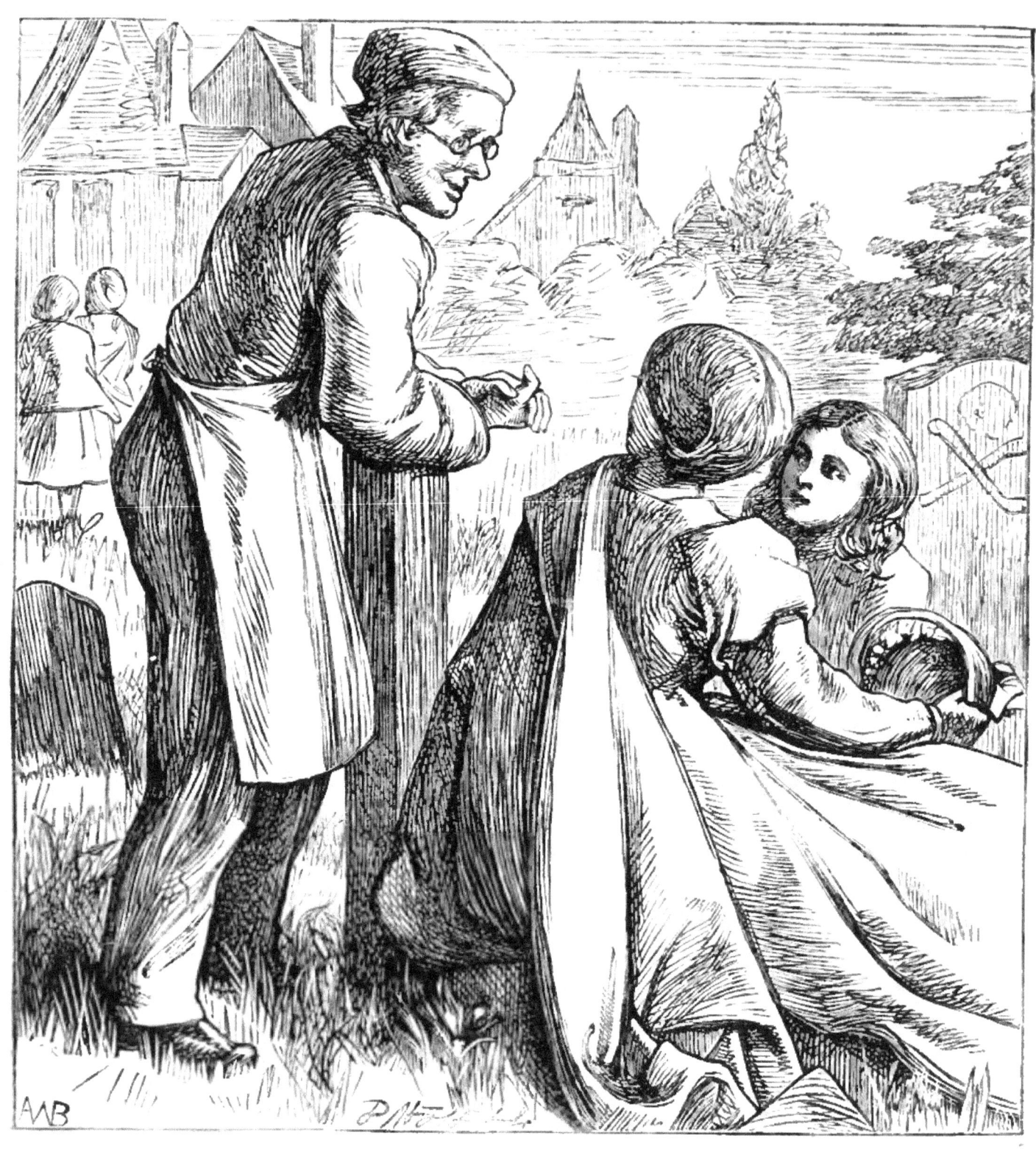

THE CHURCHYARD NARRATION.

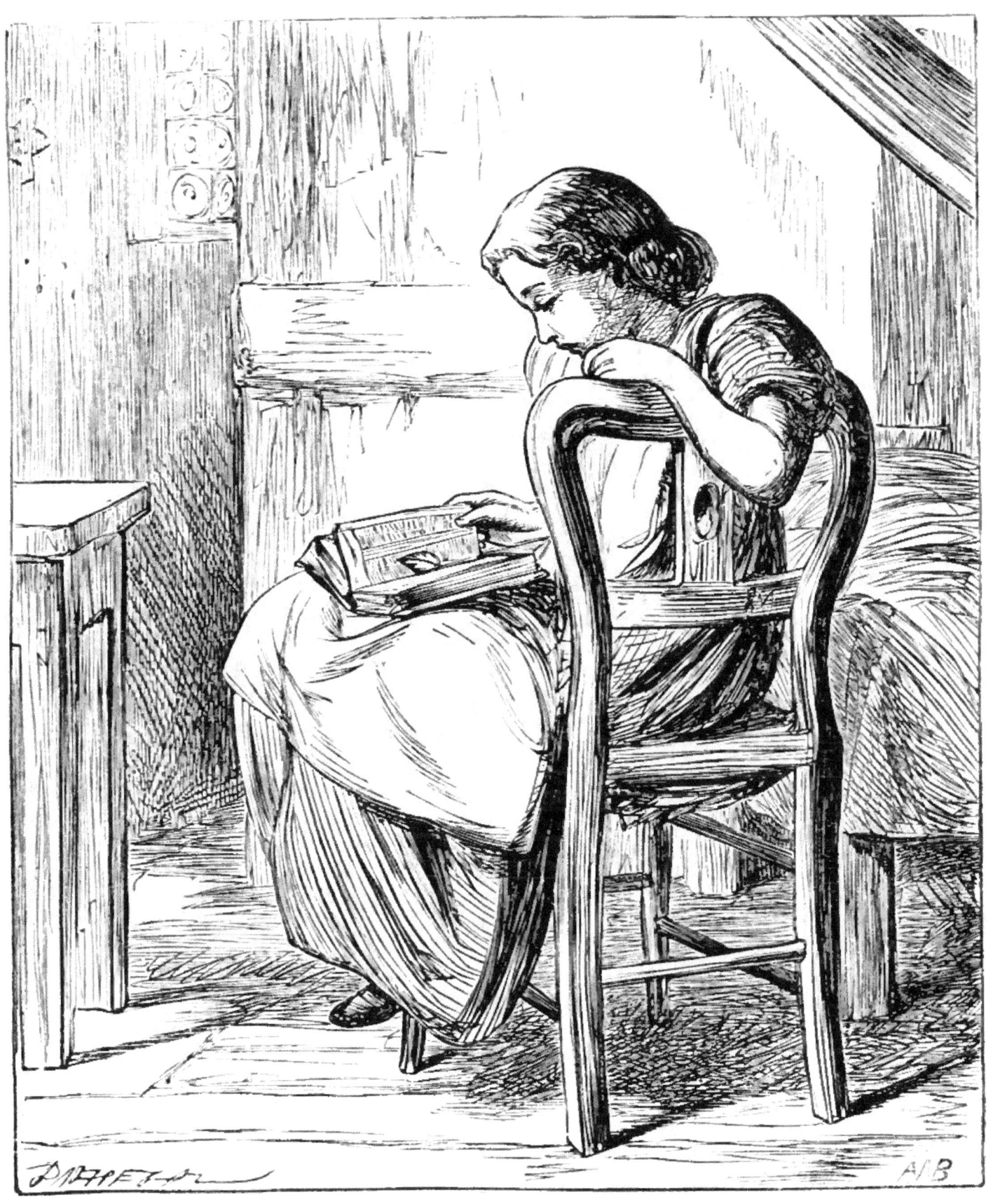

THE POOR GIRL'S TREASURE.

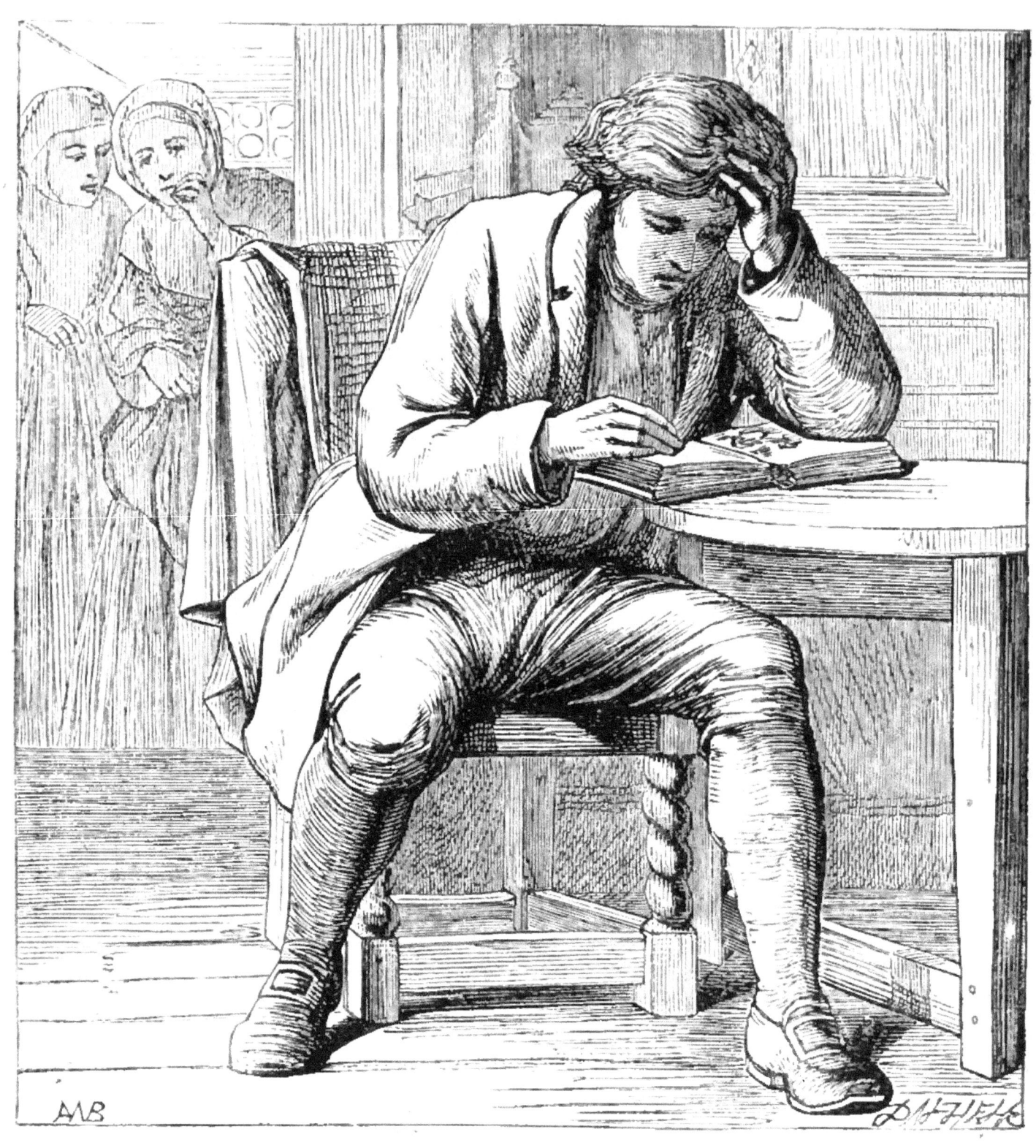

THE POWER OF THE BOOK.

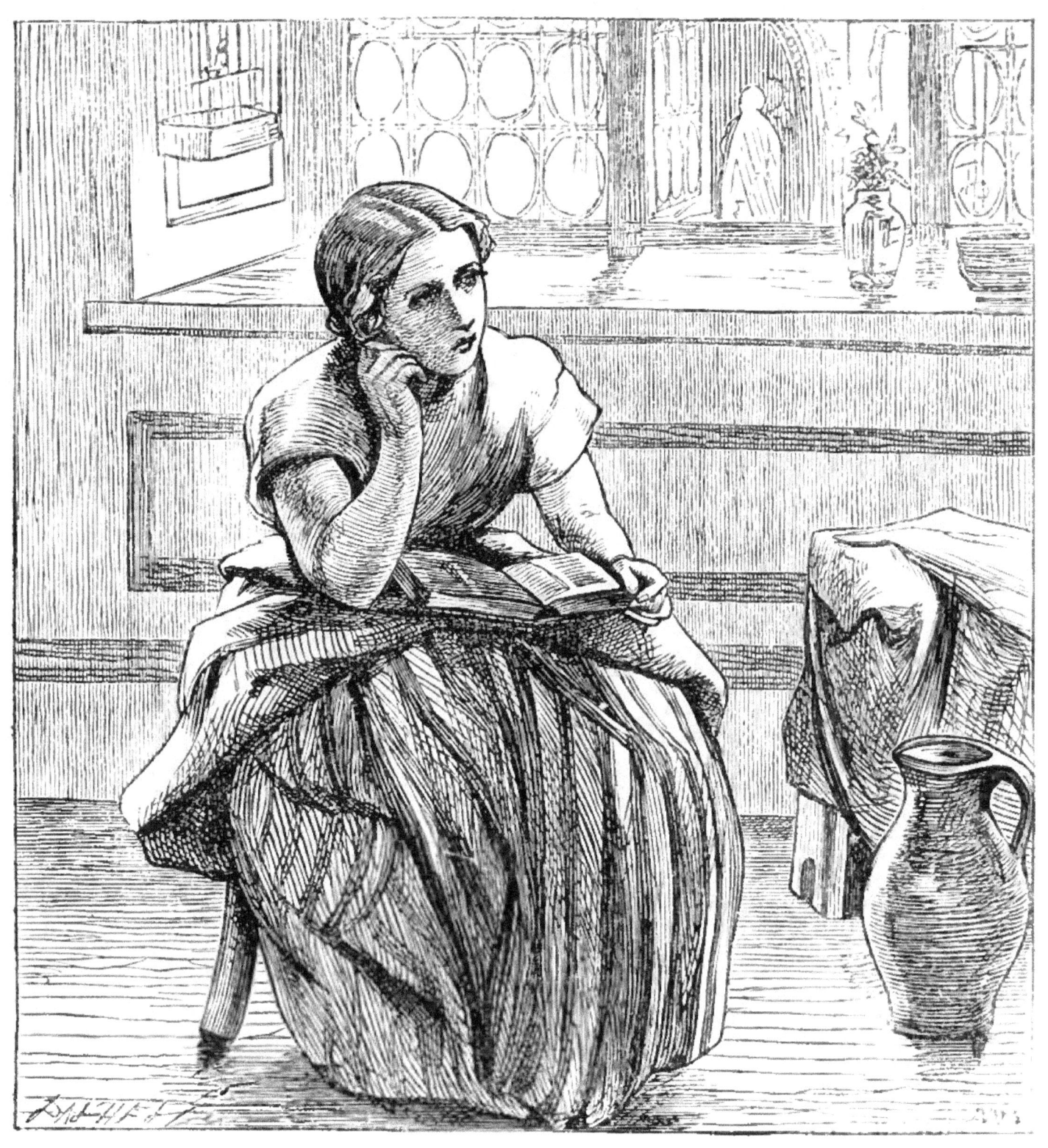

SARA LISTENING TO THE SINGING IN THE CHURCH.

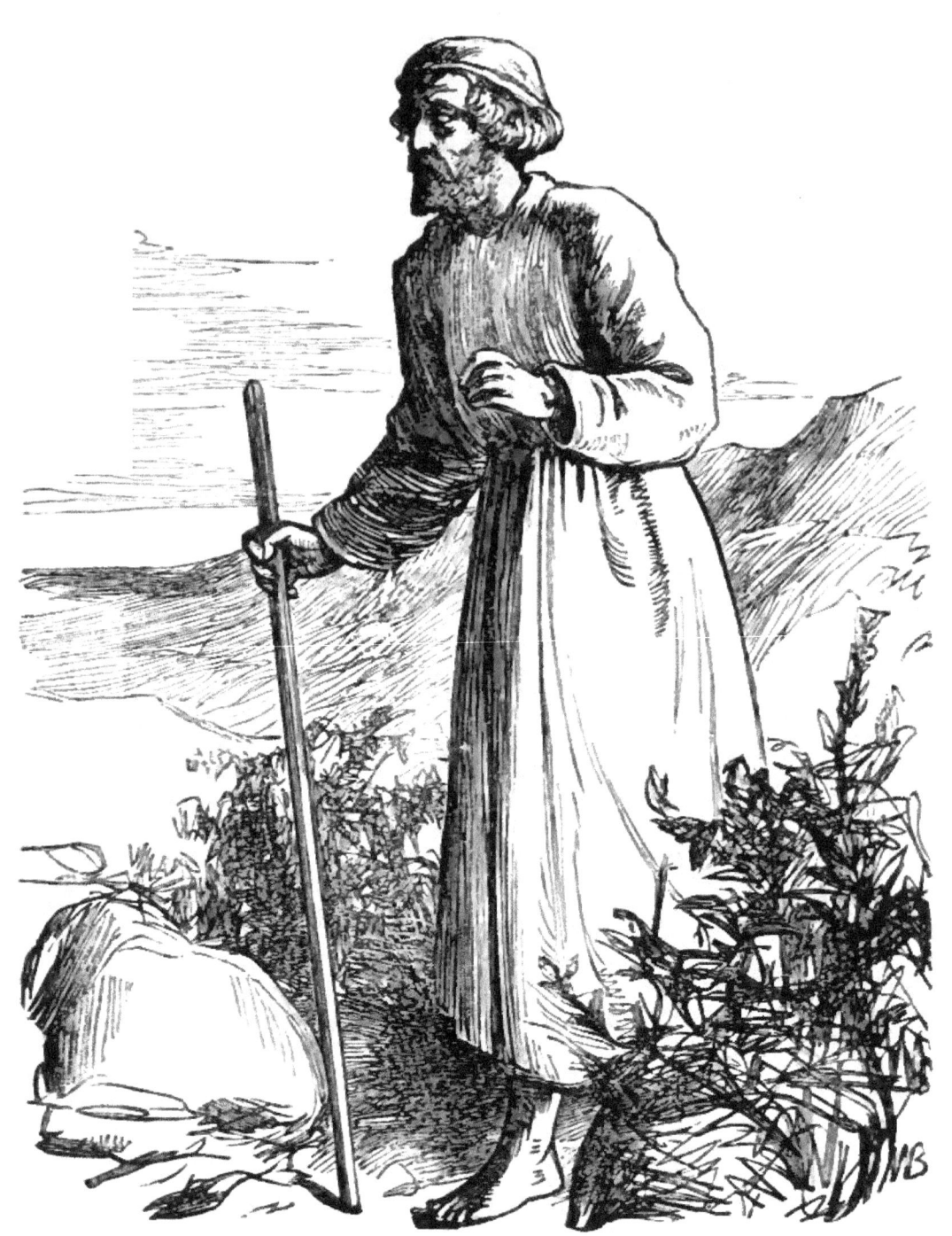

**THE KING OF POETS.**

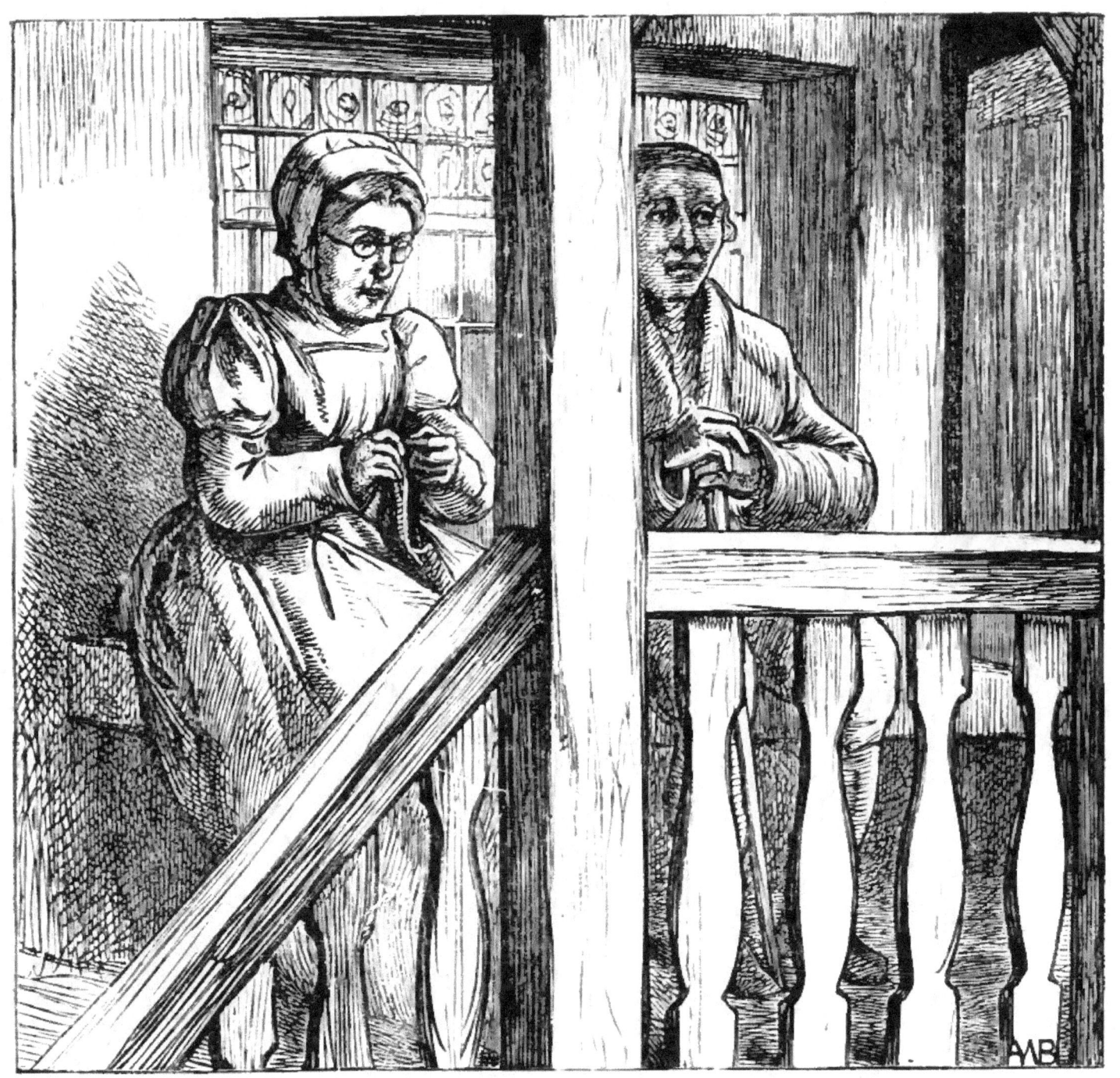

PREBEN SCHWANE AND HIS WIFE MARTHA.

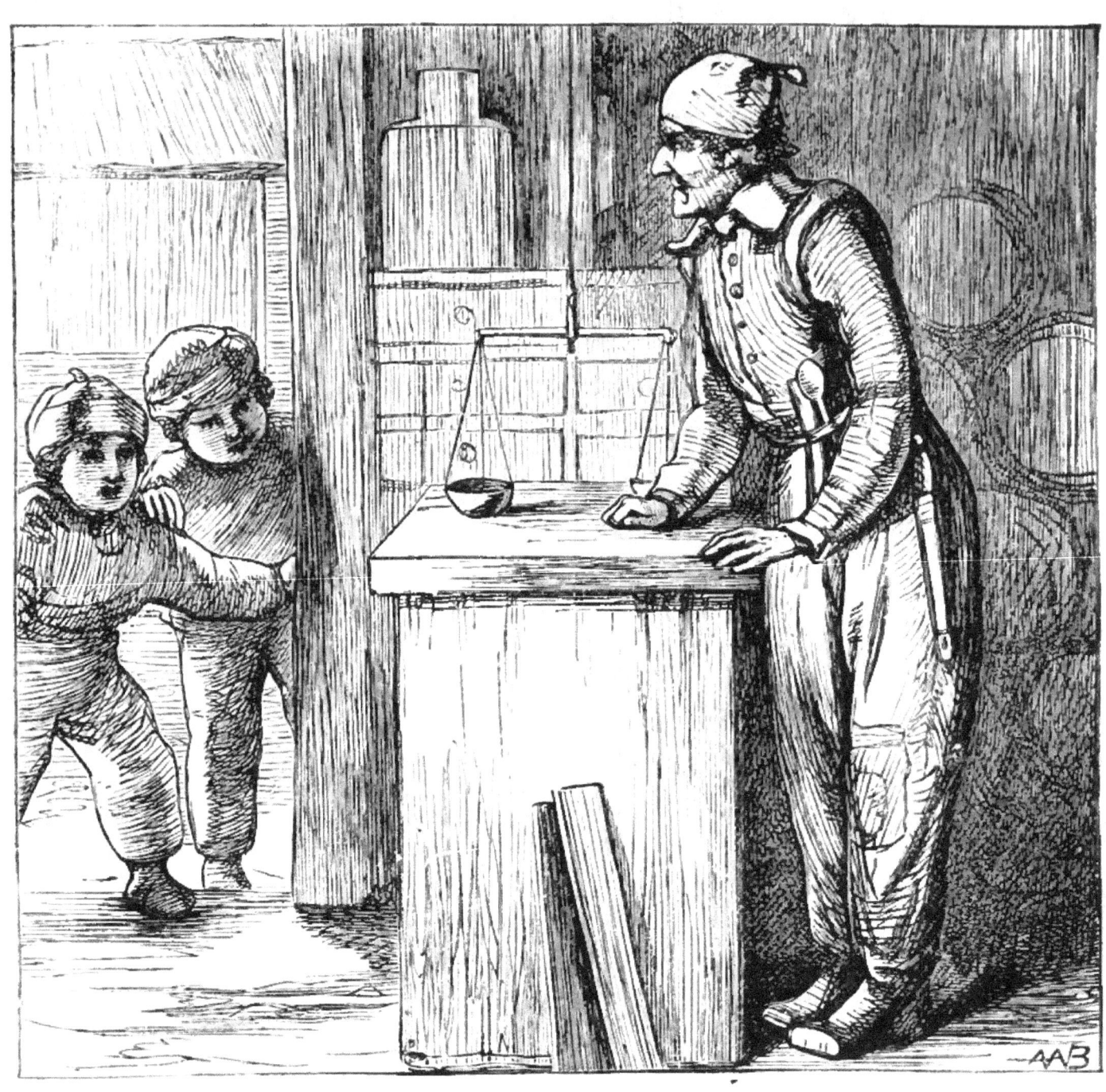

THE PEPPERER'S BOOTH.

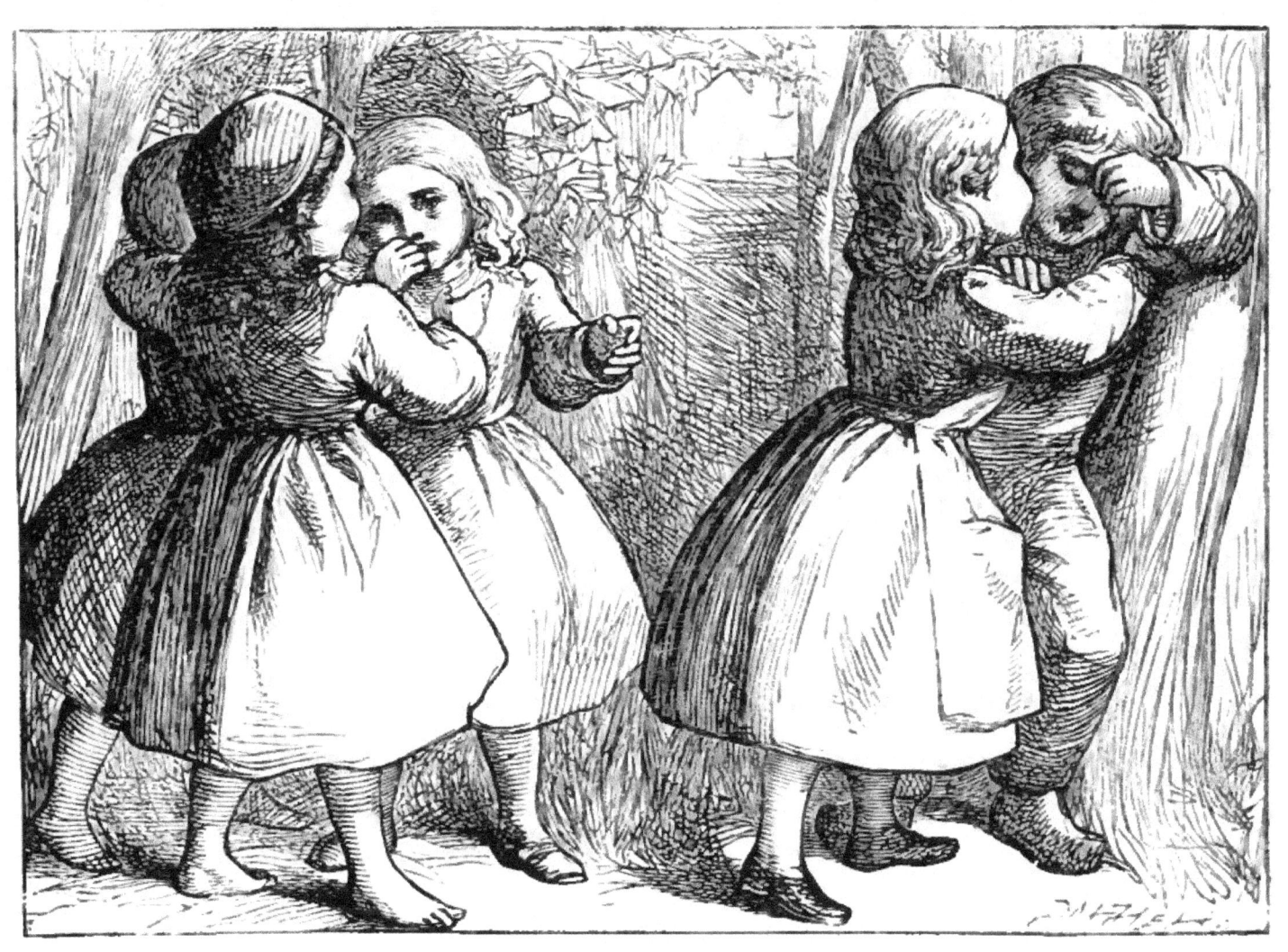

IMPERTINENT MOLLY.

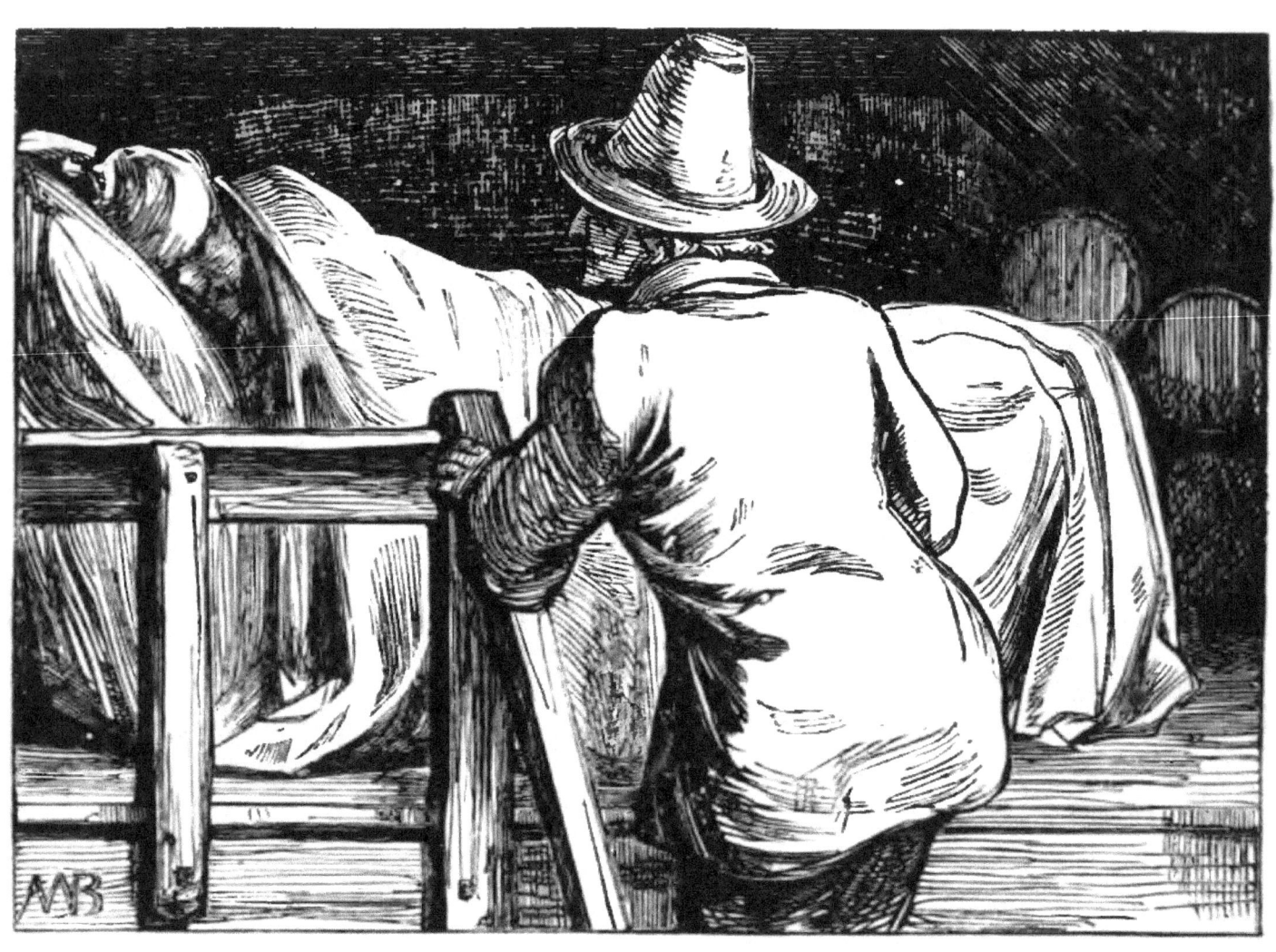

THE OPPOSITE NEIGHBOUR LOOKS AFTER OLD ANTHONY.

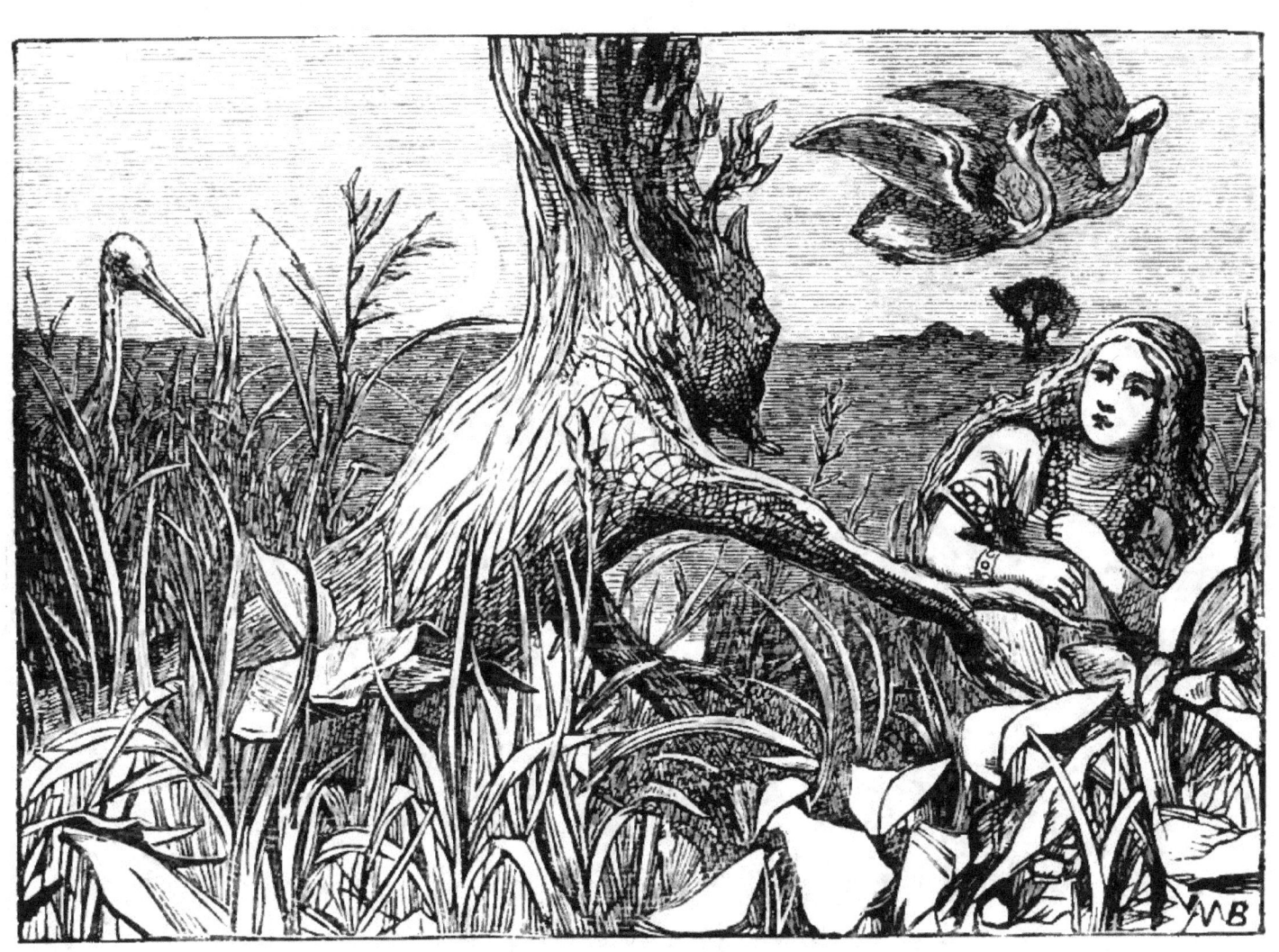

THE PRINCESS LEFT IN THE MARSH.

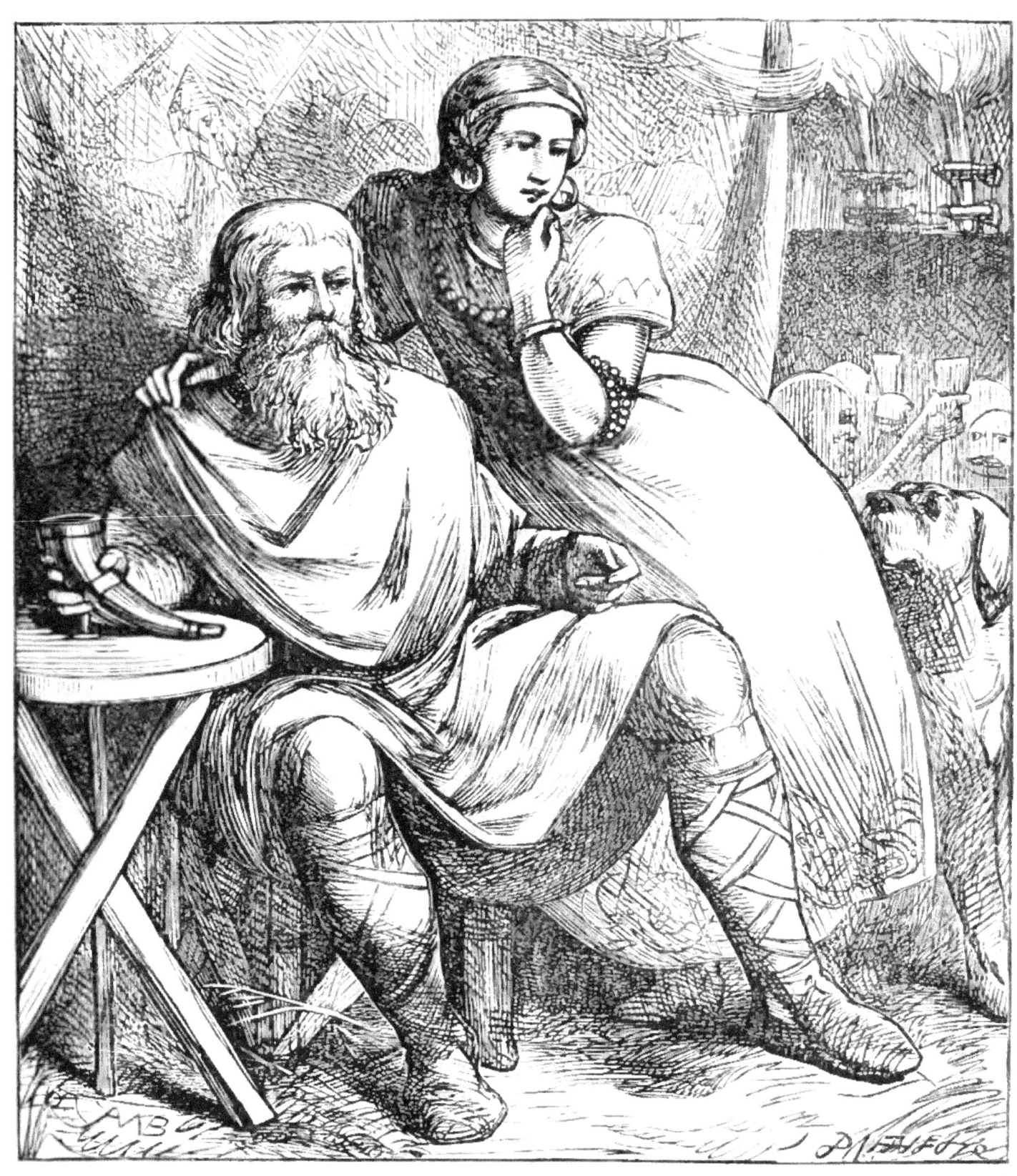

THE VIKING'S FEAST.

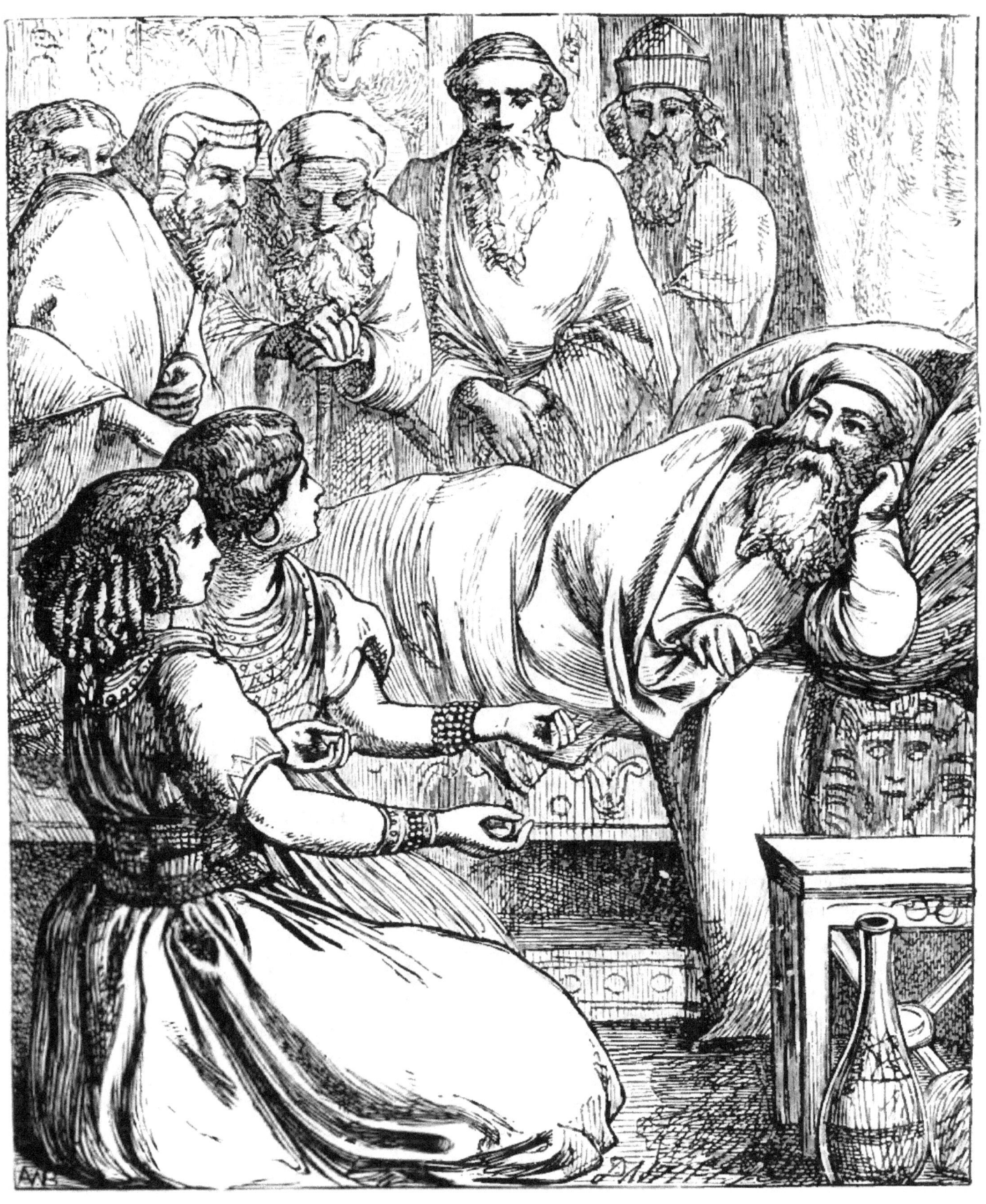

THE KING OF EGYPT DECEIVED BY THE PRINCESSES.

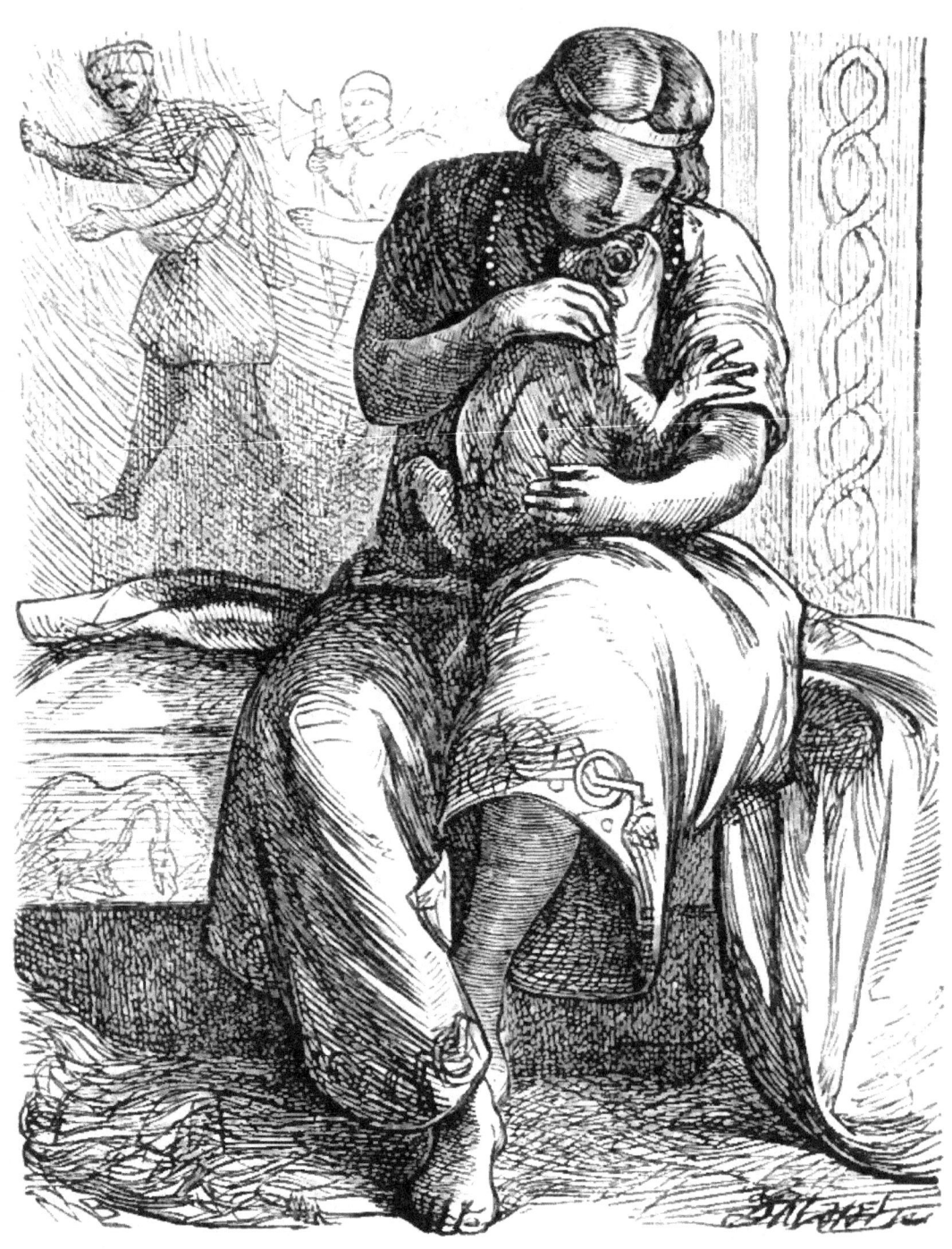

THE TRANSFORMED PRINCESS.

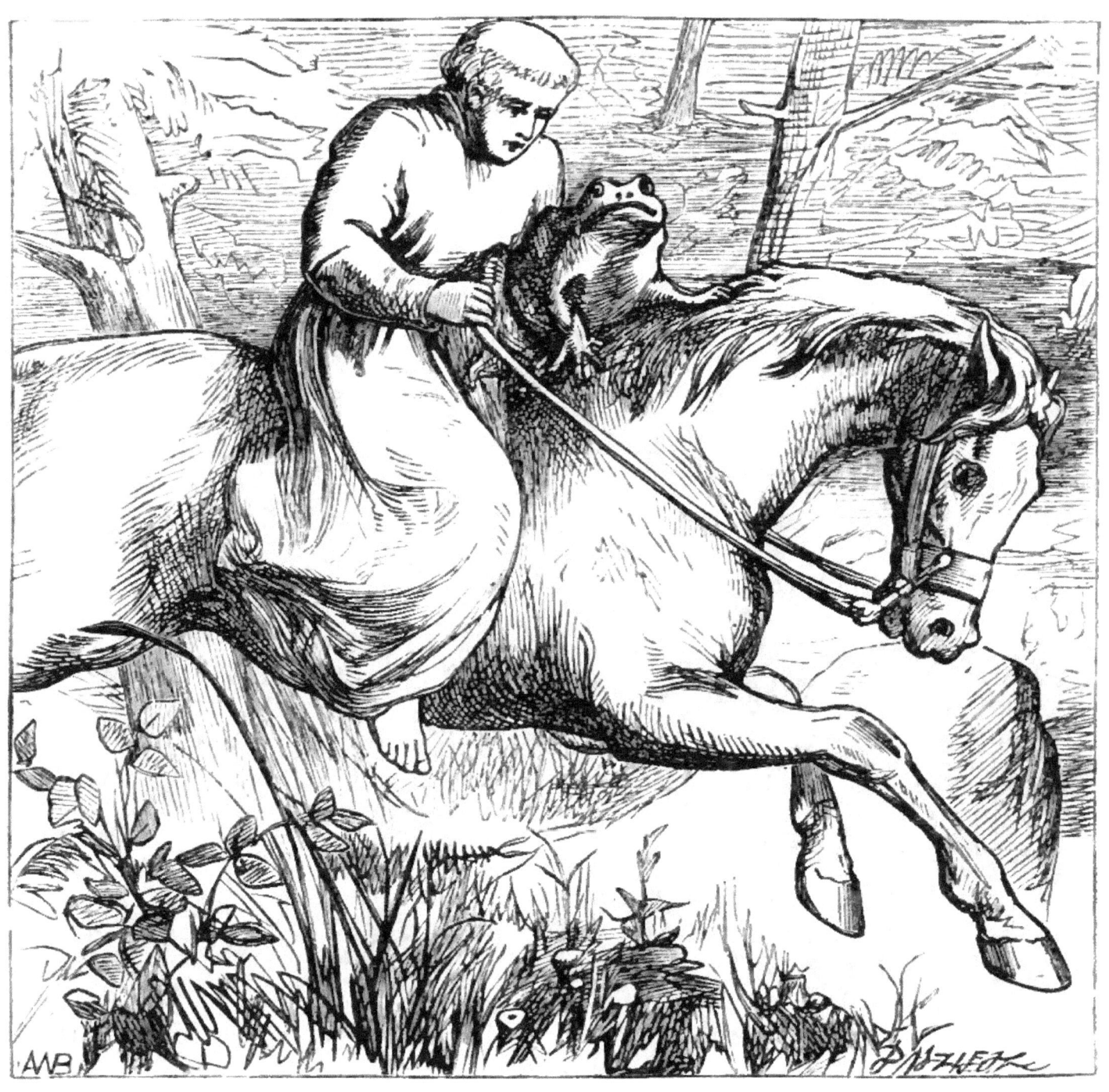

THE FLIGHT.

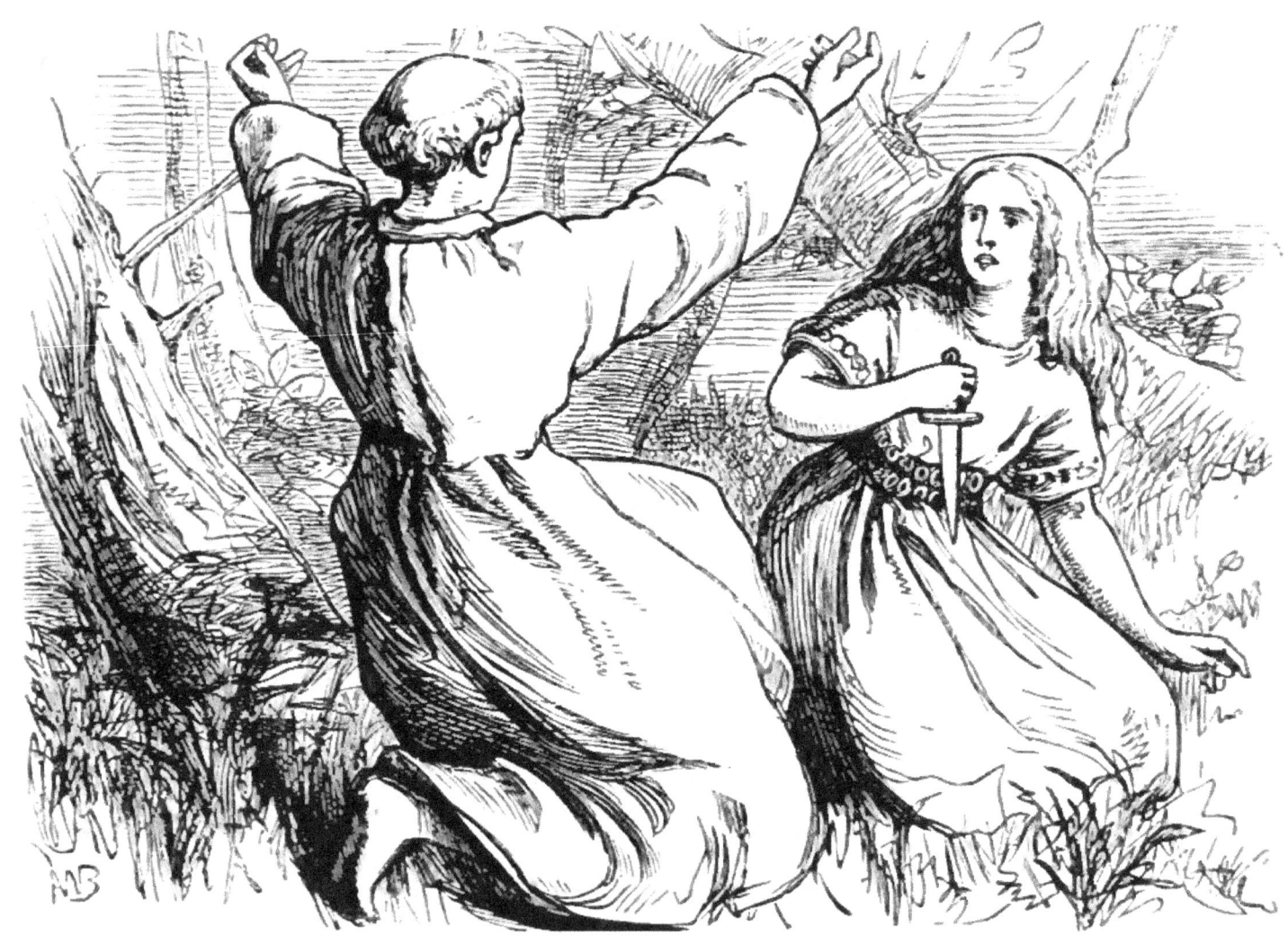

THE CHRISTIAN PRIEST'S SPELL.

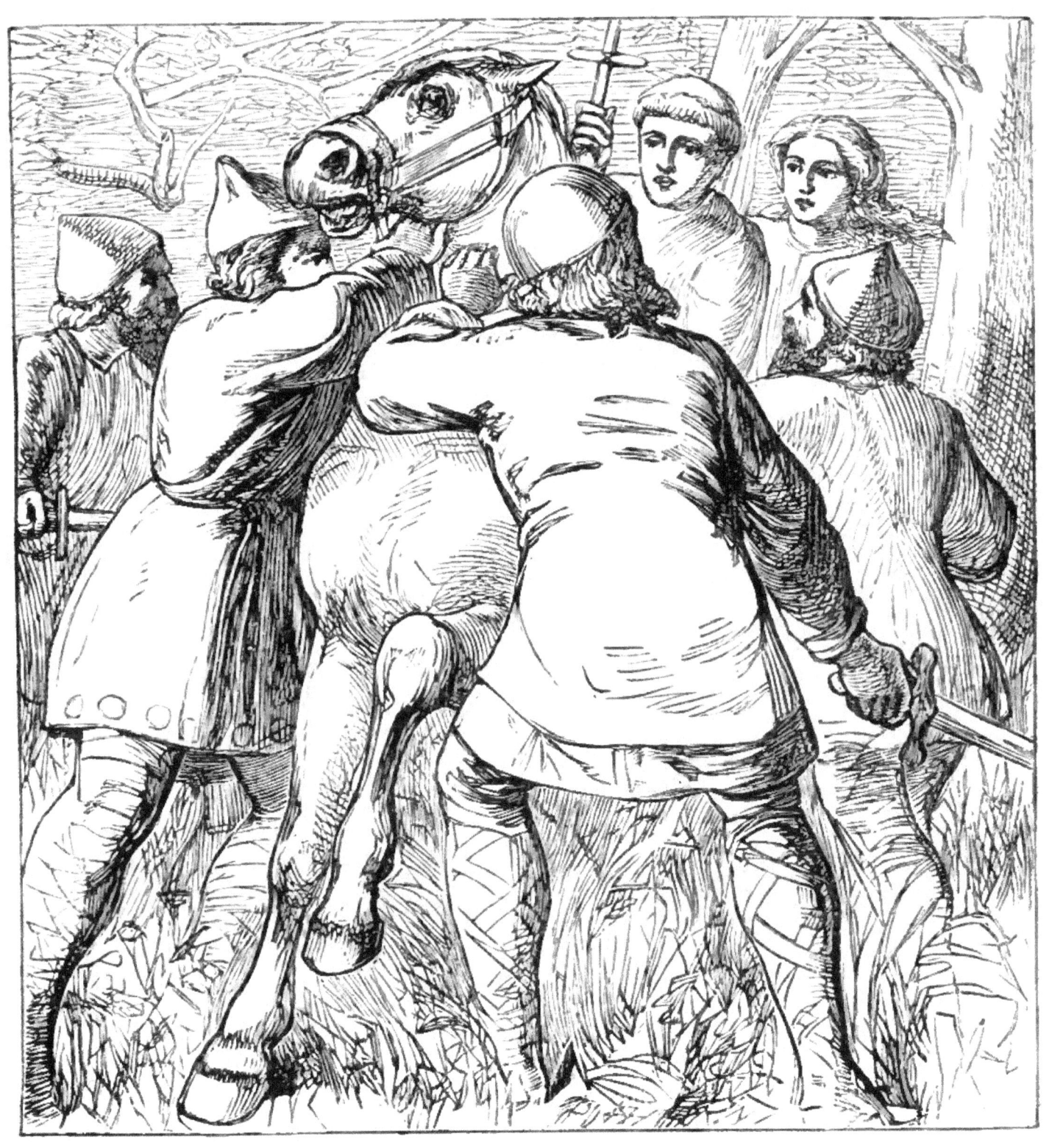

HELGA AND THE PRIEST ATTACKED BY ROBBERS.

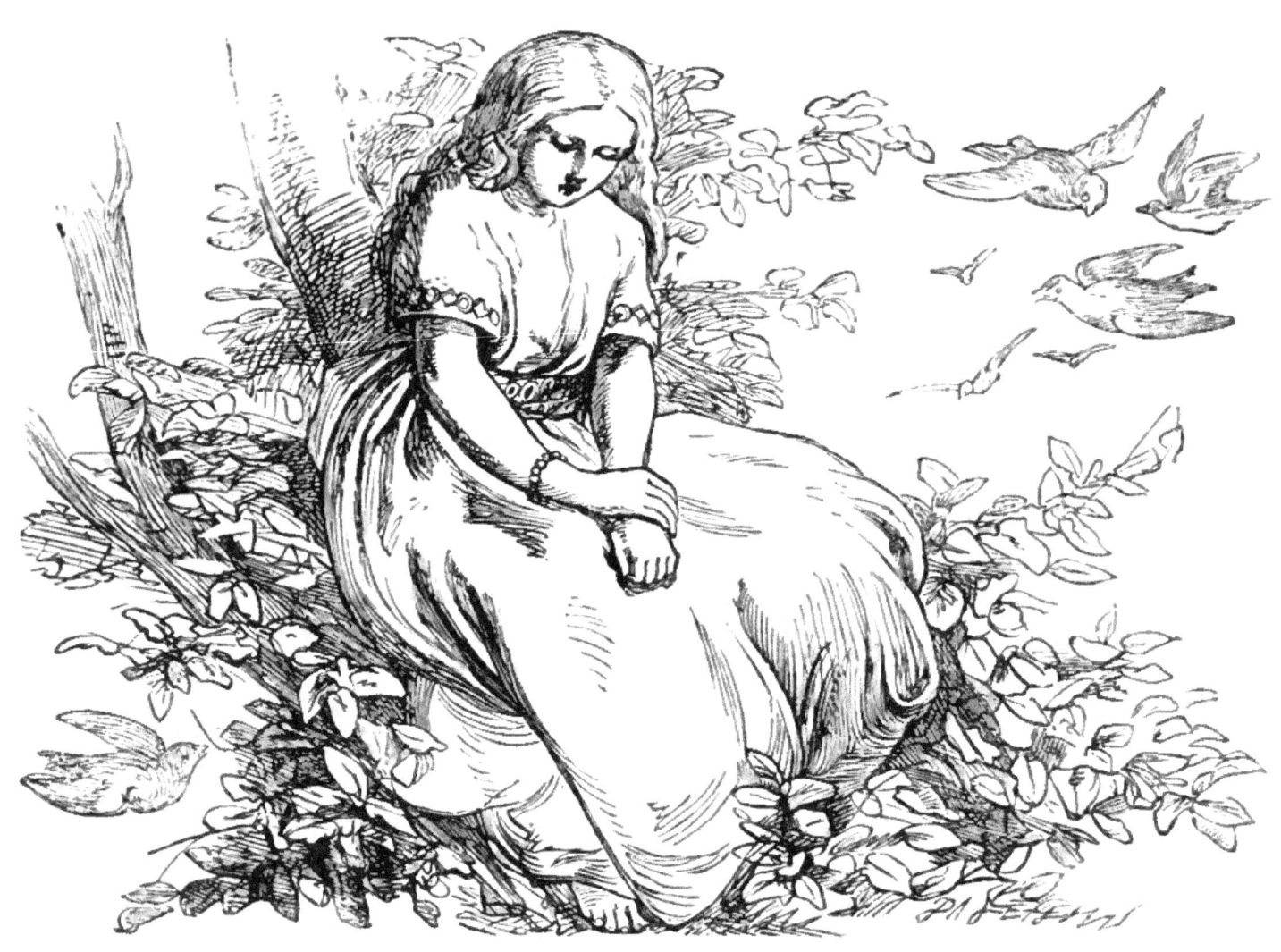

HELGA IN THE TREE.

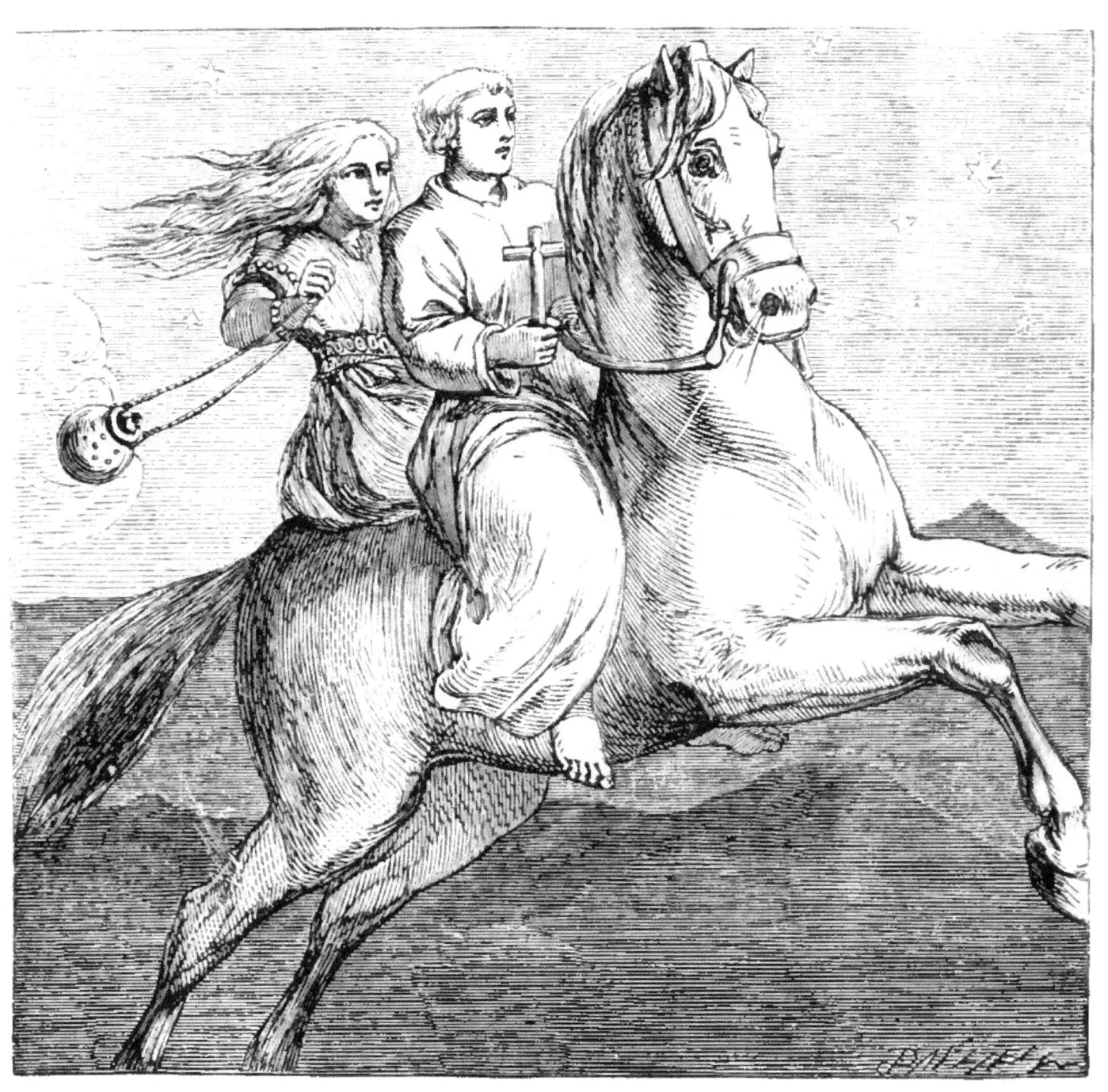

HELGA IS TAKEN BACK TO THE MARSH.

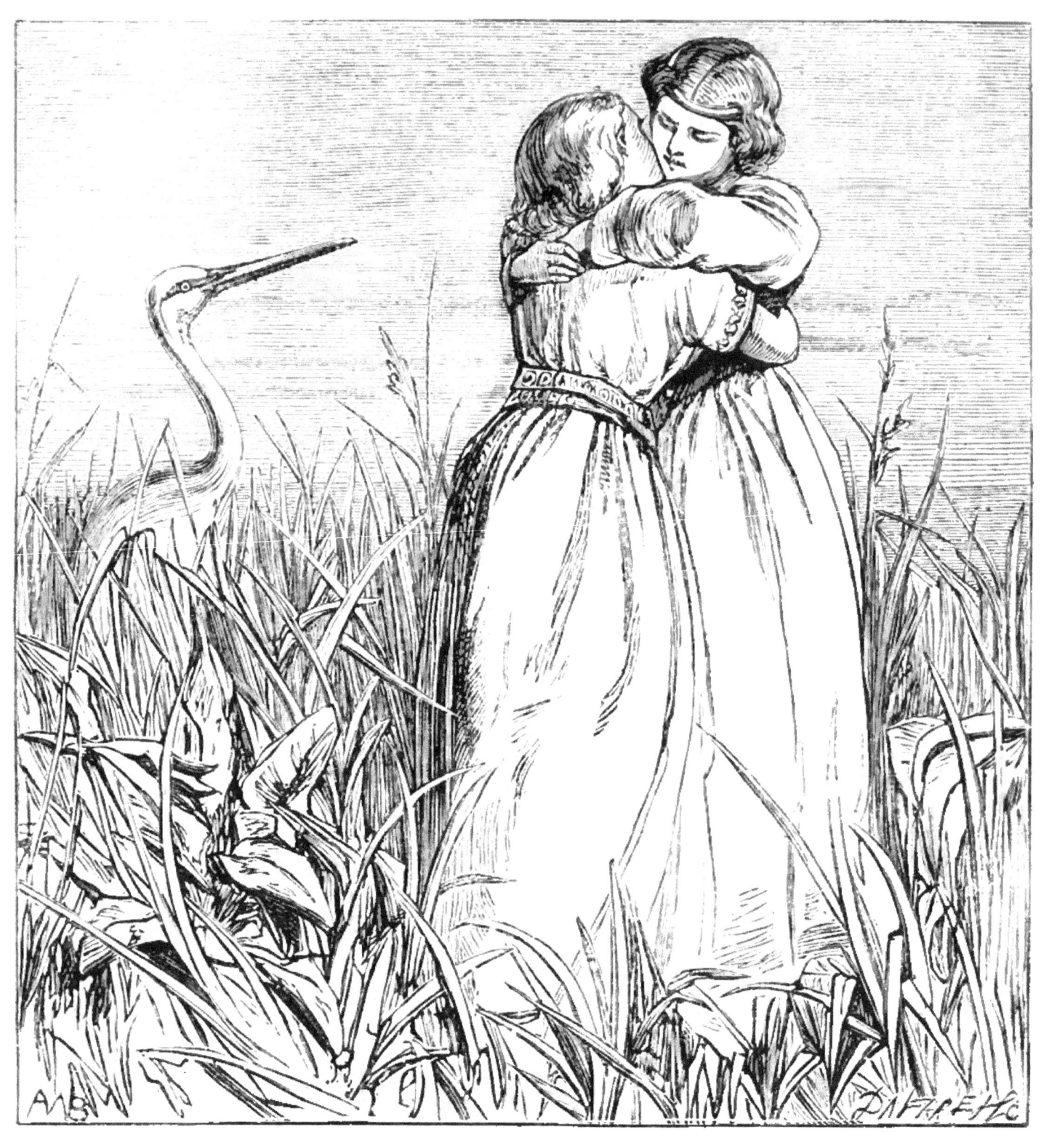

HELGA MEETS WITH HER MOTHER IN THE MARSH.

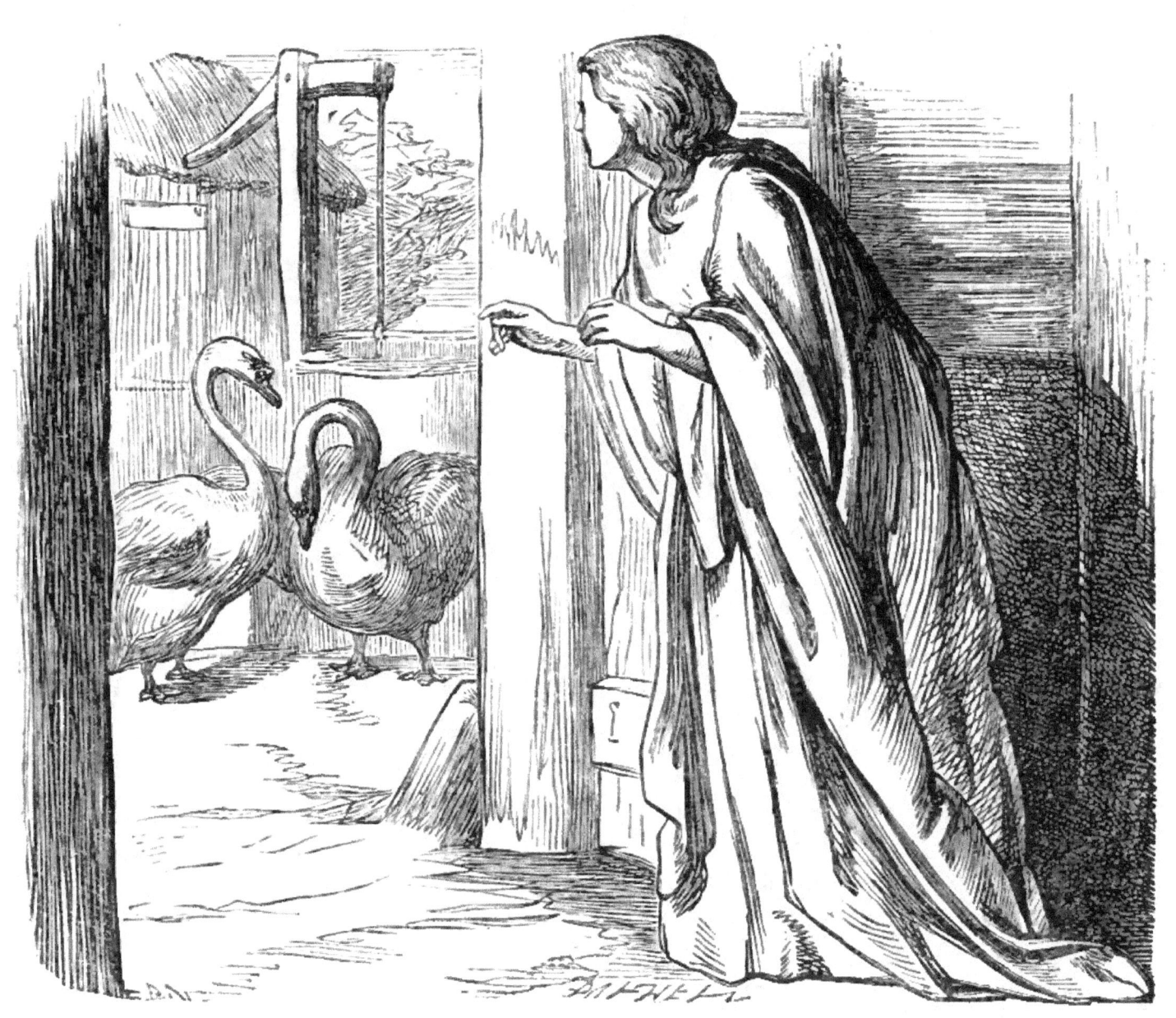

THE DISGUISED PRINCESSES BID FAREWELL TO THE VIKING WOMAN.

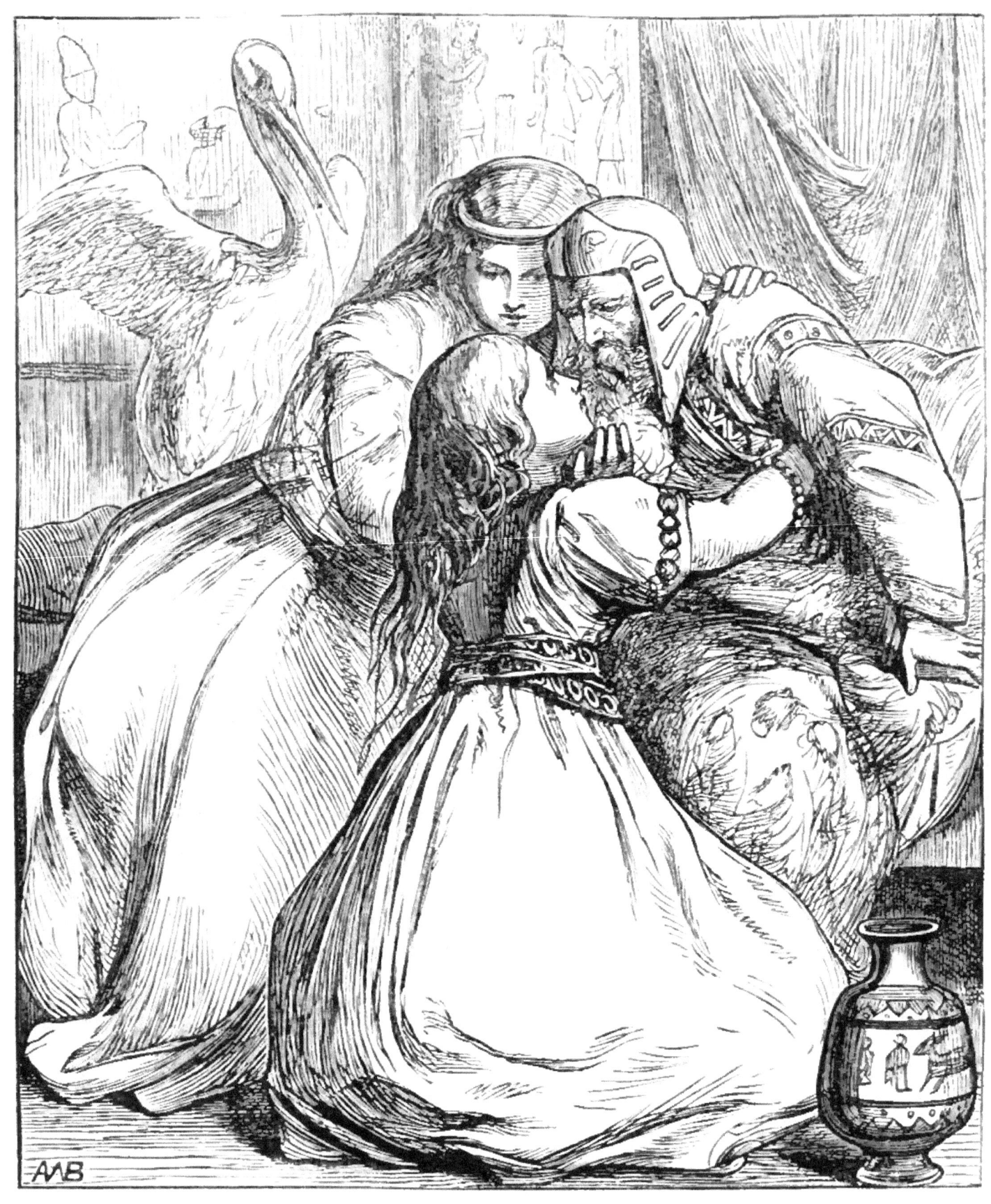

THE KING OF EGYPT'S RECOVERY.

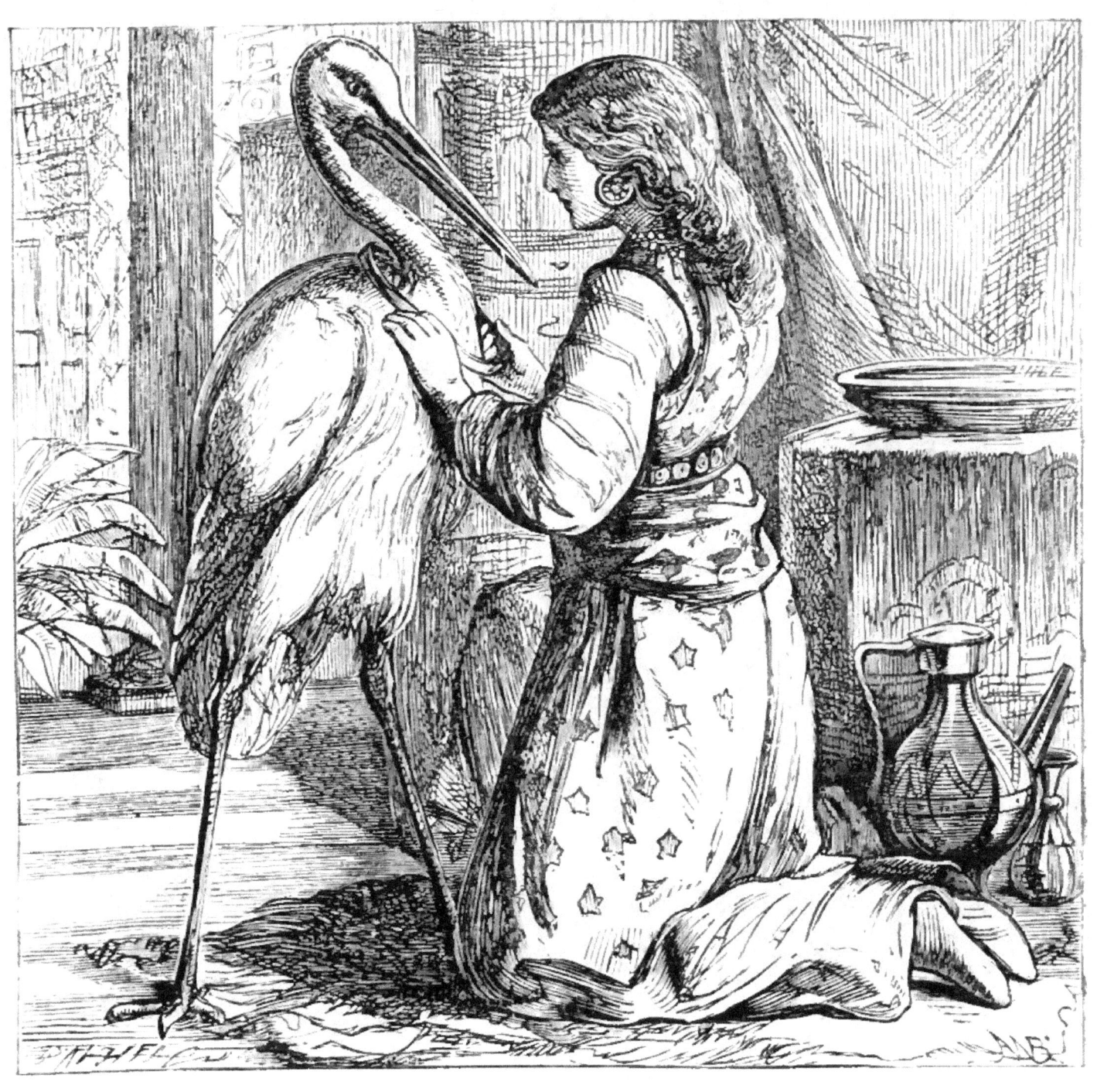

A MESSAGE TO THE VIKING WOMAN.

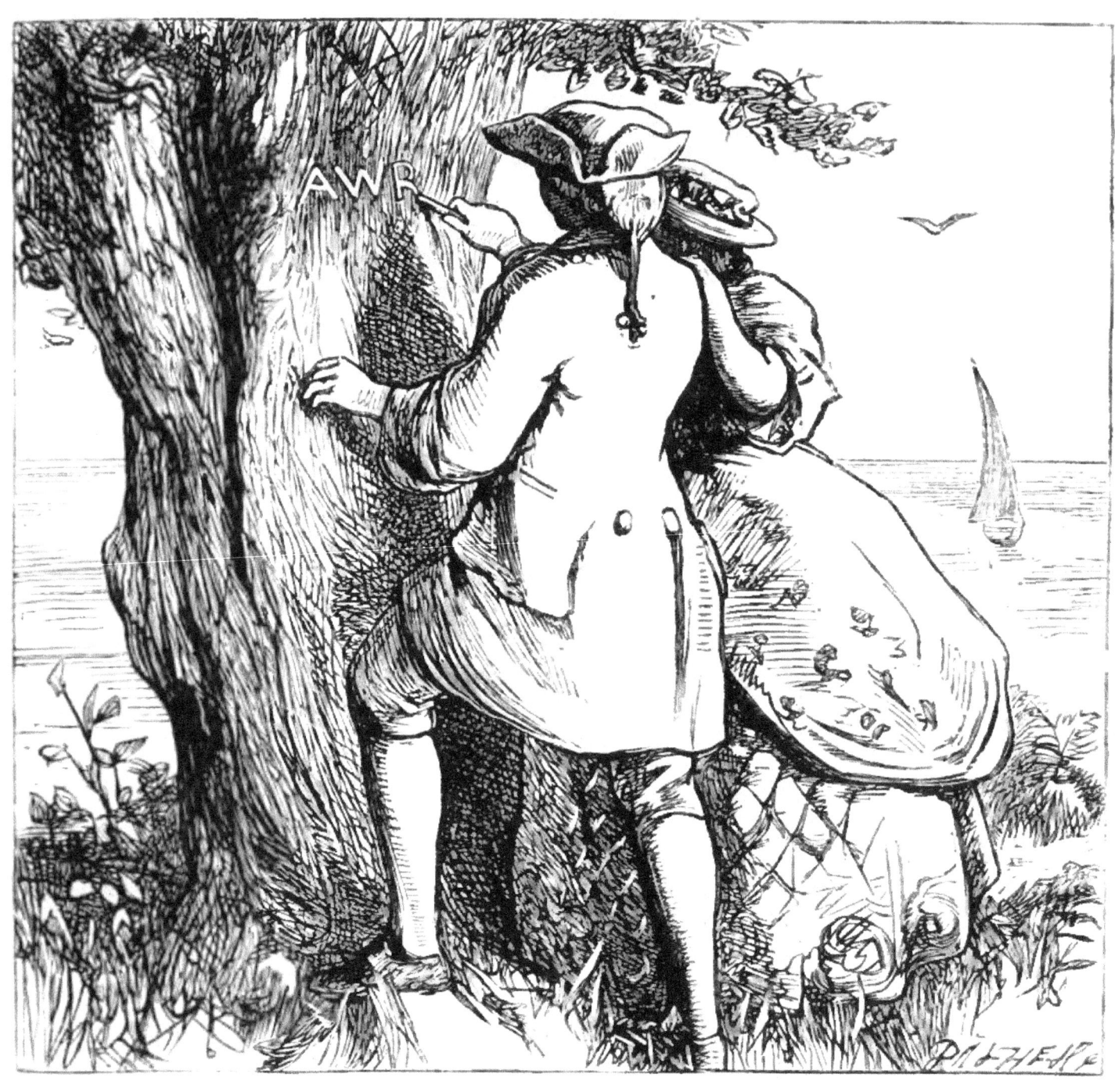

THE LOVERS AT THE OLD OAK TREE.

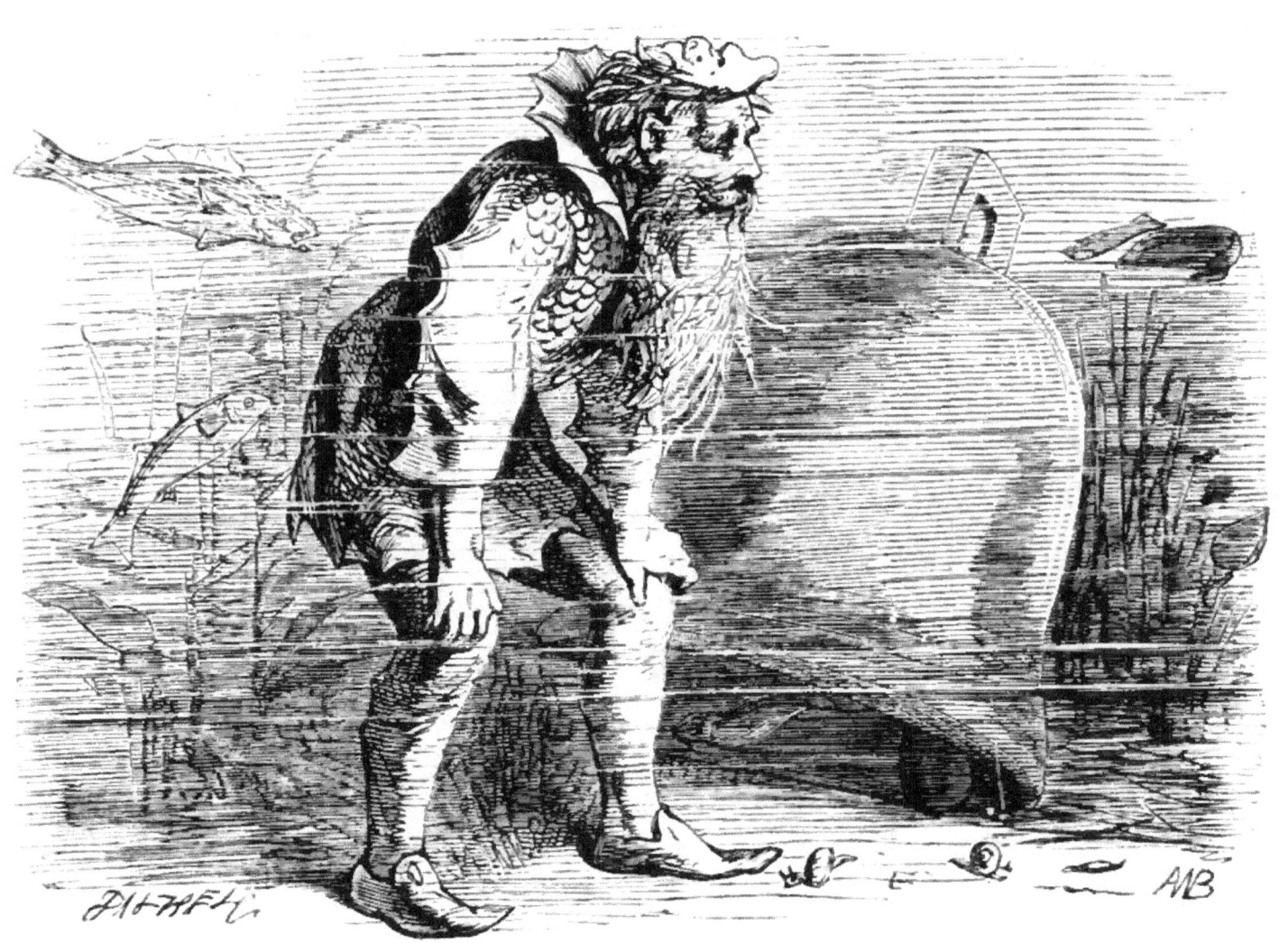

THE AU-MANN LISTENING TO THE BELL.

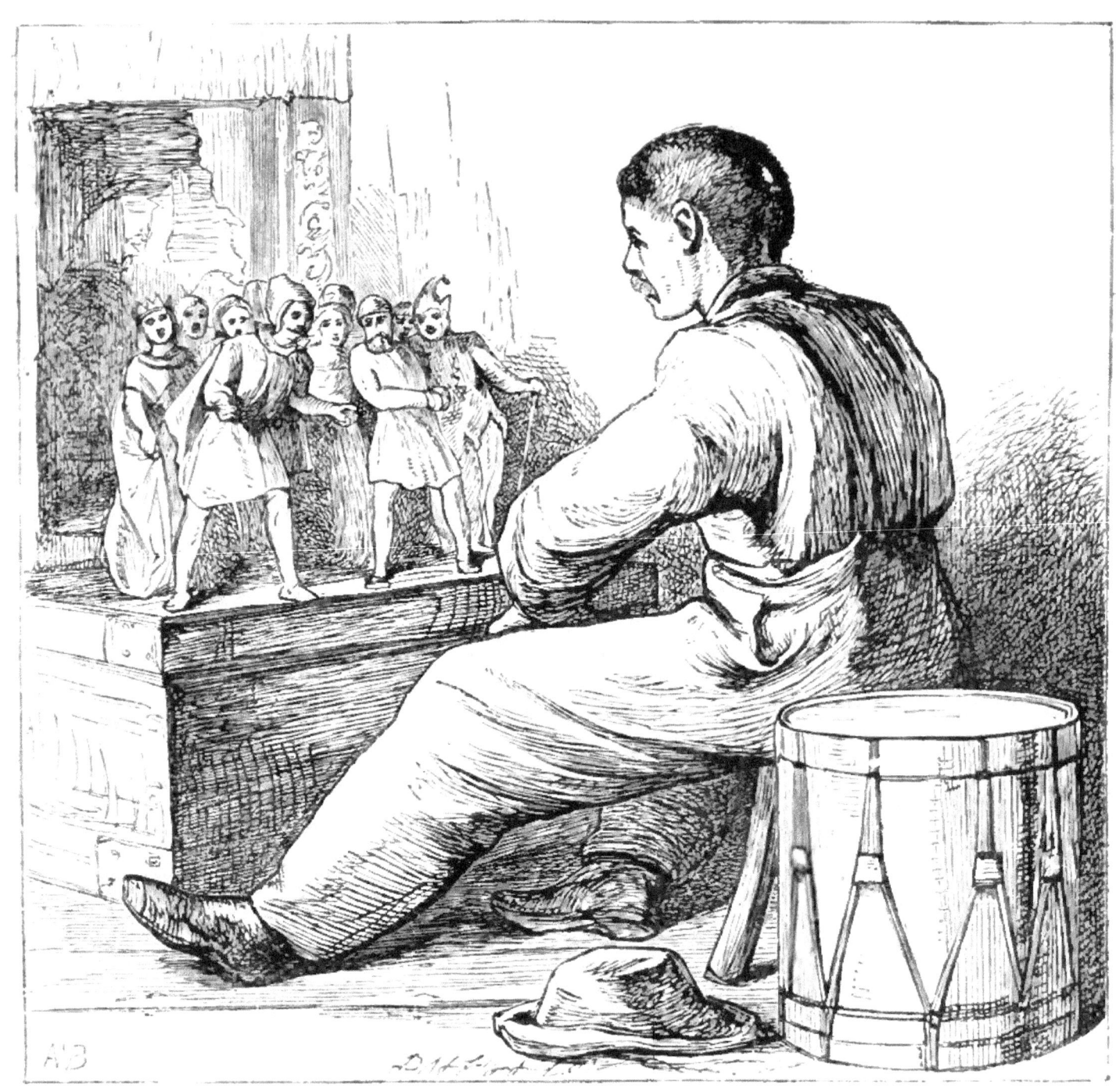

THE ANIMATED PUPPETS.

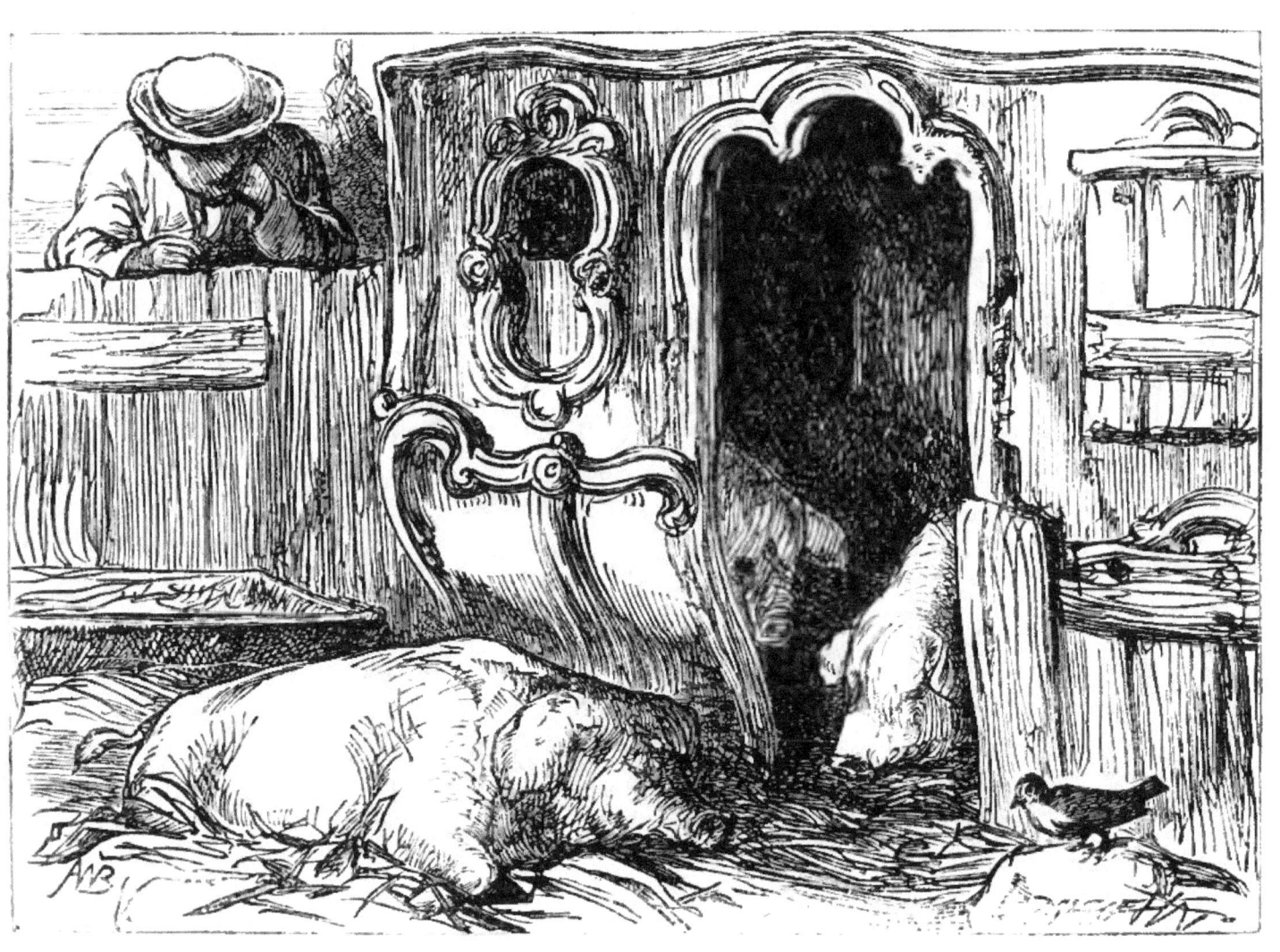

THE PIGS AT HOME IN THE OLD STATE COACH.

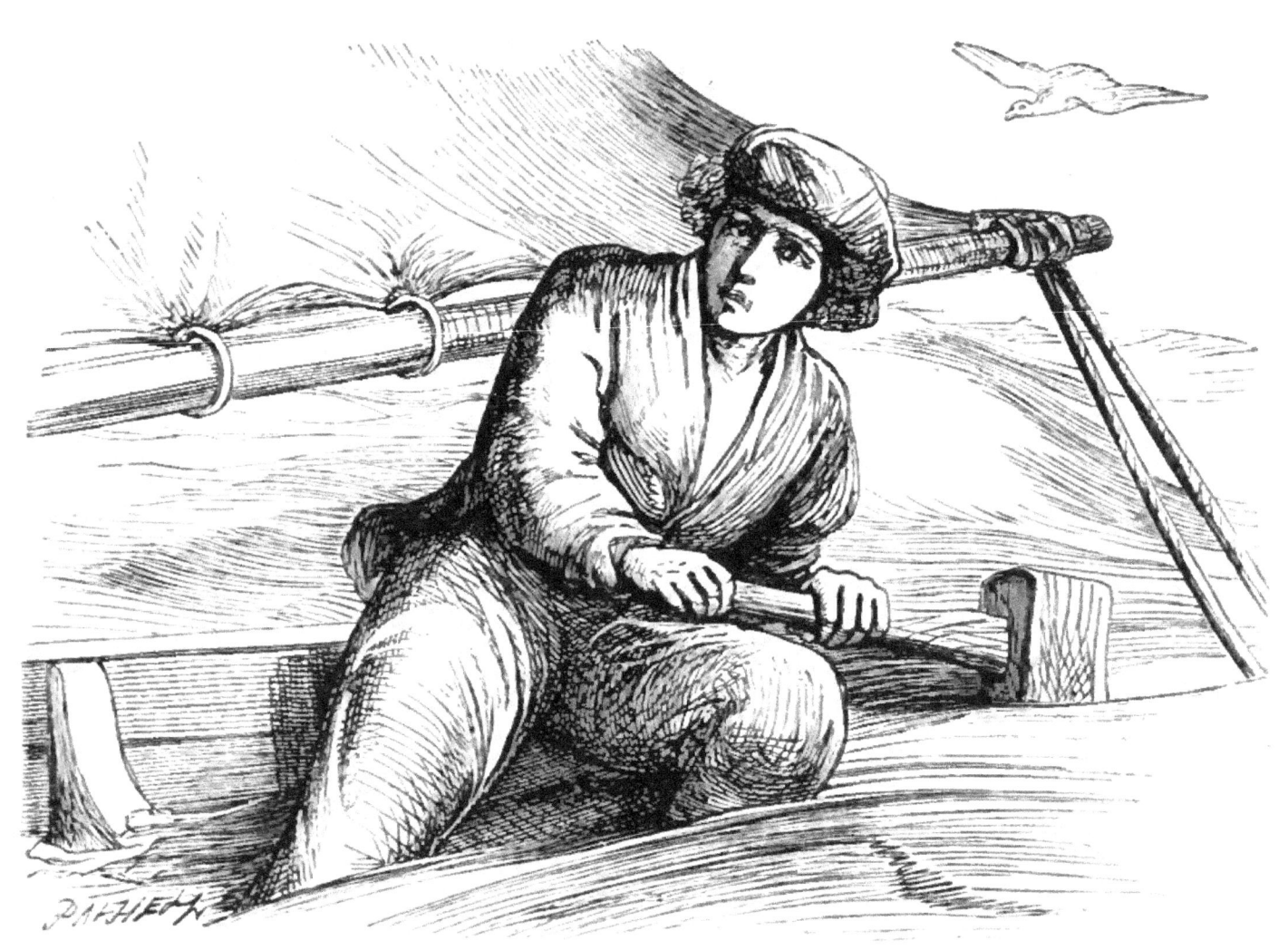

ANNE LISBETH'S BOY.

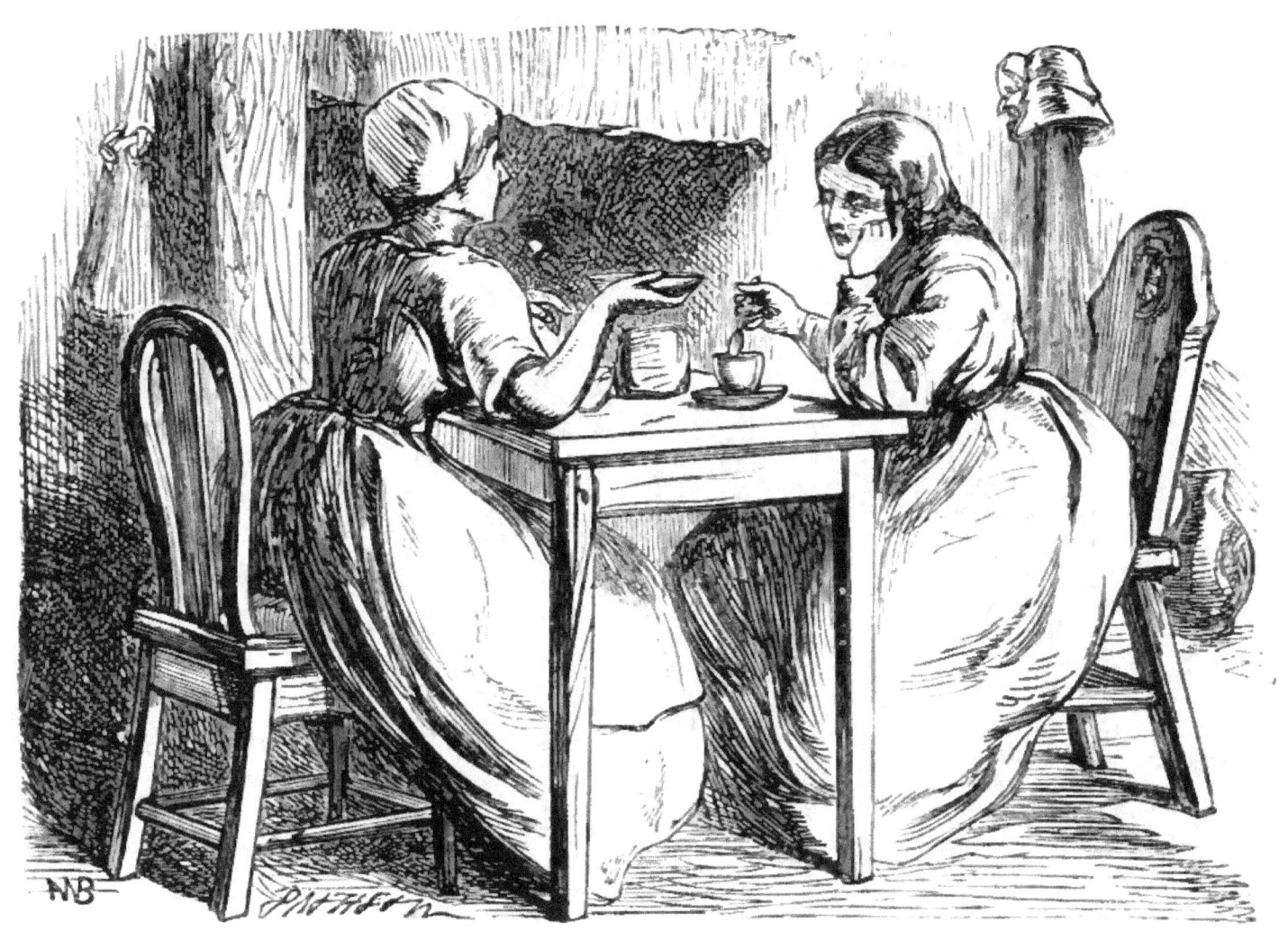

ANNE LISBETH AT THE LABOURER'S COTTAGE.

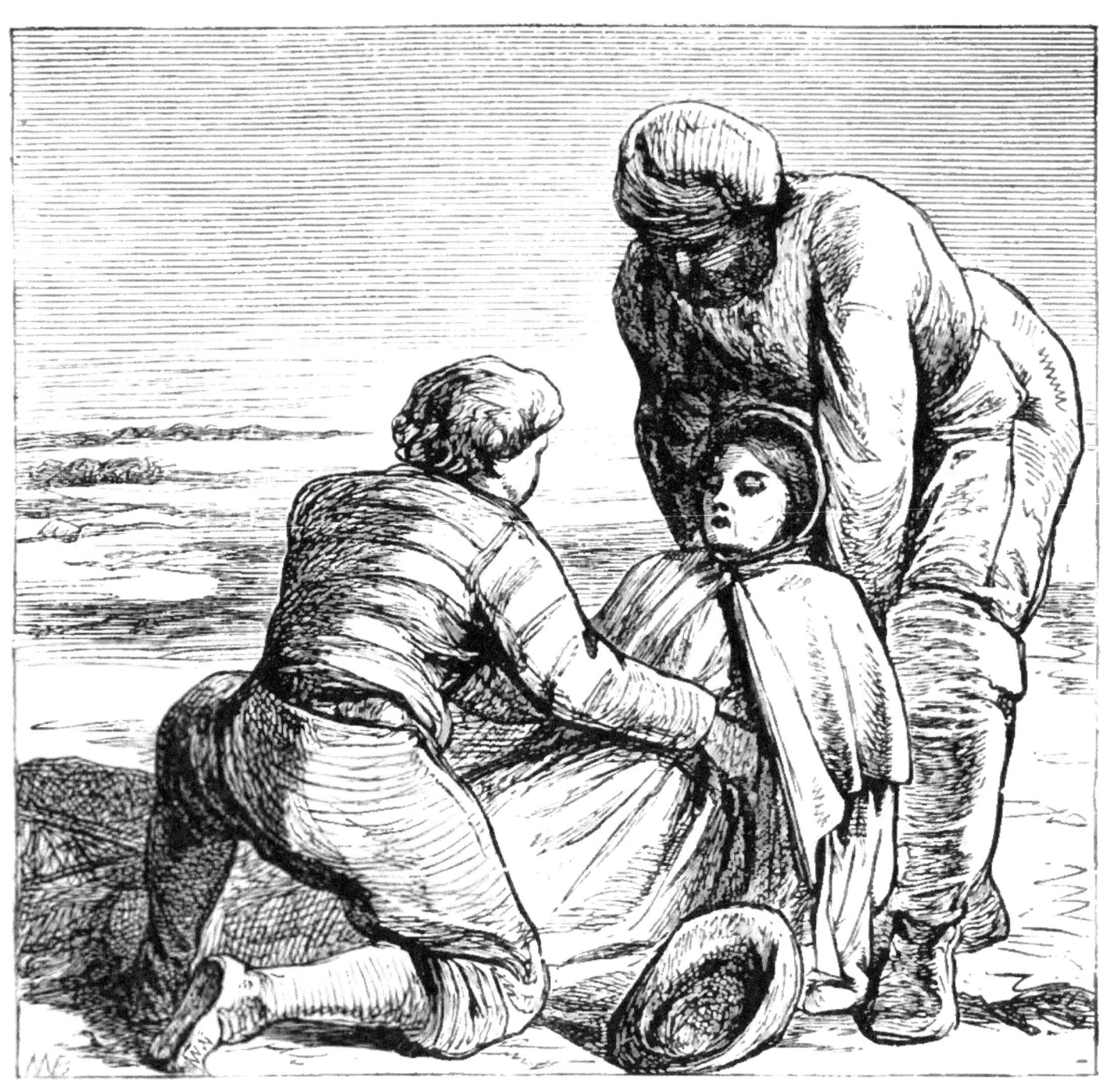

ANNE LISBETH FOUND ON THE SEA SHORE.

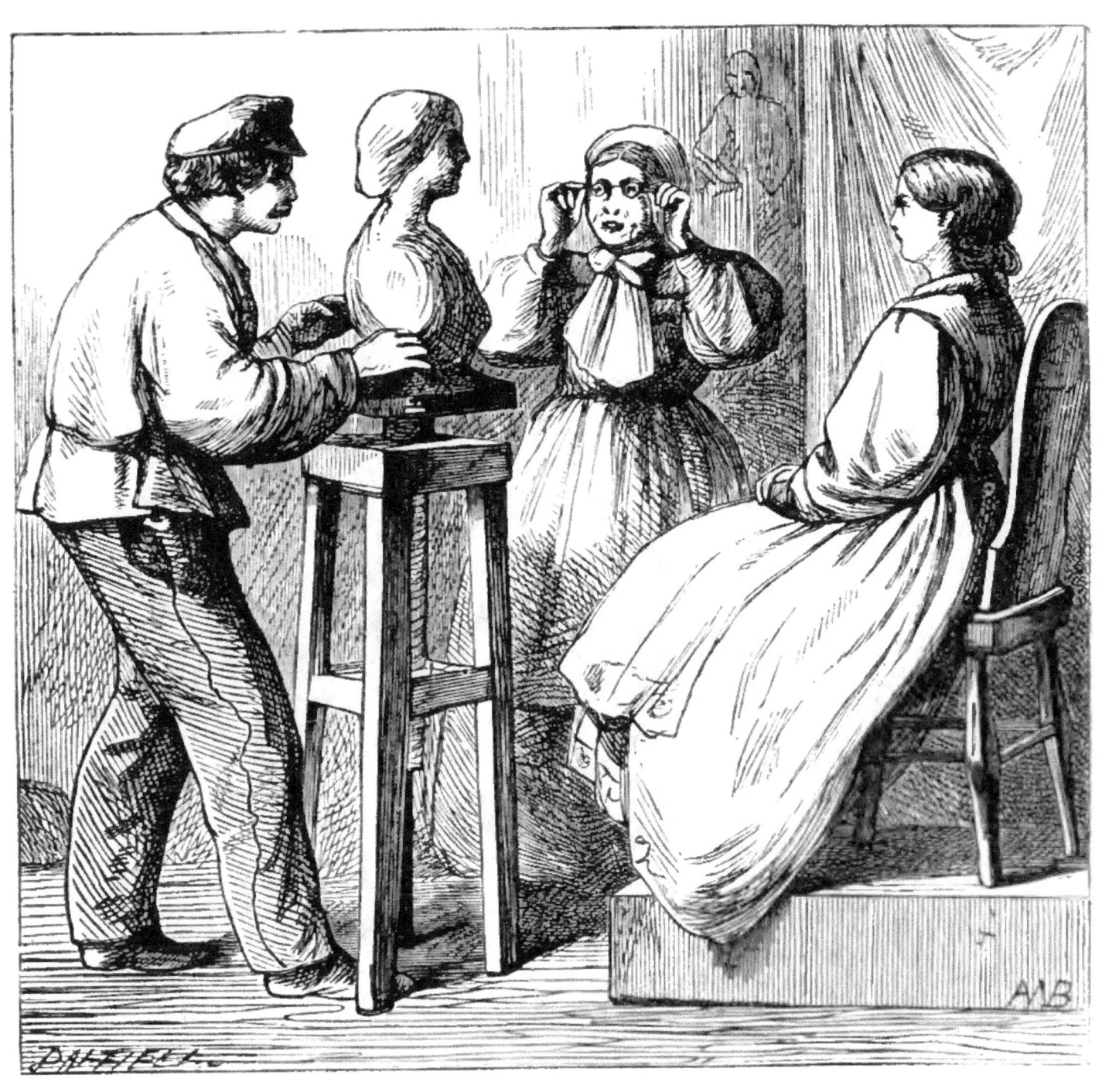

KALA'S BUST.

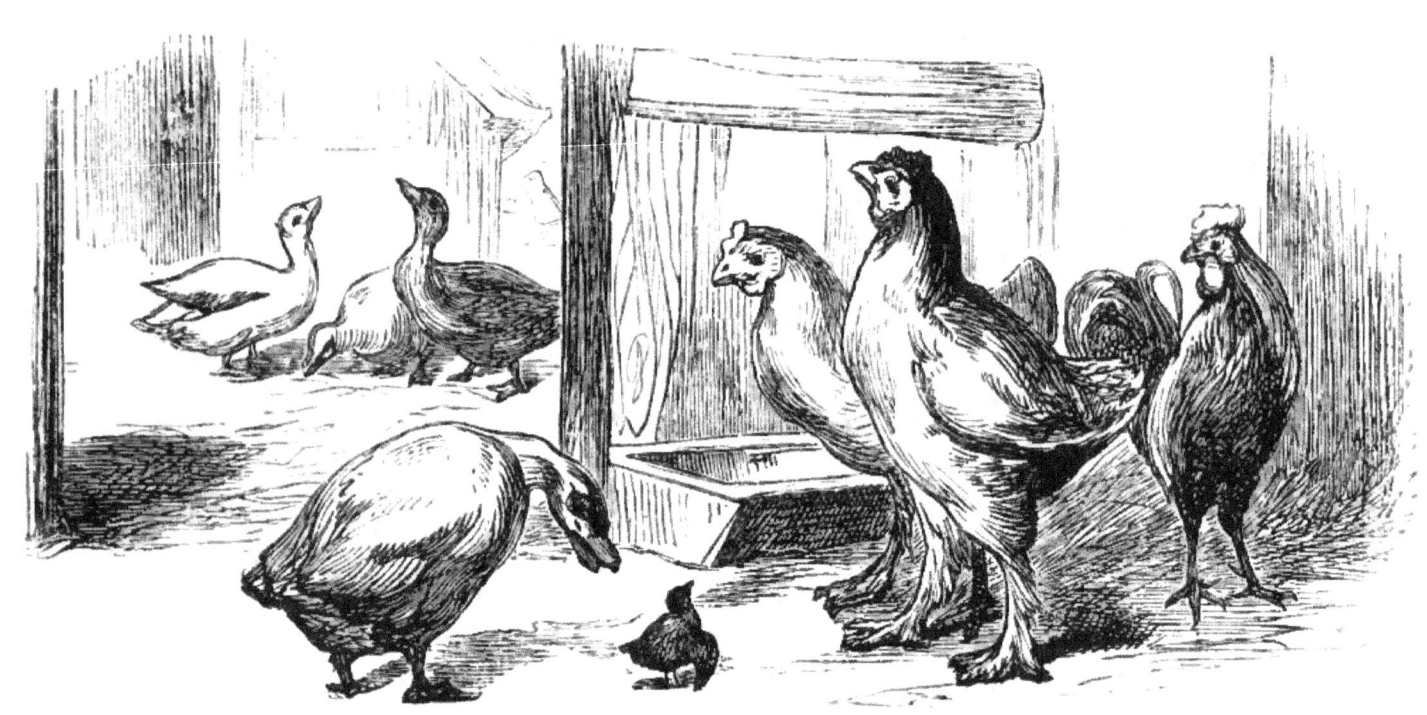

THE LITTLE SINGING BIRD RECEIVES DISTINGUISHED PATRONAGE.

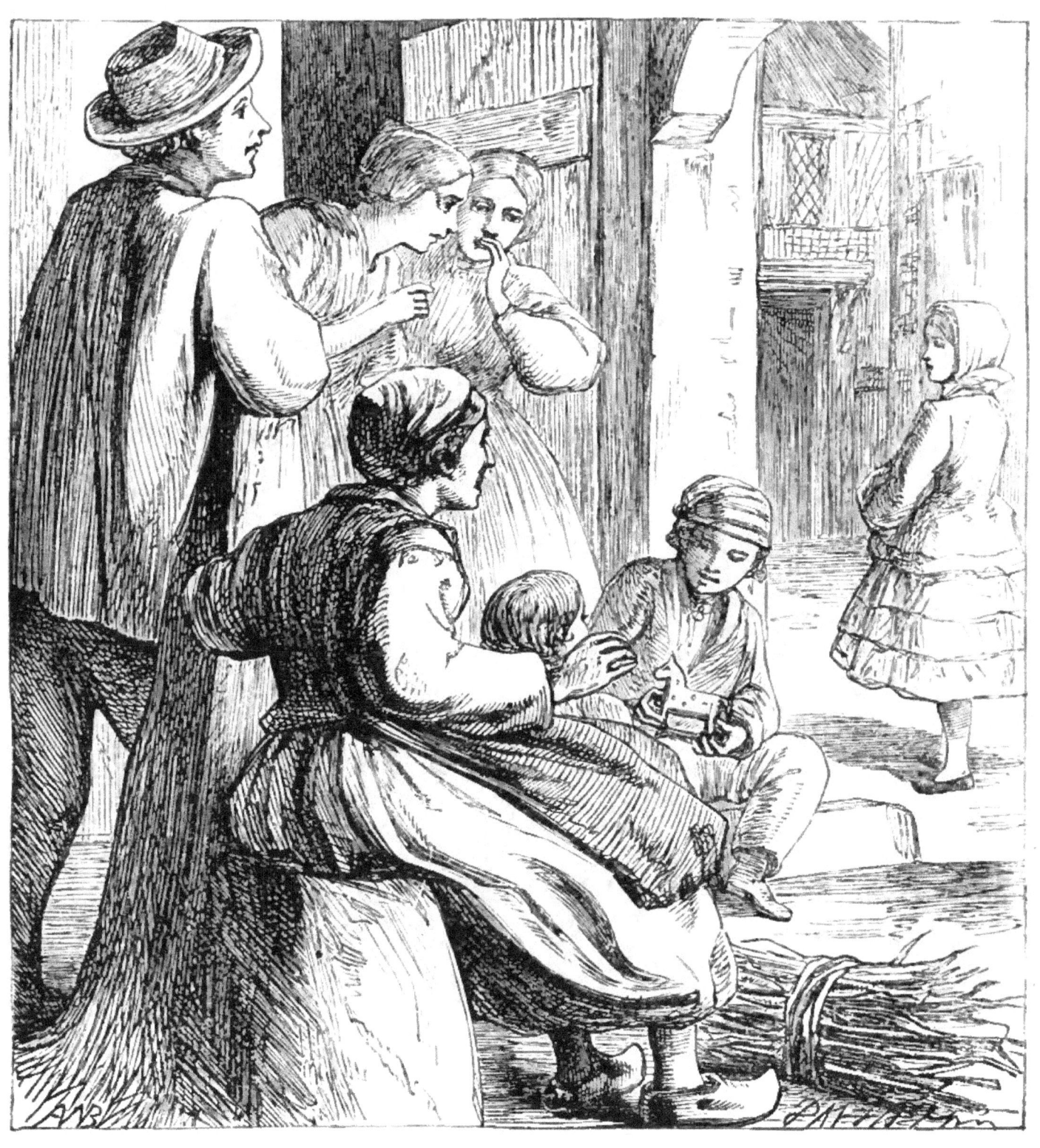

INGÉ TURNS BACK AT THE SIGHT OF HER POOR MOTHER.

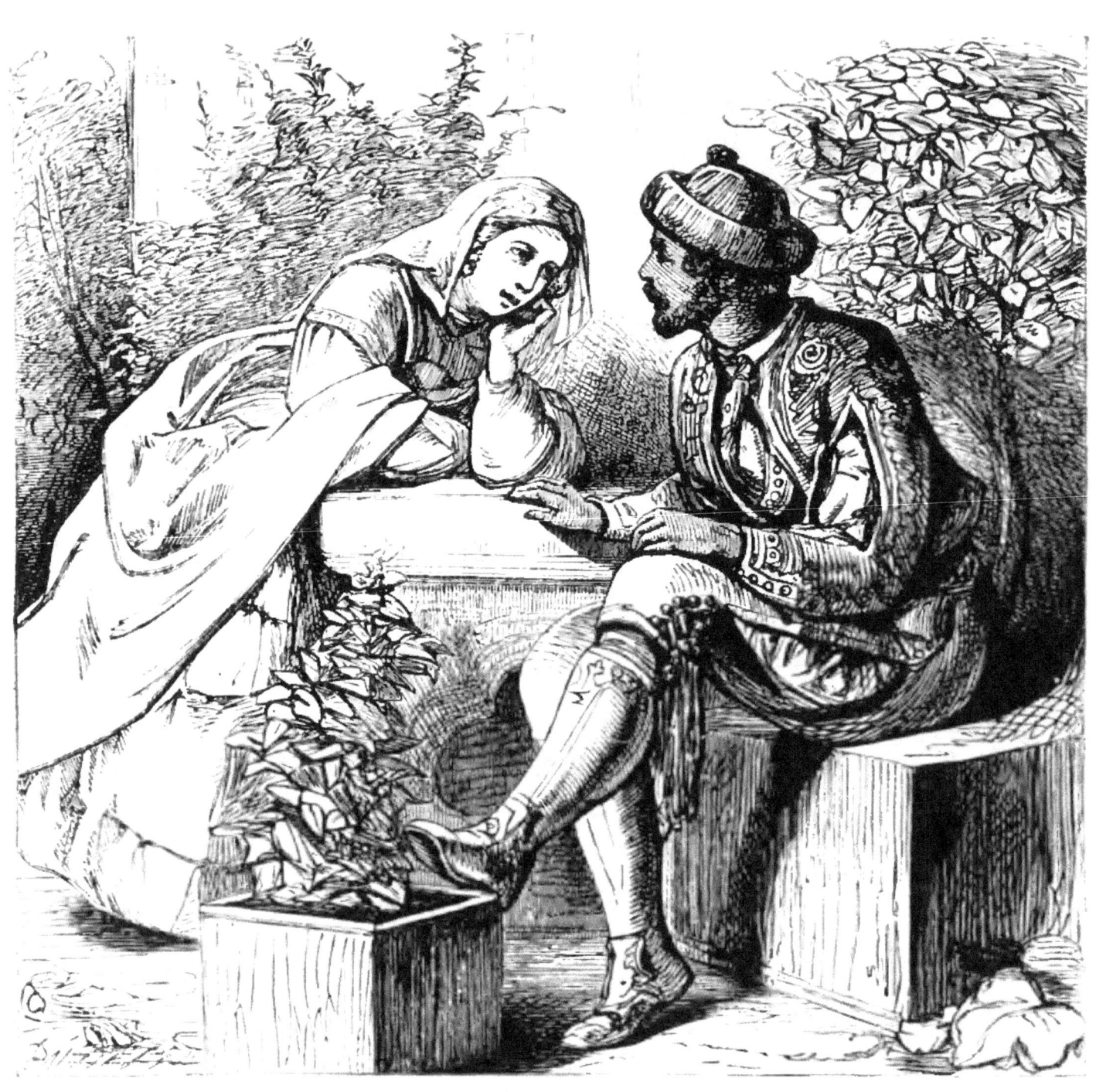

IN SPAIN.

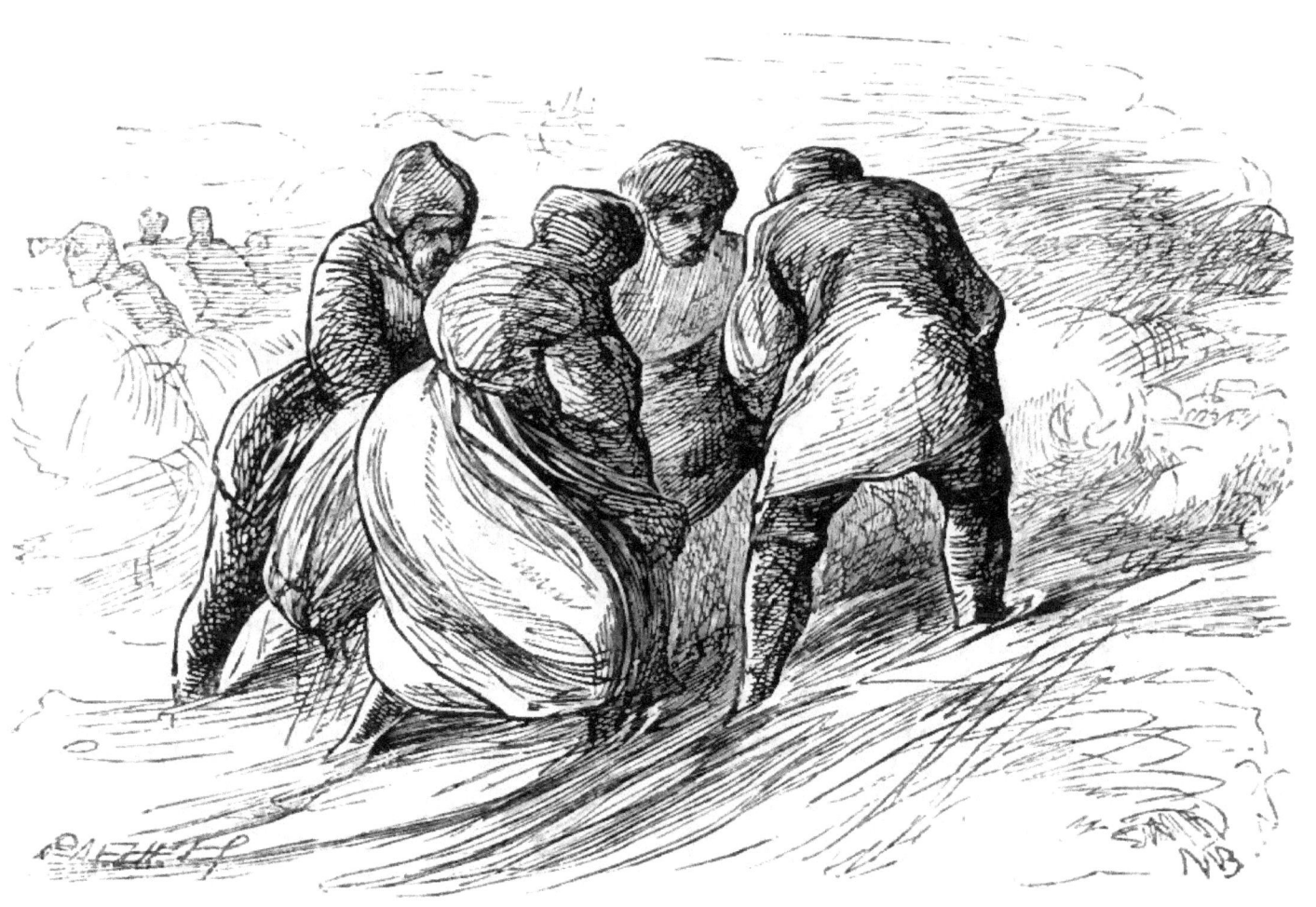

SAVED FROM THE WRECK.

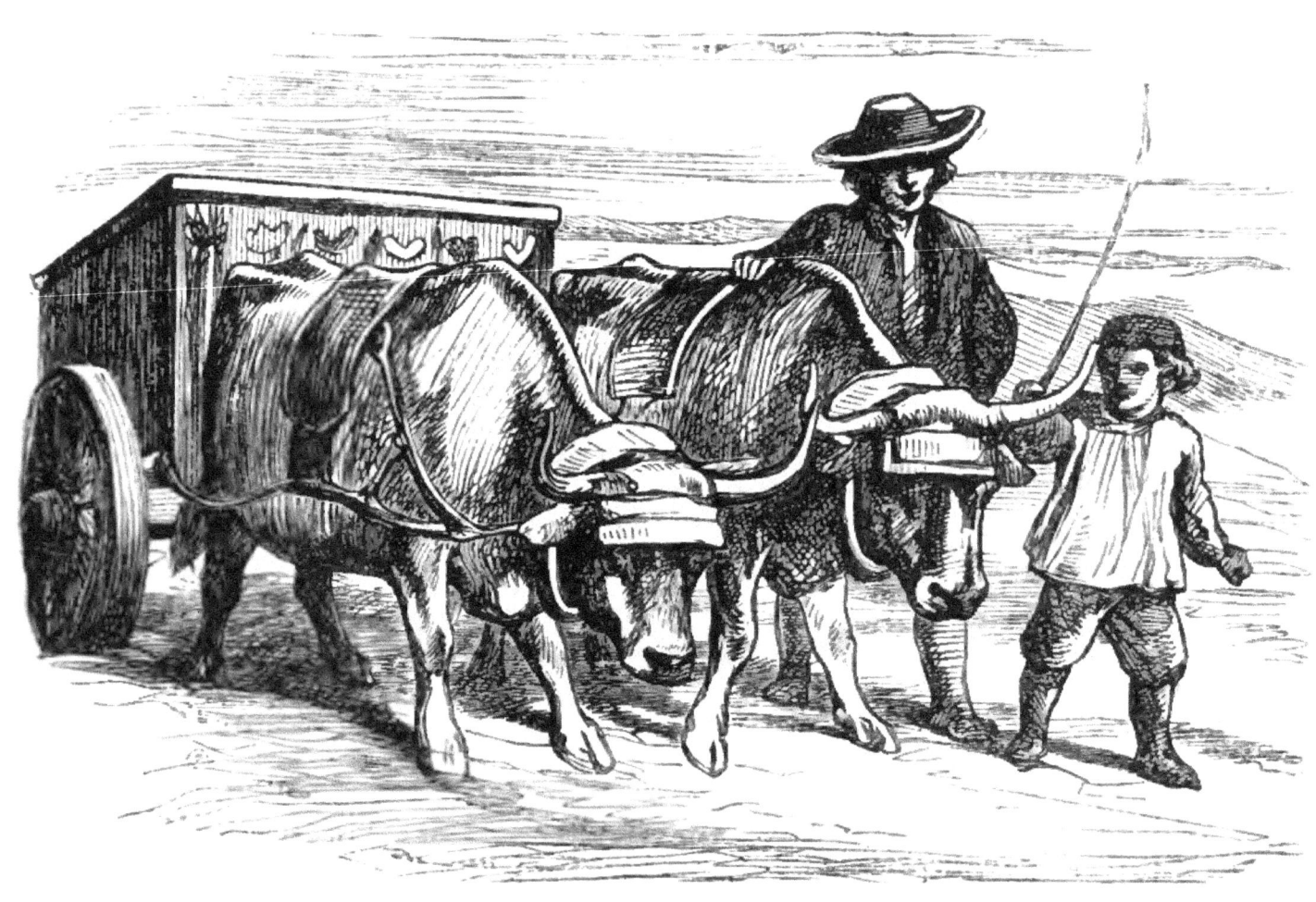

THE EEL BREEDER'S VISIT.

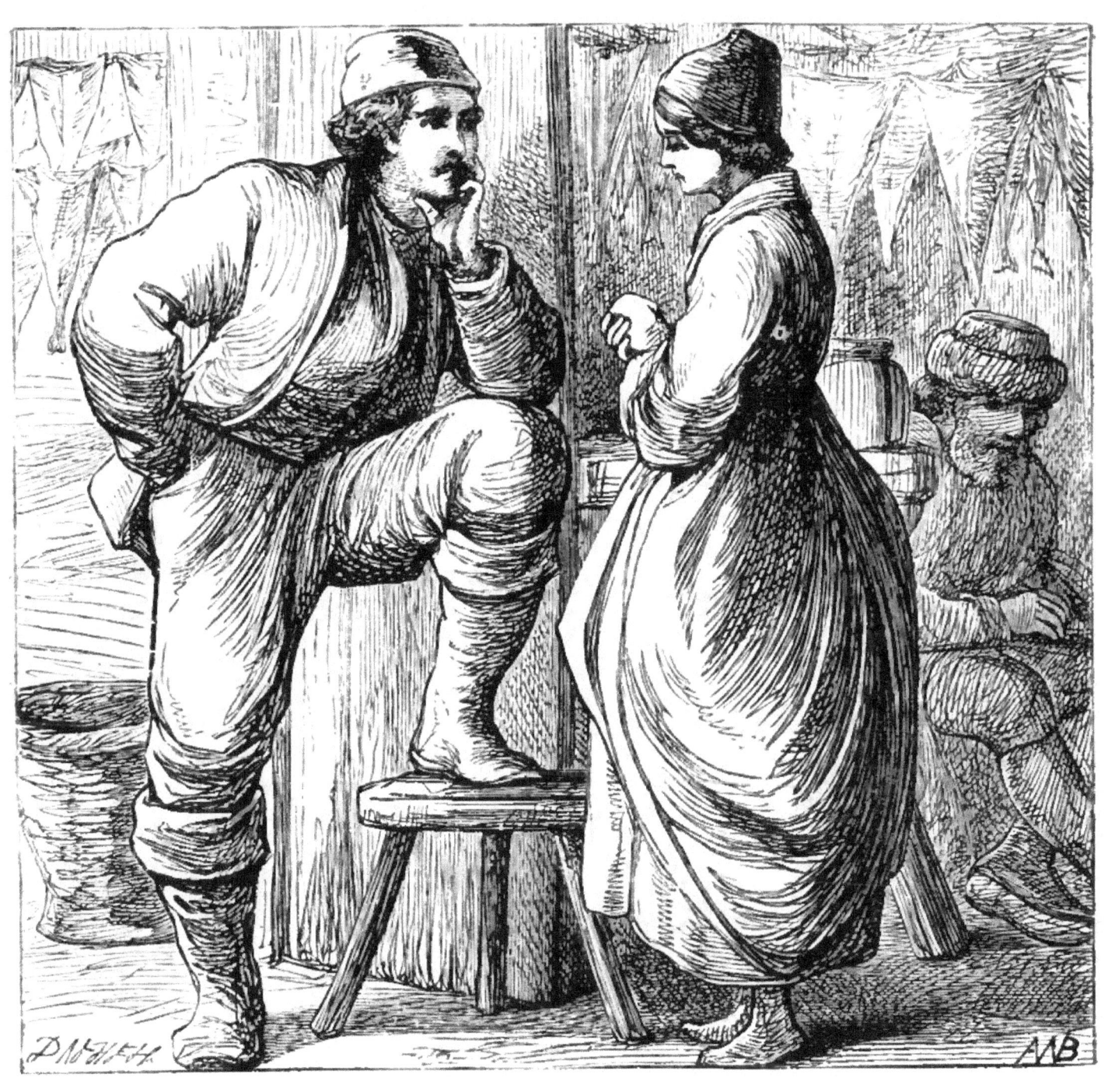

ELSE AFFIRMS HER PREFERENCE FOR MARTIN.

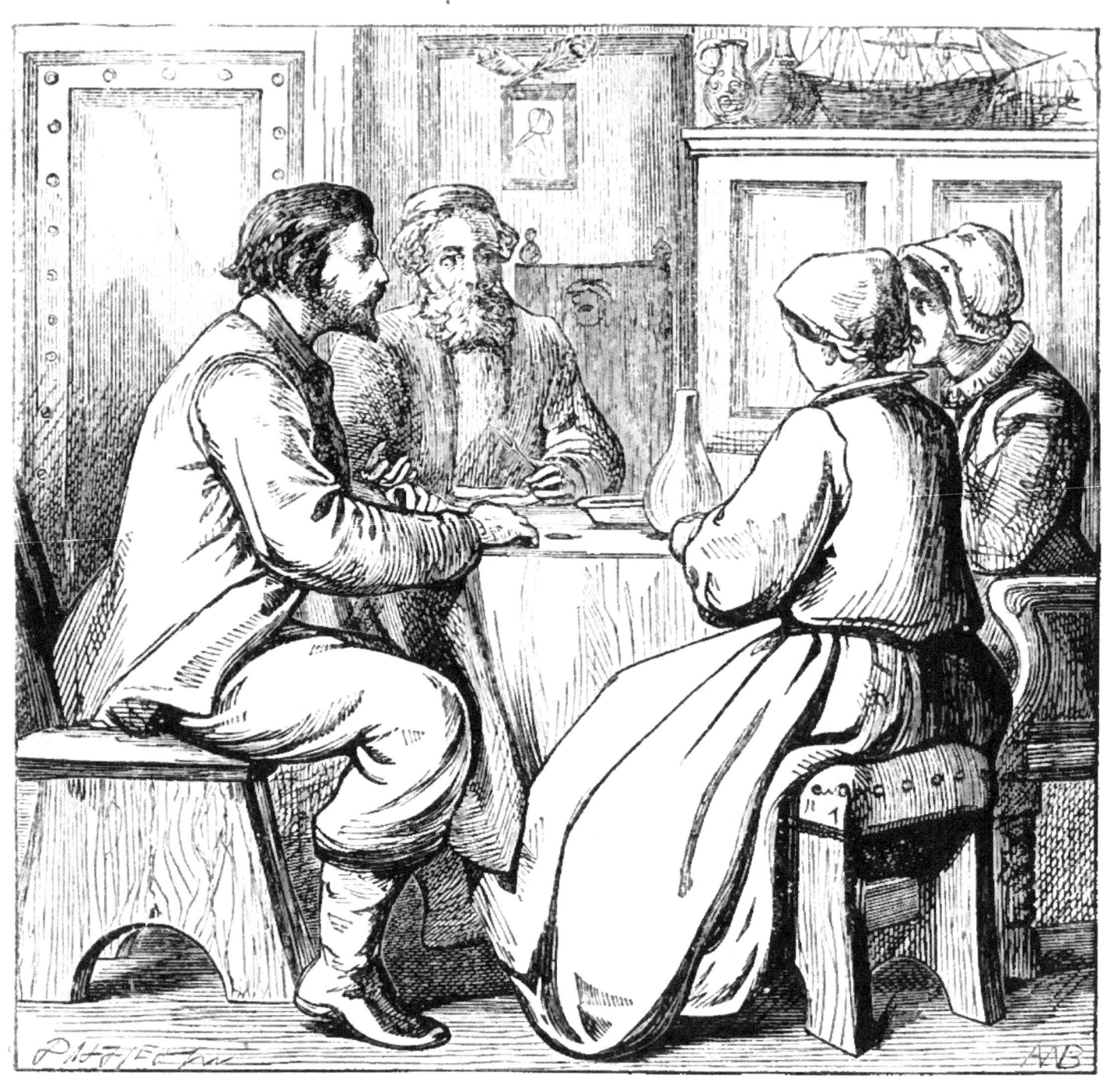

JÜRGEN'S BETTER FORTUNE.

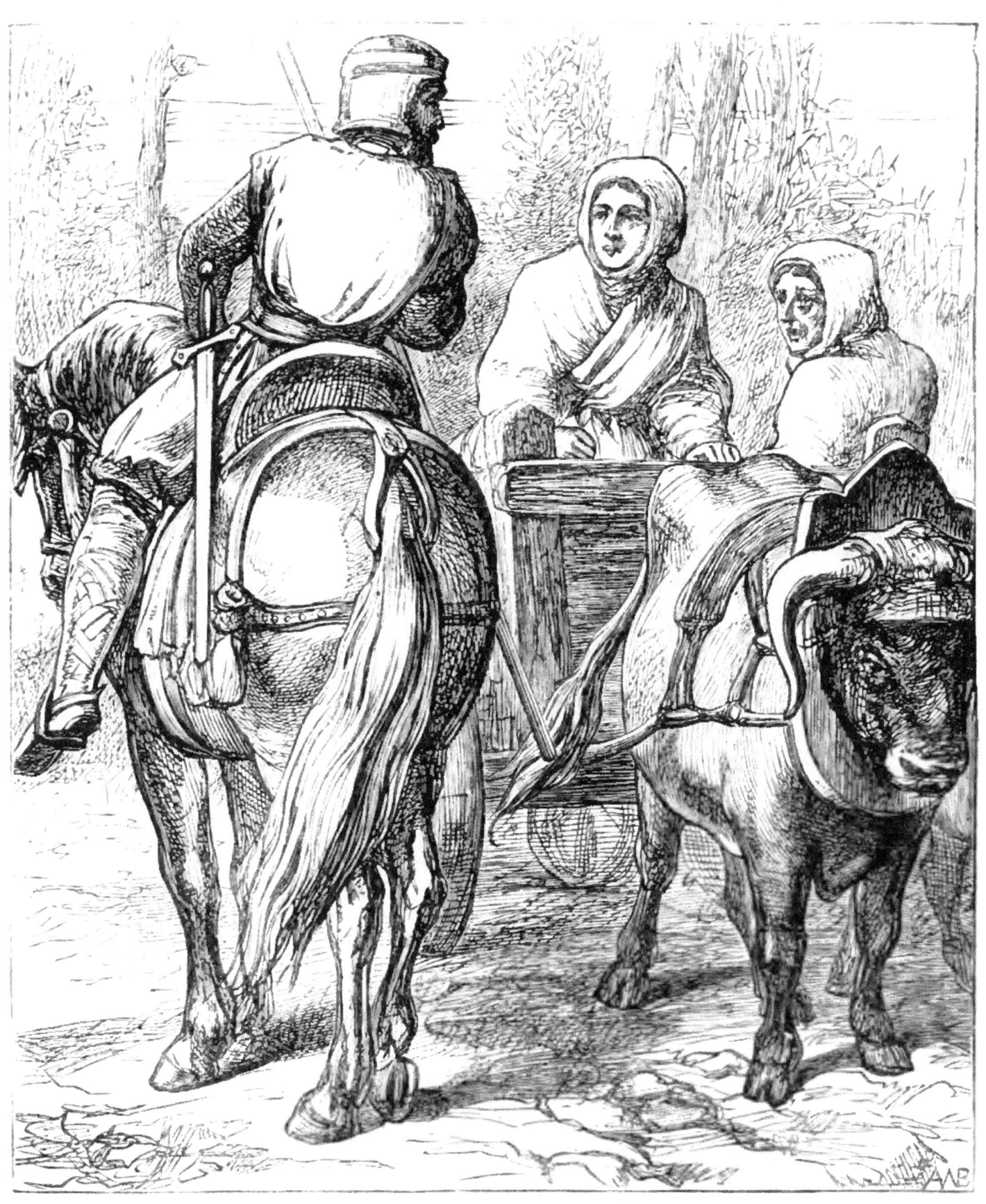

JENS GLOB MEETS HIS MOTHER.

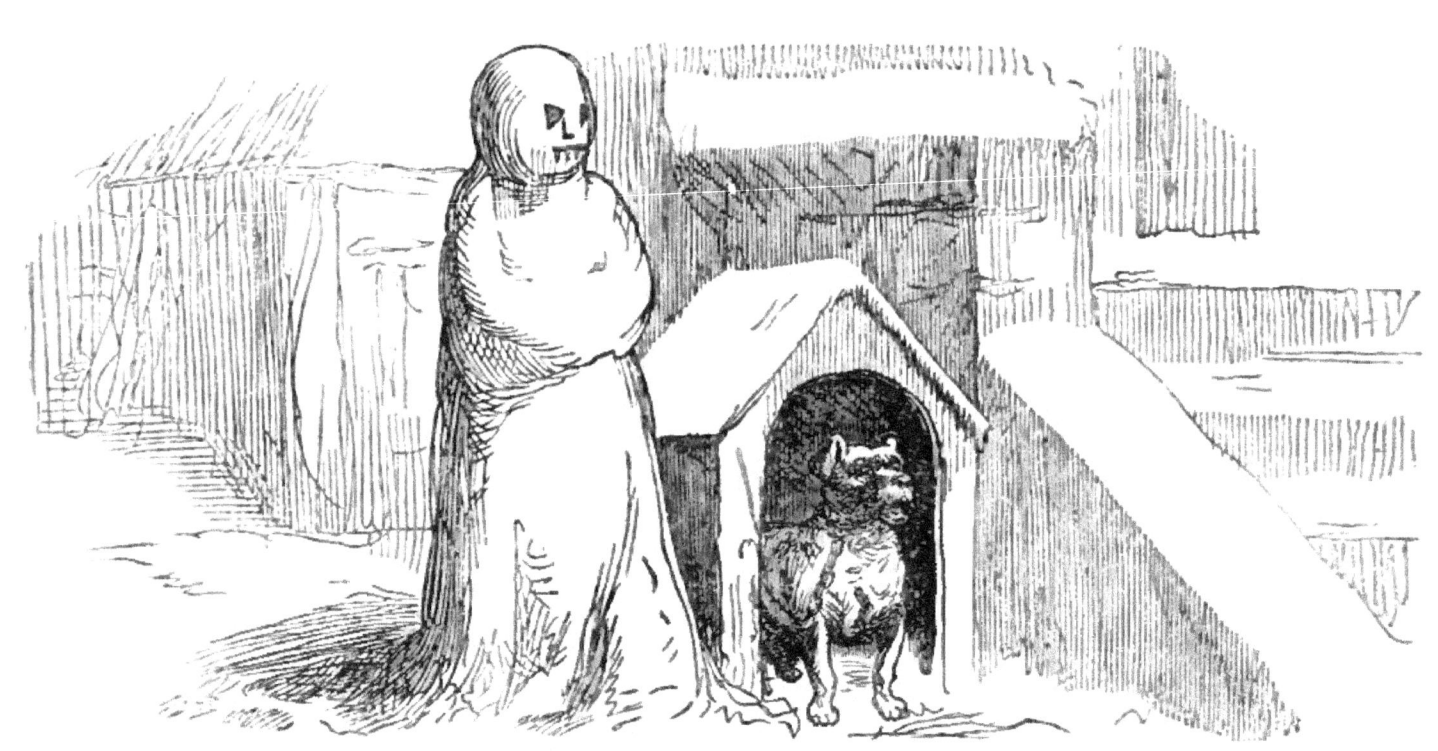

THE SNOW MAN AND THE YARD DOG.

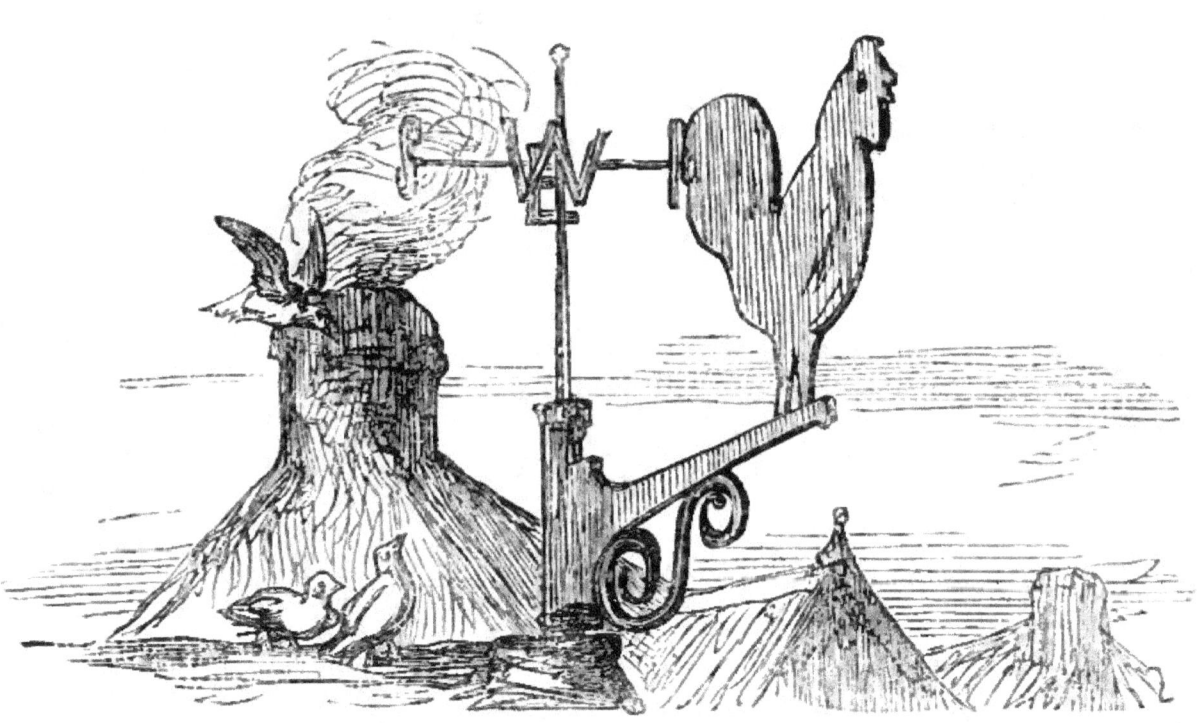

THE WEATHERCOCK.

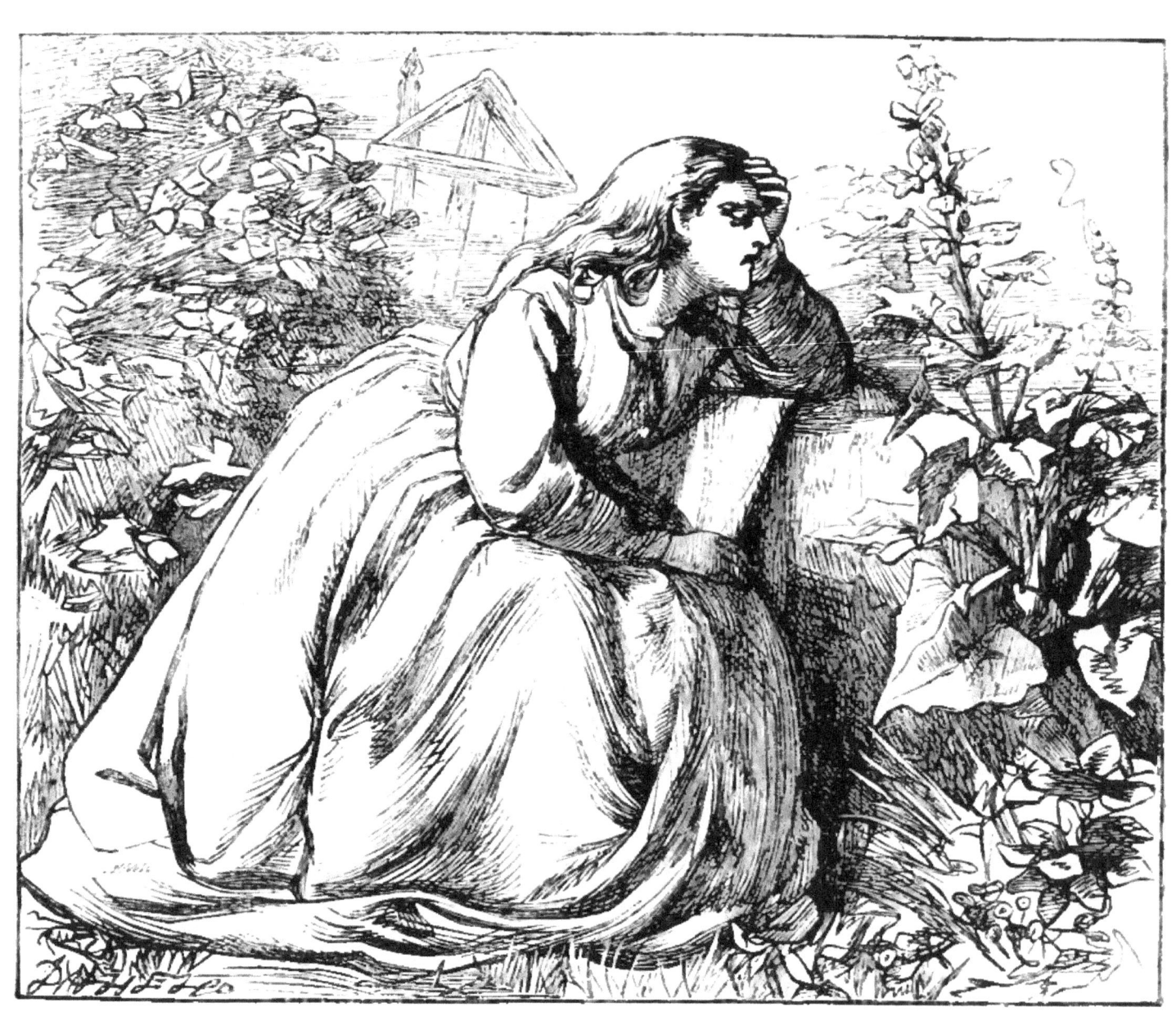

THE MOTHER AT THE GRAVE.

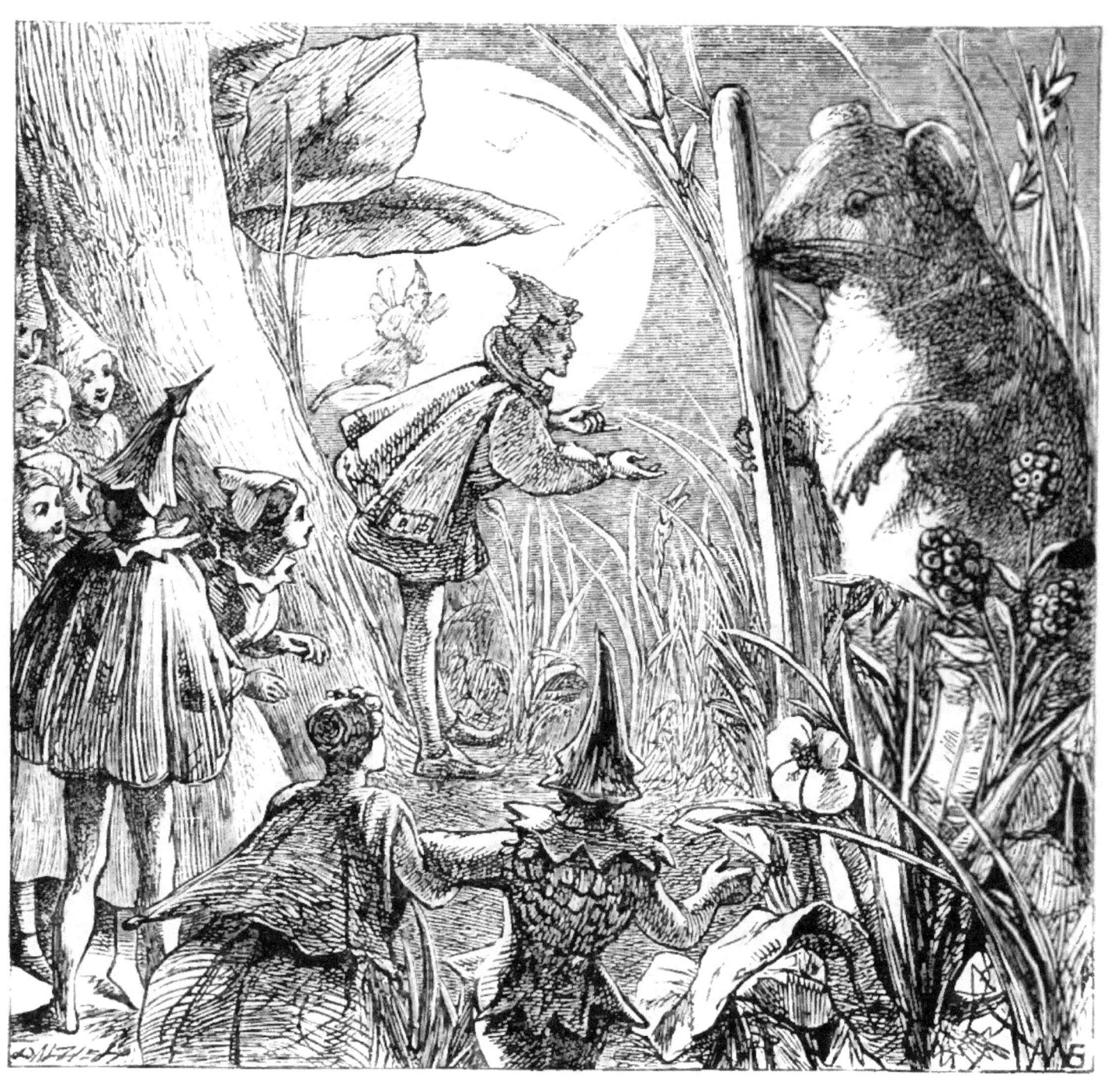

THE ELVES APPLY FOR THE LOAN OF THE SAUSAGE-PEG.

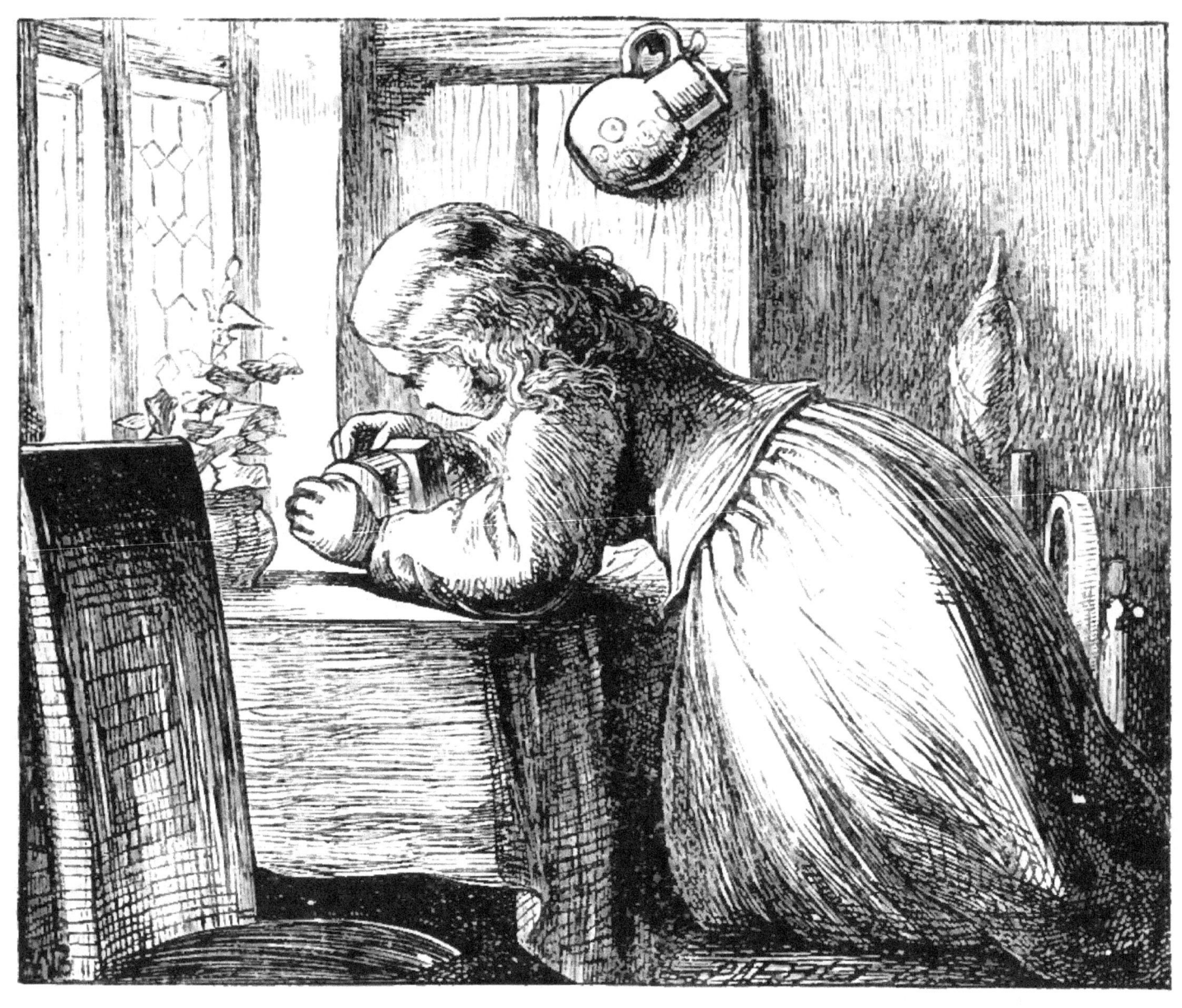

THE GAOLER'S GRANDDAUGHTER TAKES PITY ON THE LITTLE MOUSE.

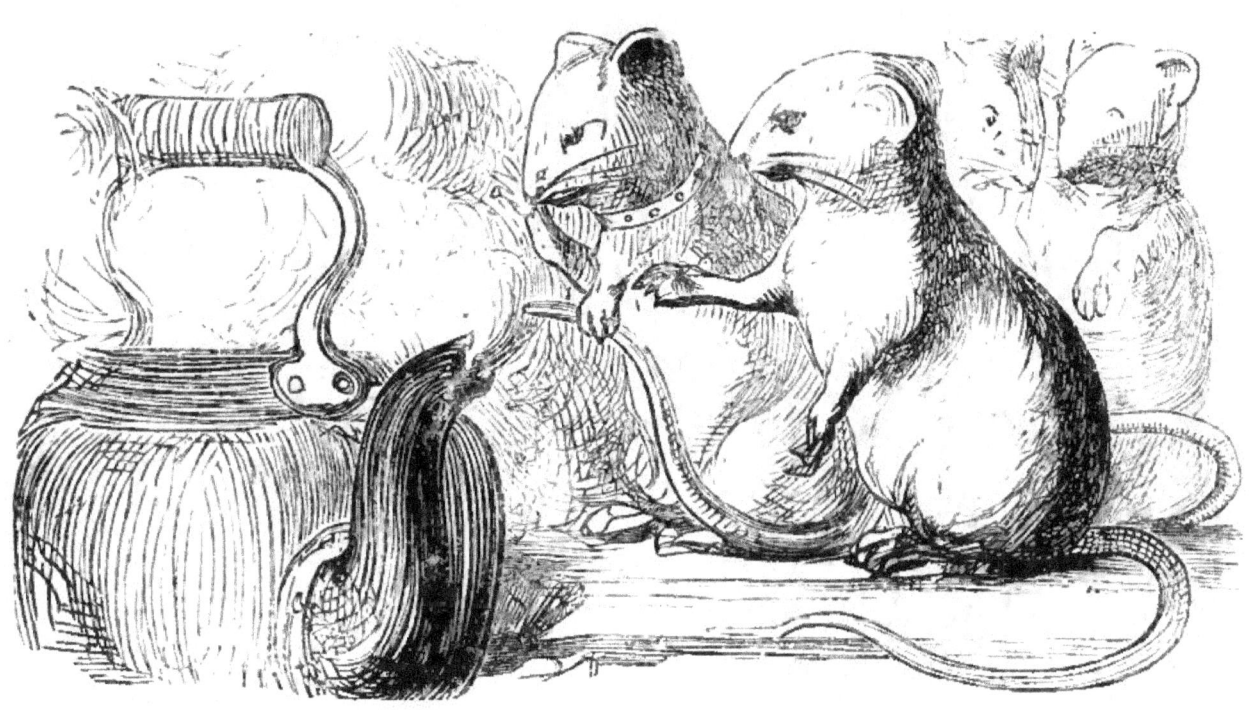

THE MOUSE KING UNDERSTANDS HOW THE SOUP IS MADE.

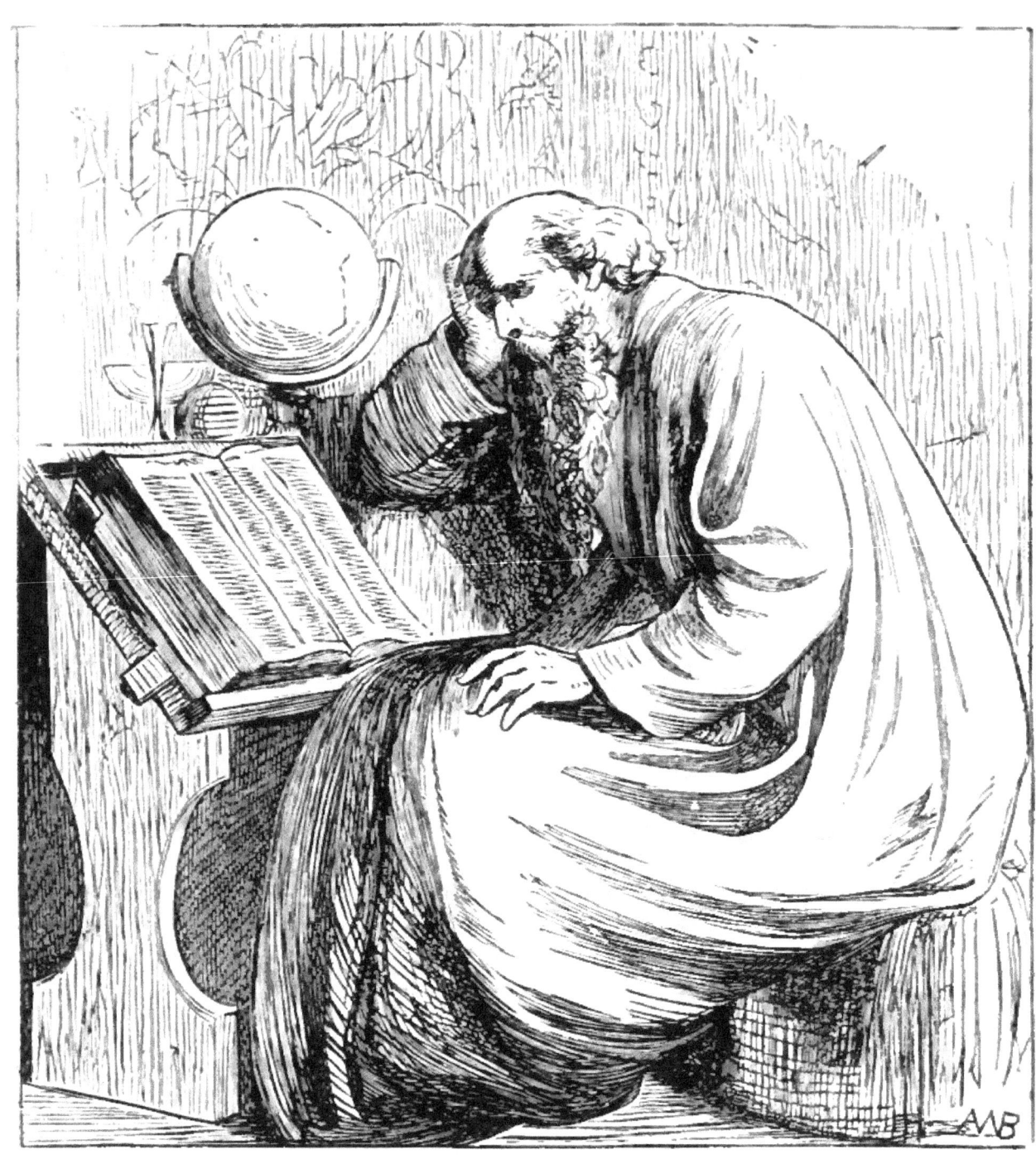

THE BOOK OF TRUTH.

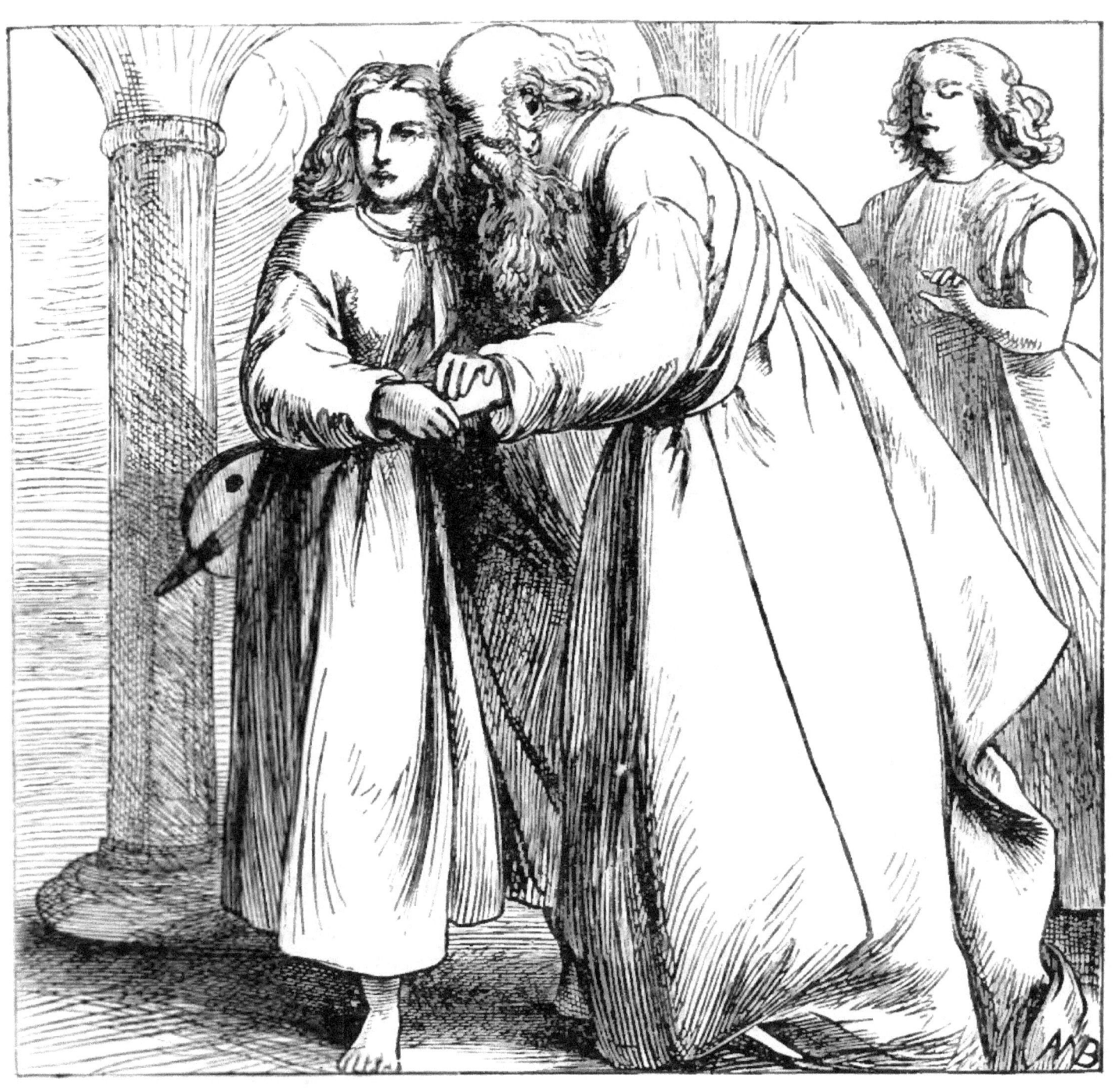

THE DEPARTURE OF THE THIRD BROTHER.

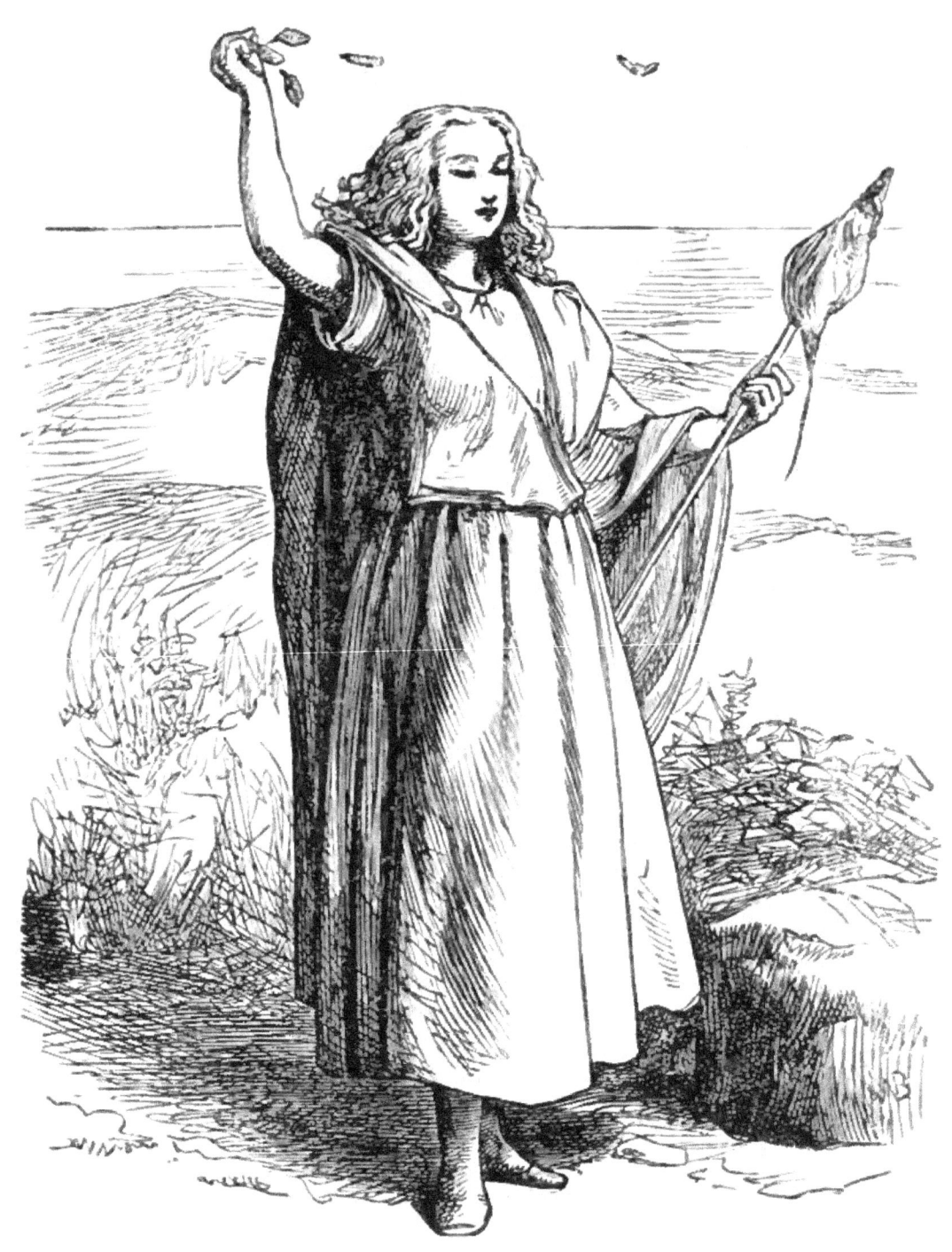

THE BLIND GIRL'S MESSENGERS.

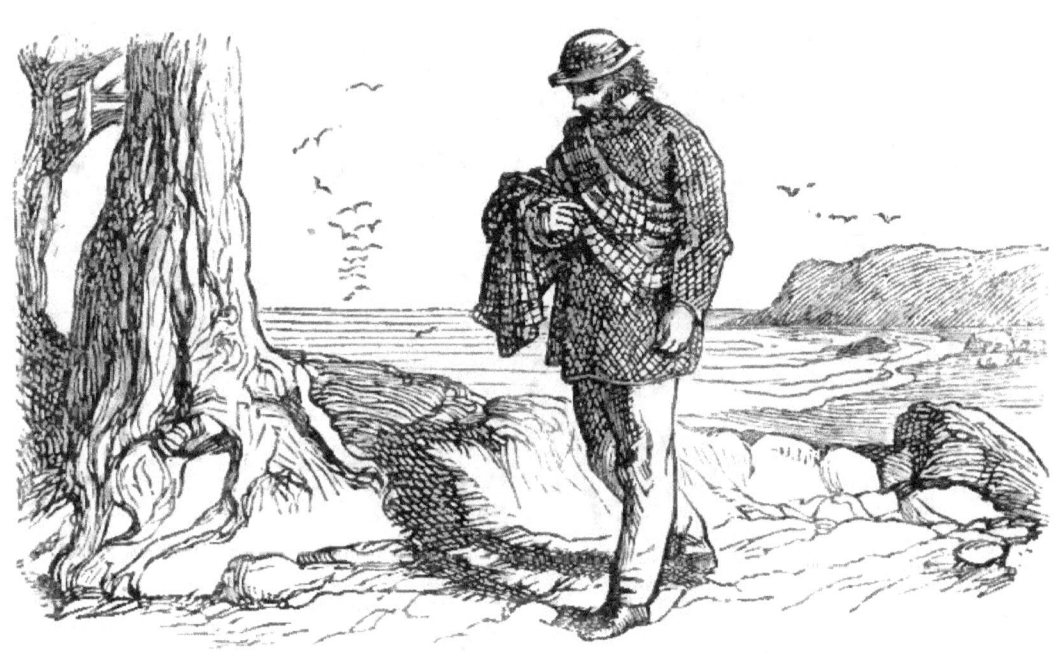

IN SEARCH OF THE STORY.

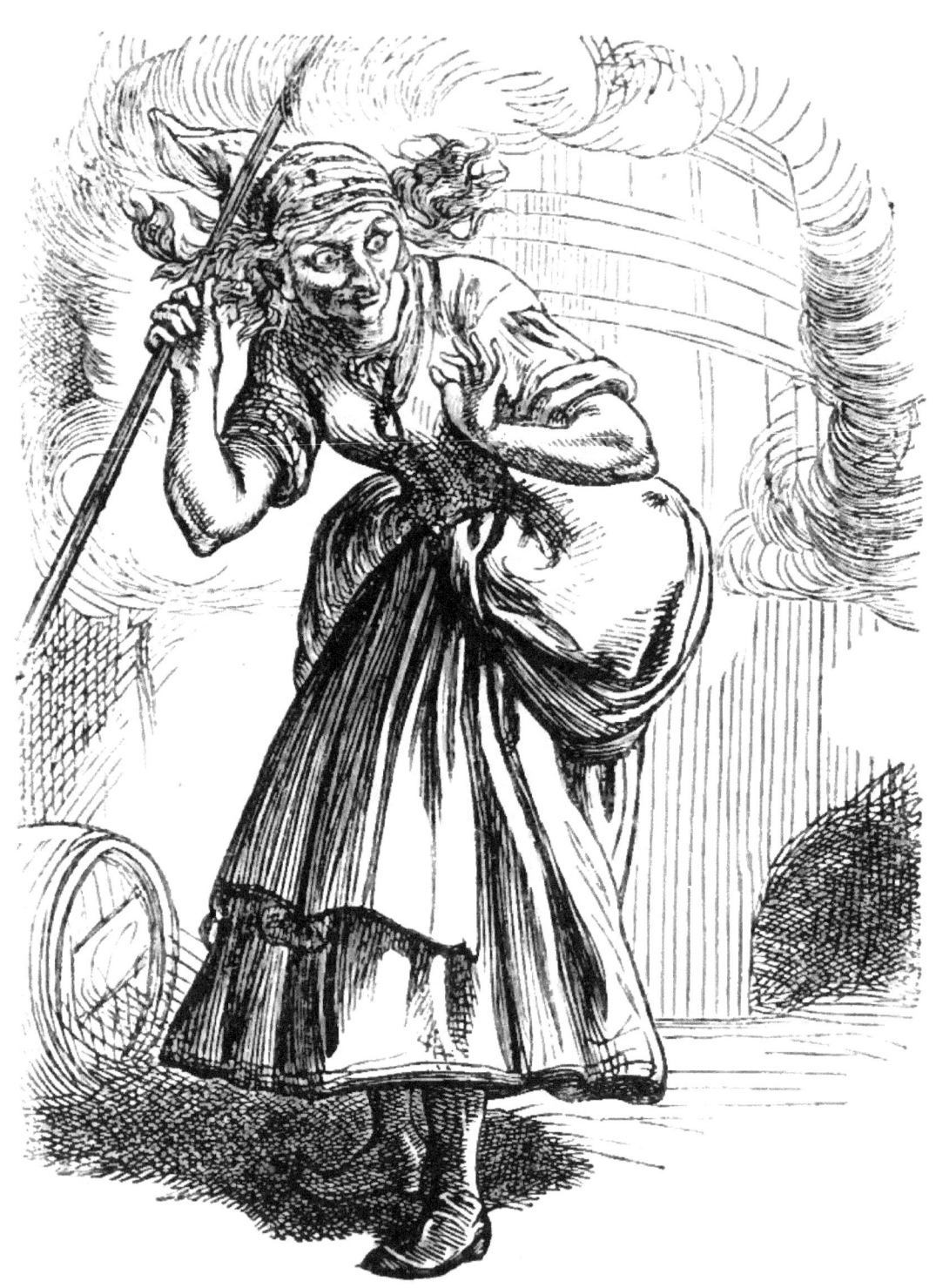

THE MOOR-WOMAN BREWING.

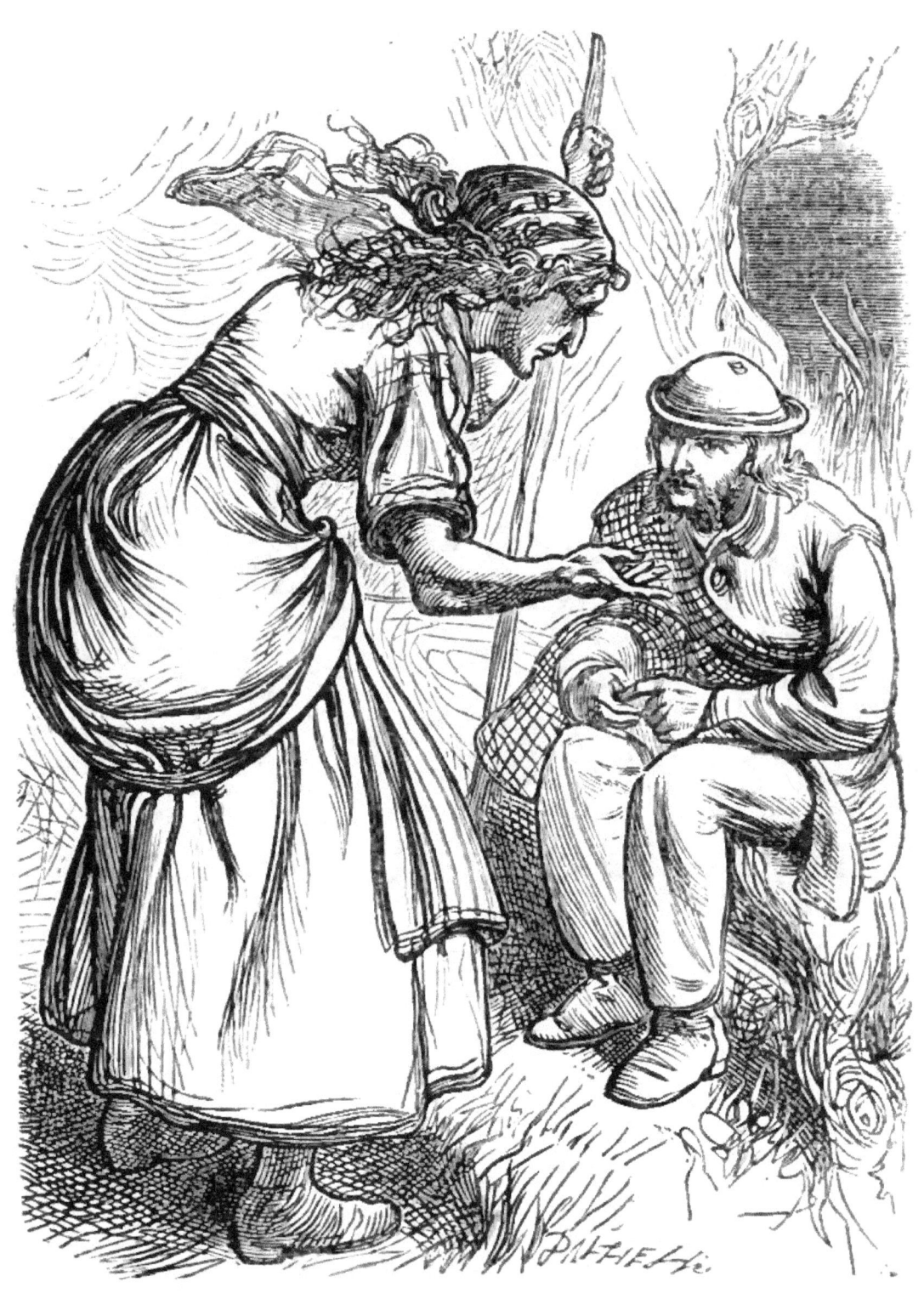

THE MOOR-WOMAN TELLING THE STORY.

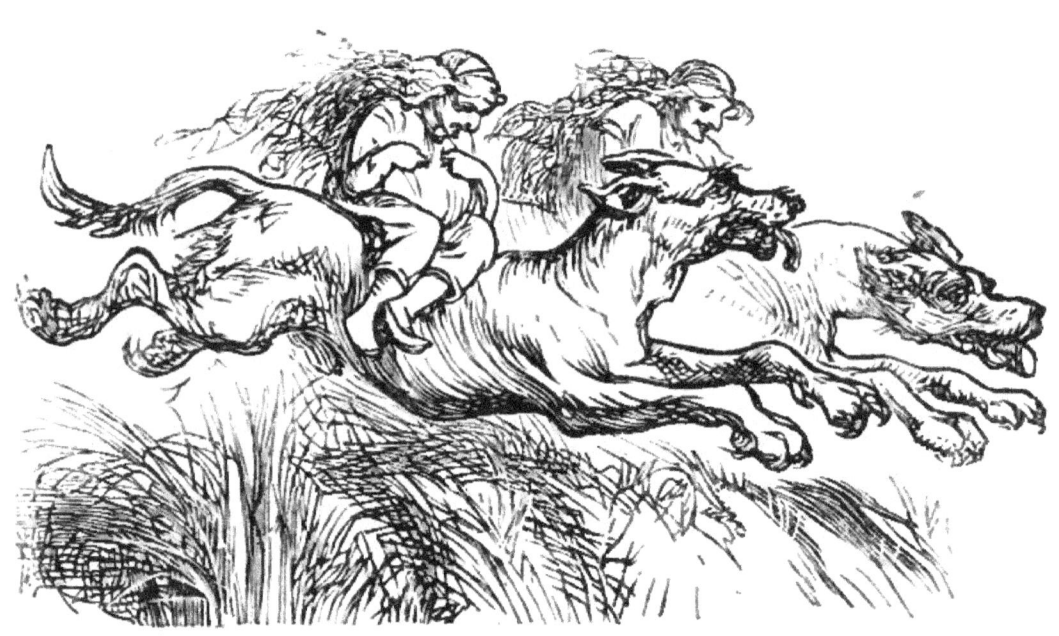

KING WALDEMAR'S GIFT.

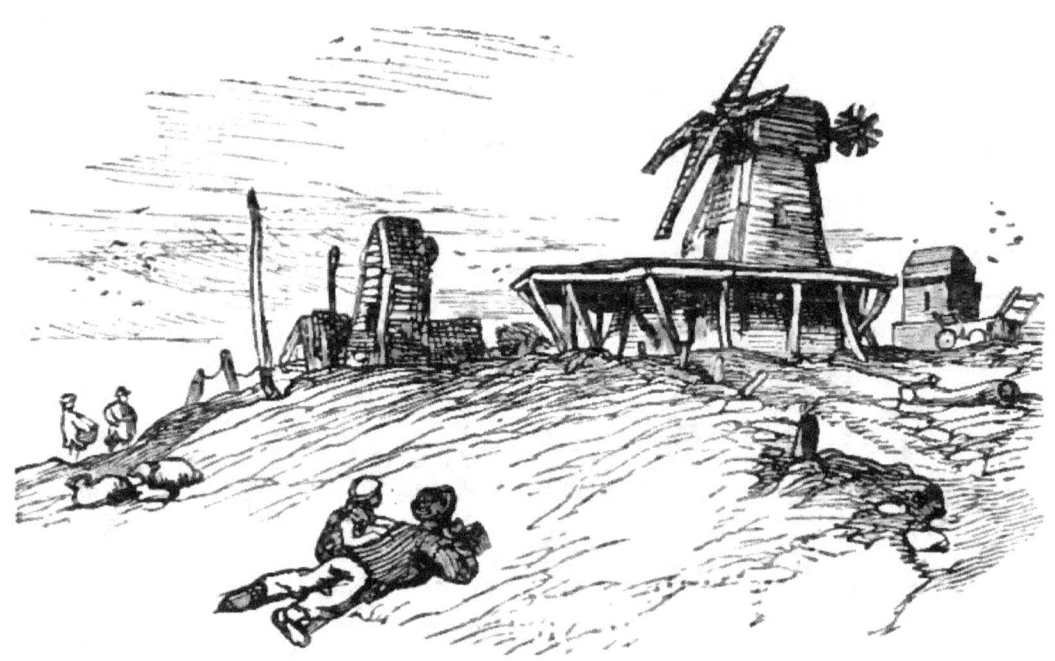

THE PROUD WINDMILL.

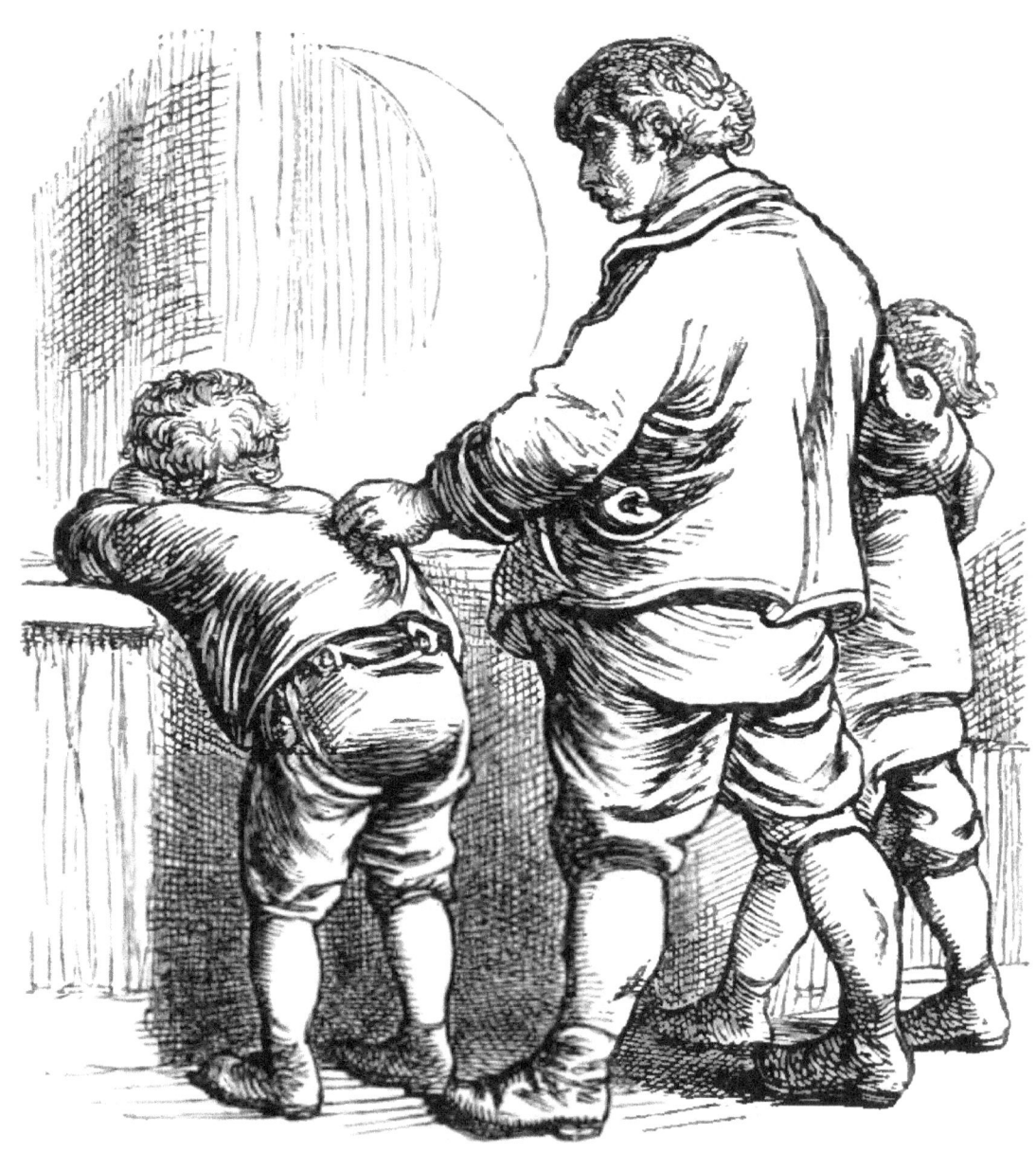

EXAMINING THE MILL.

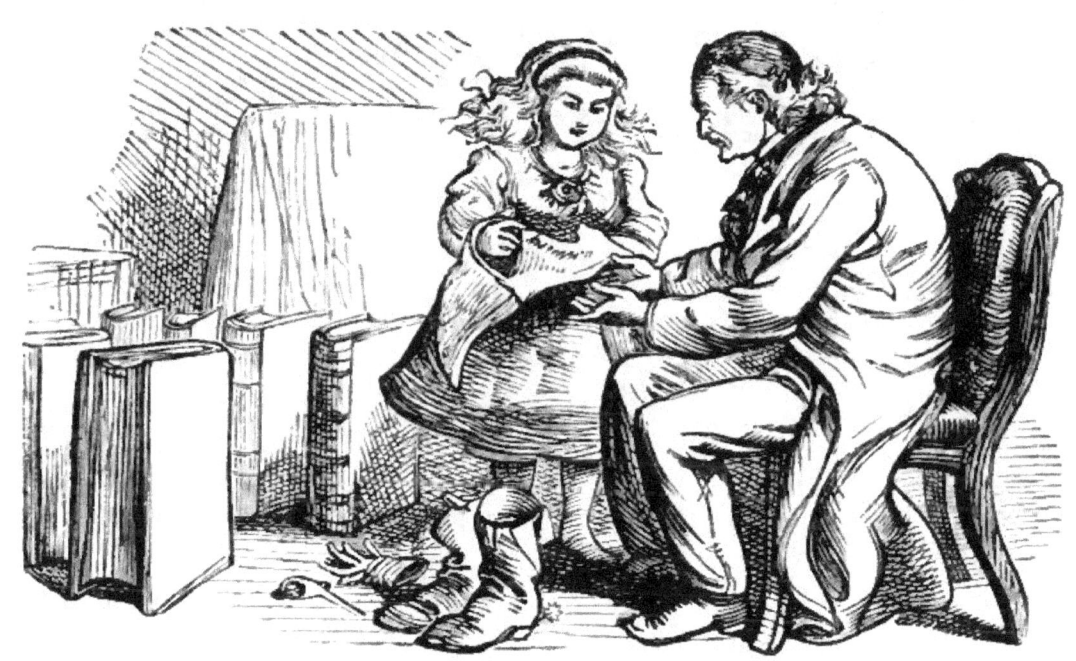

THE PLAY.

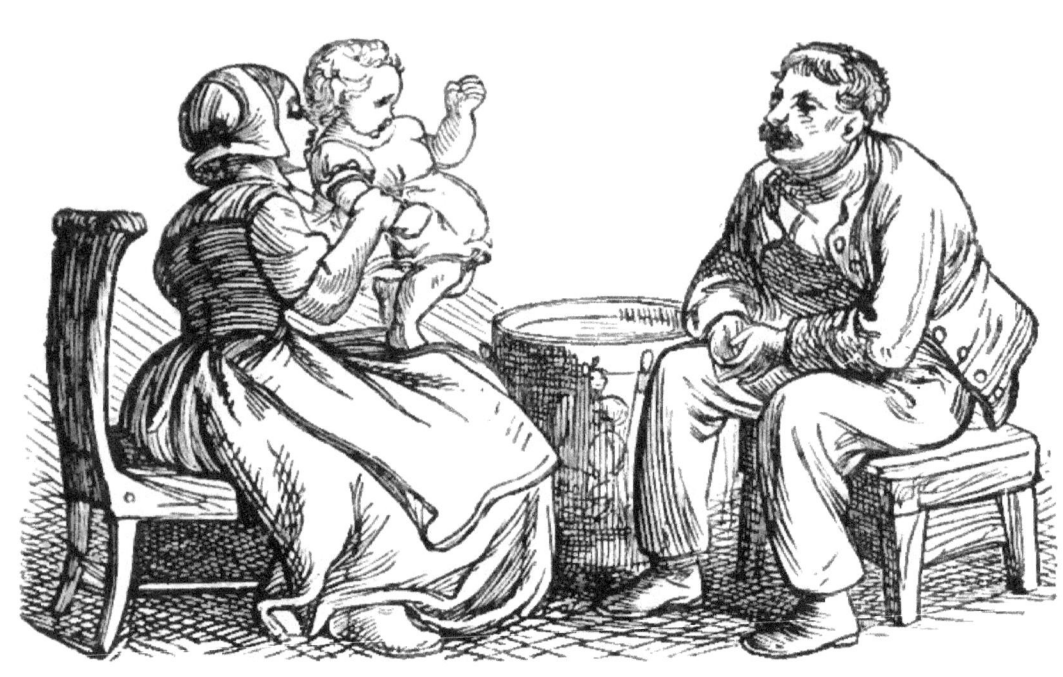

PETER'S MOTHER.

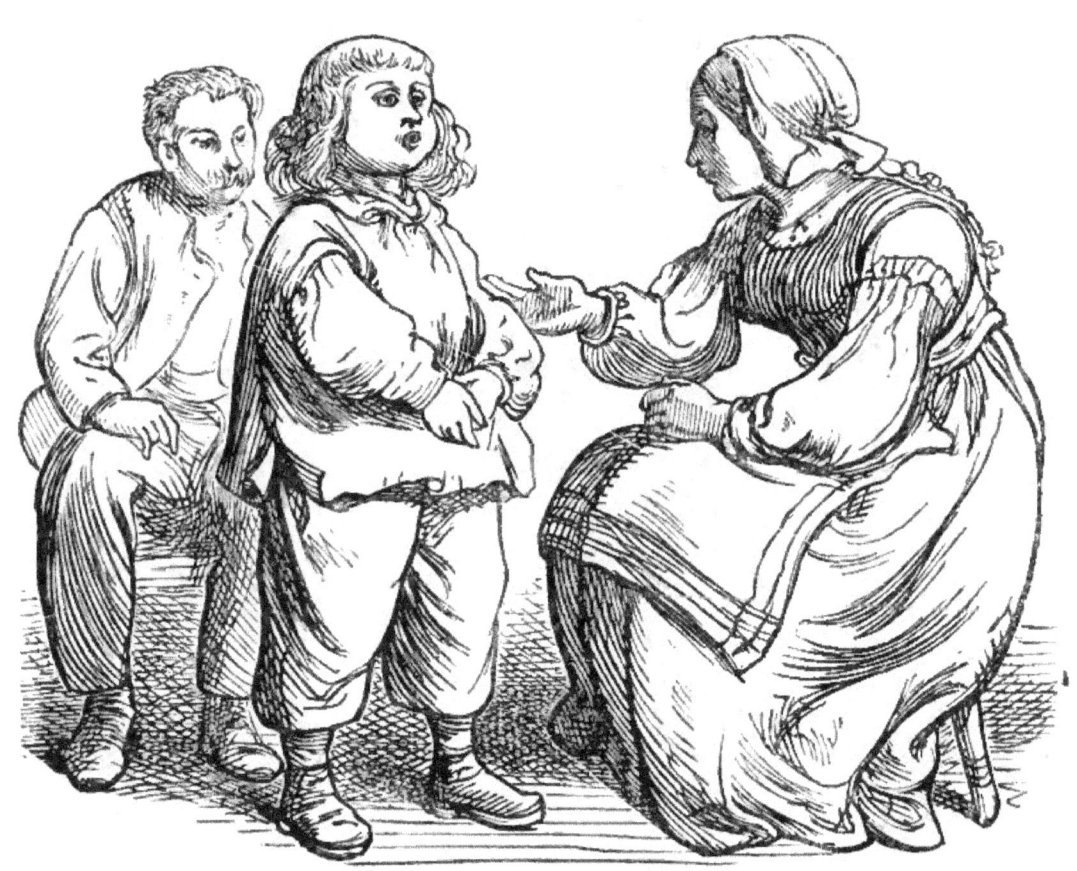

PETER SINGING.

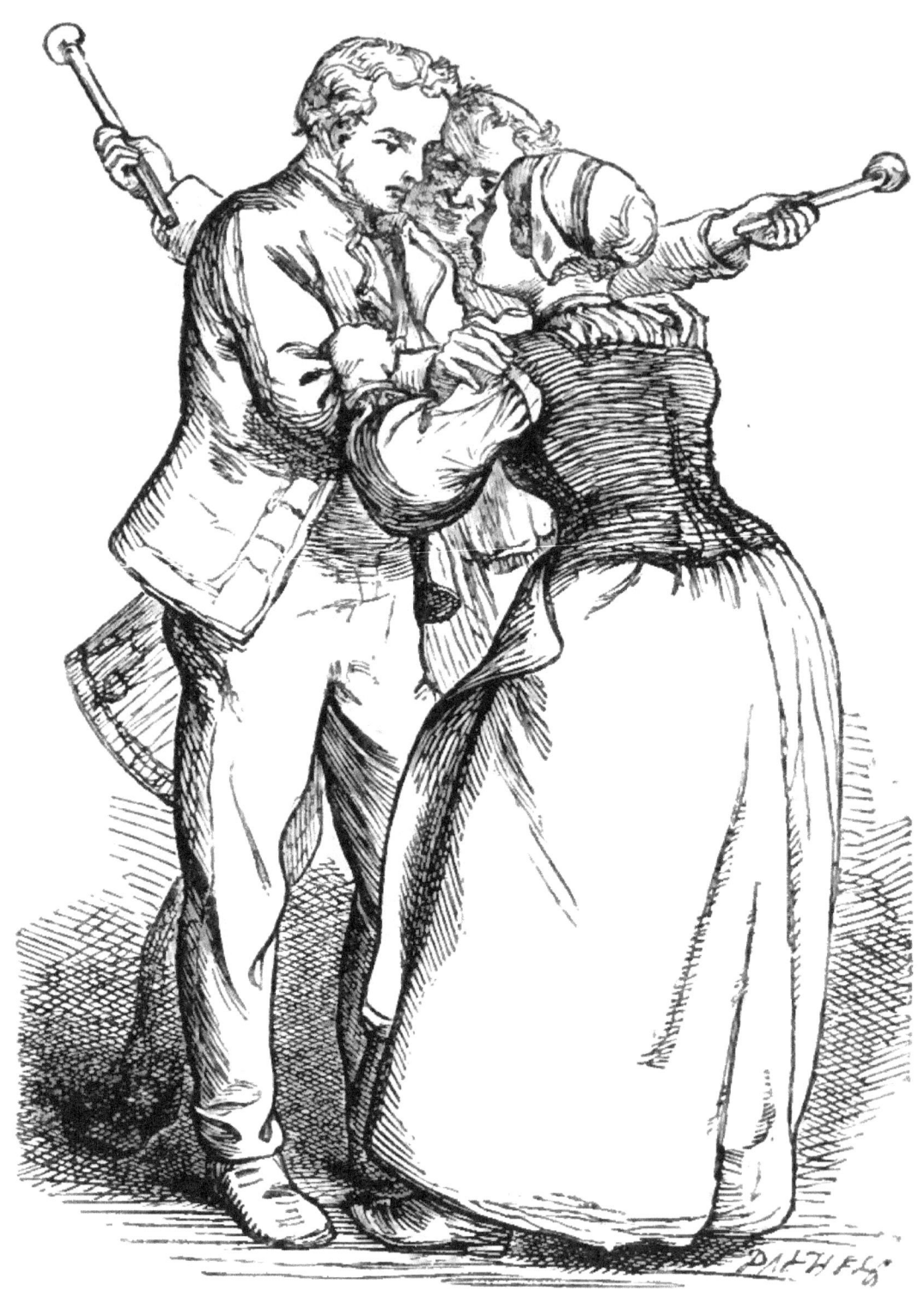

PETER'S RETURN.

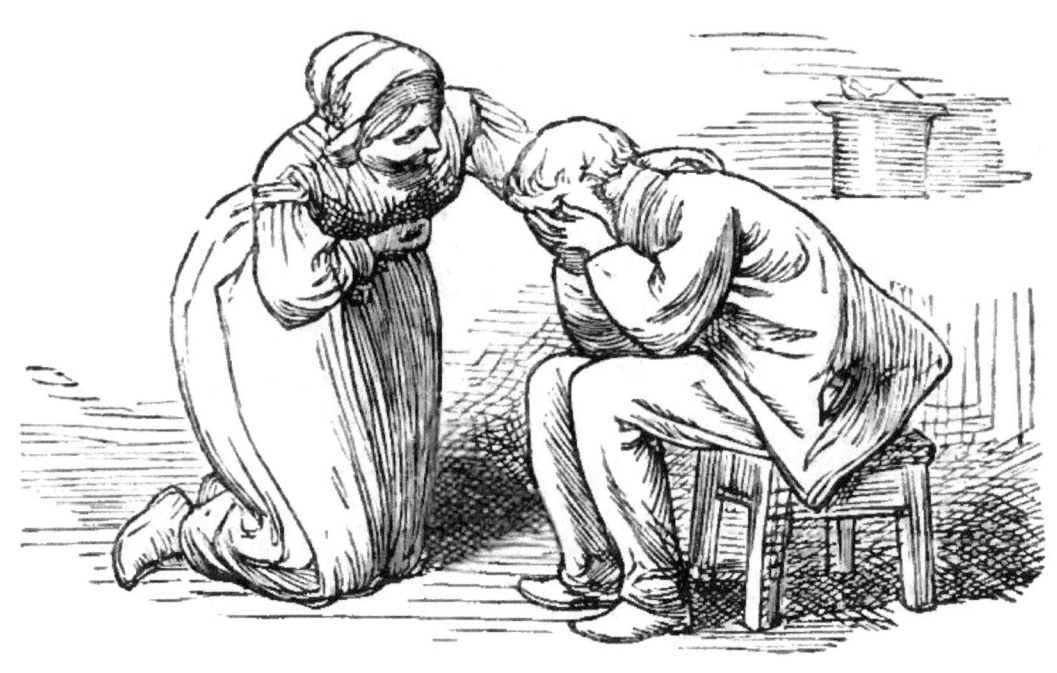

PETER'S GRIEF.

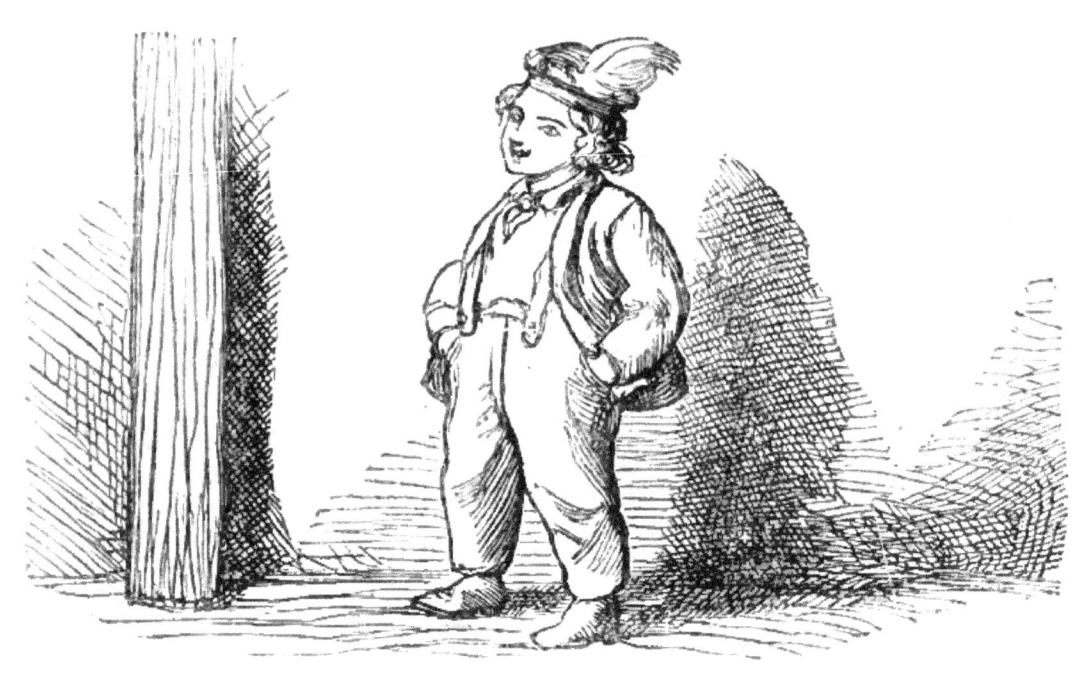

HOW GRANDPAPA LOOKED WHEN A BOY.

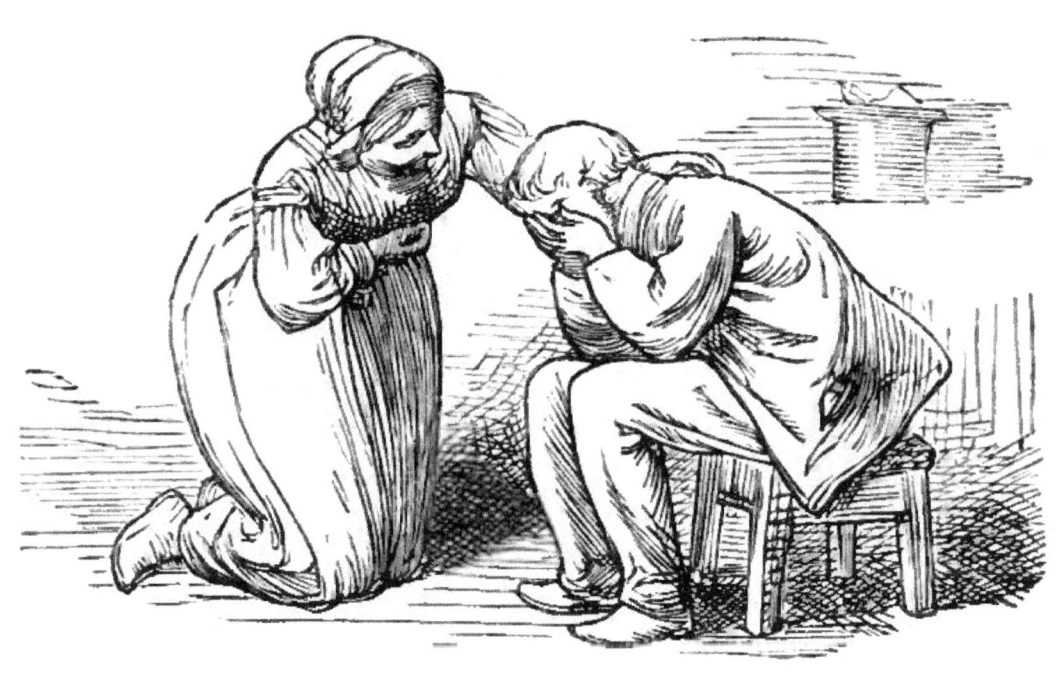

PETER'S GRIEF.

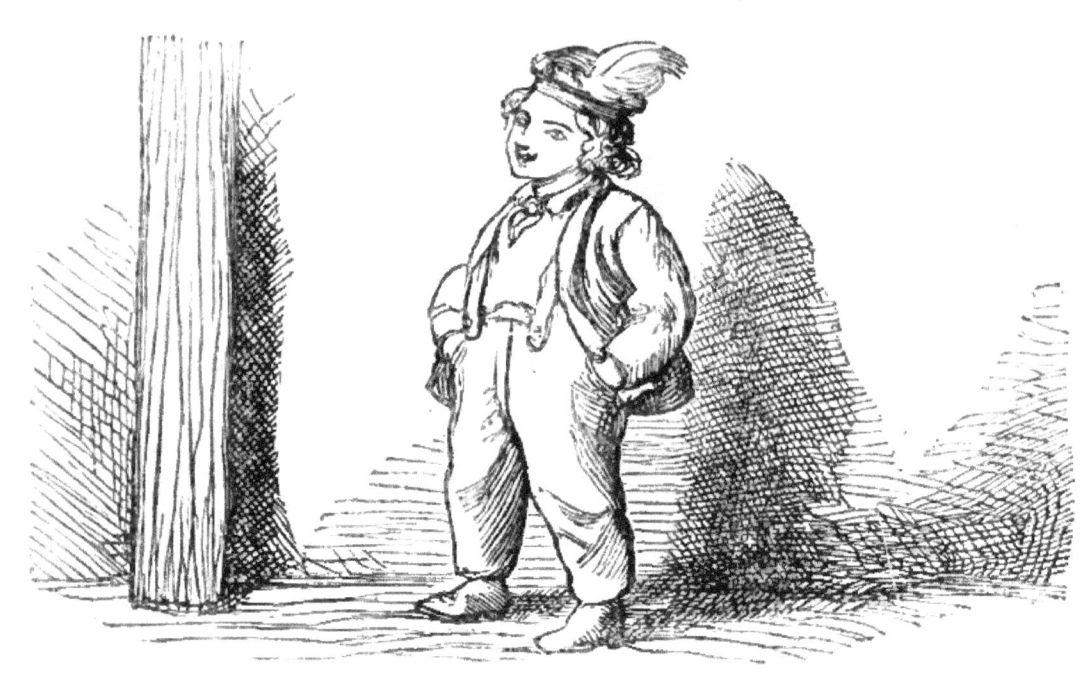

HOW GRANDPAPA LOOKED WHEN A BOY.

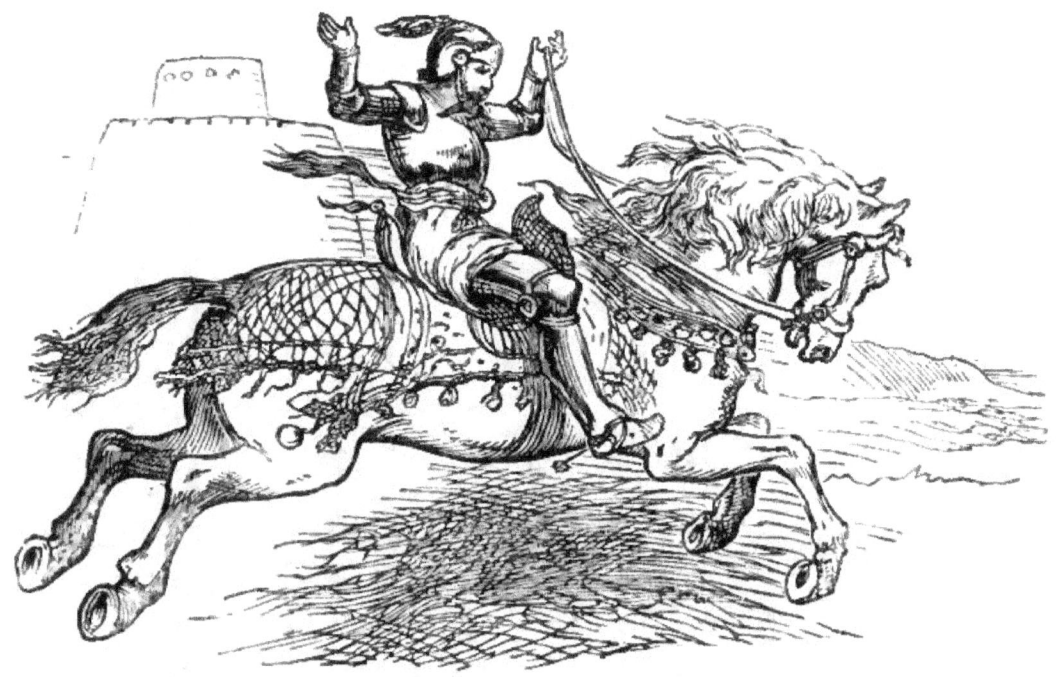

THE KNIGHT'S ESCAPE.

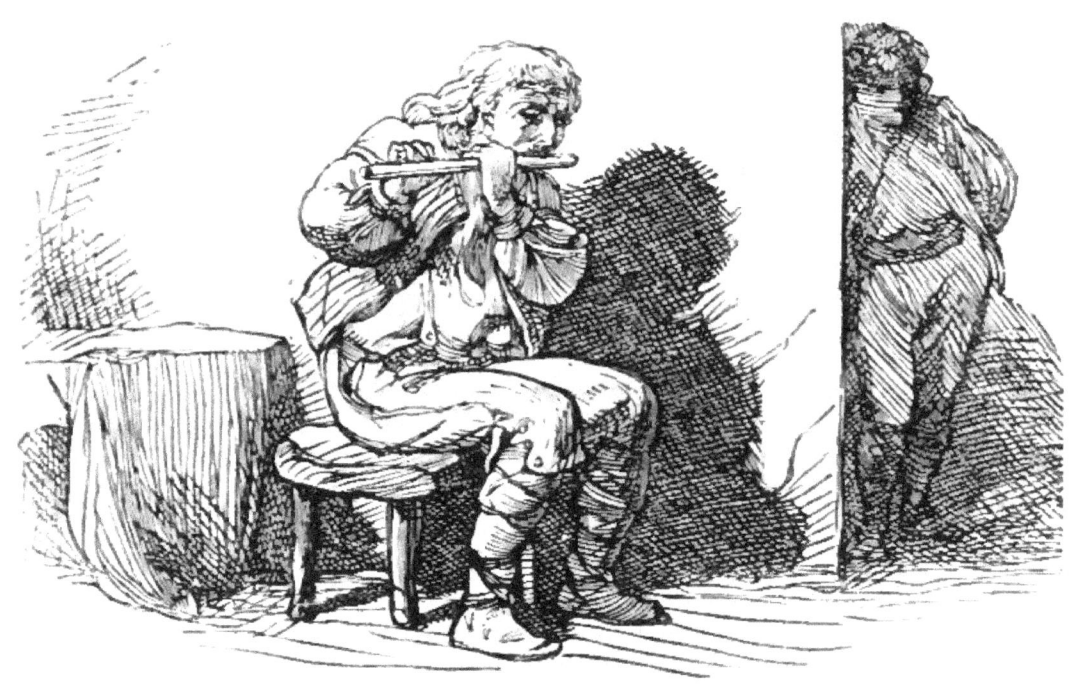

THE OLD PEASANT.

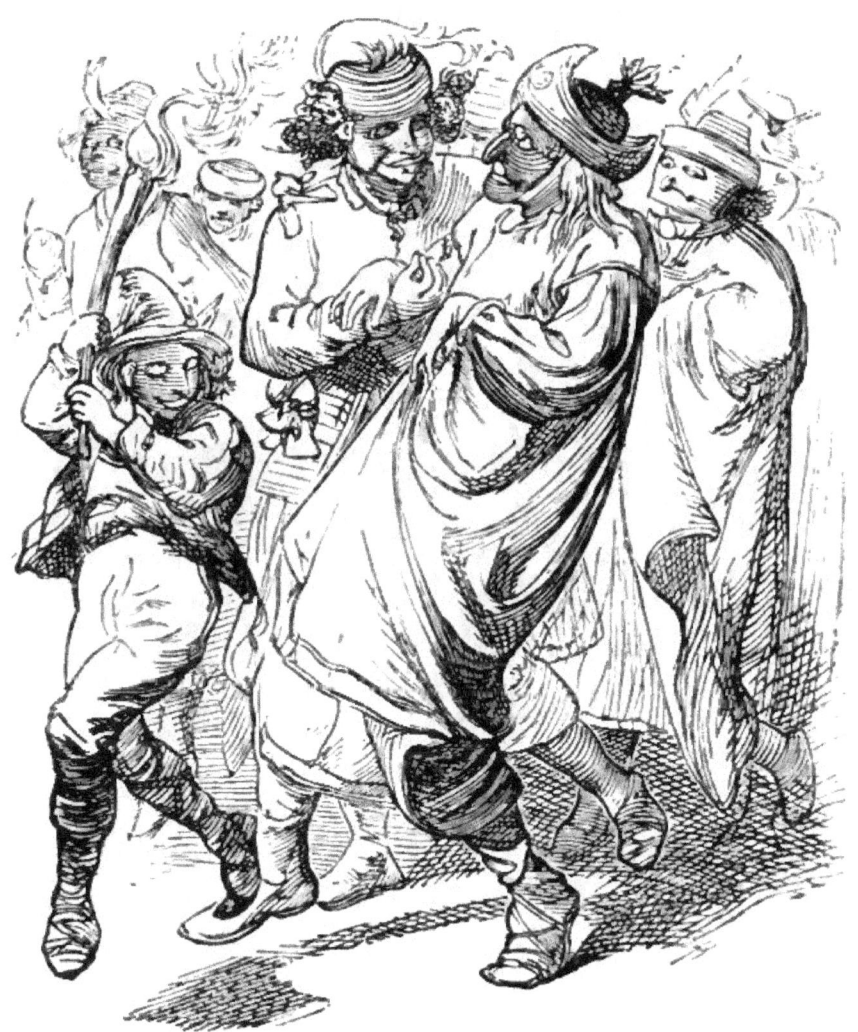

IN THE STREETS.

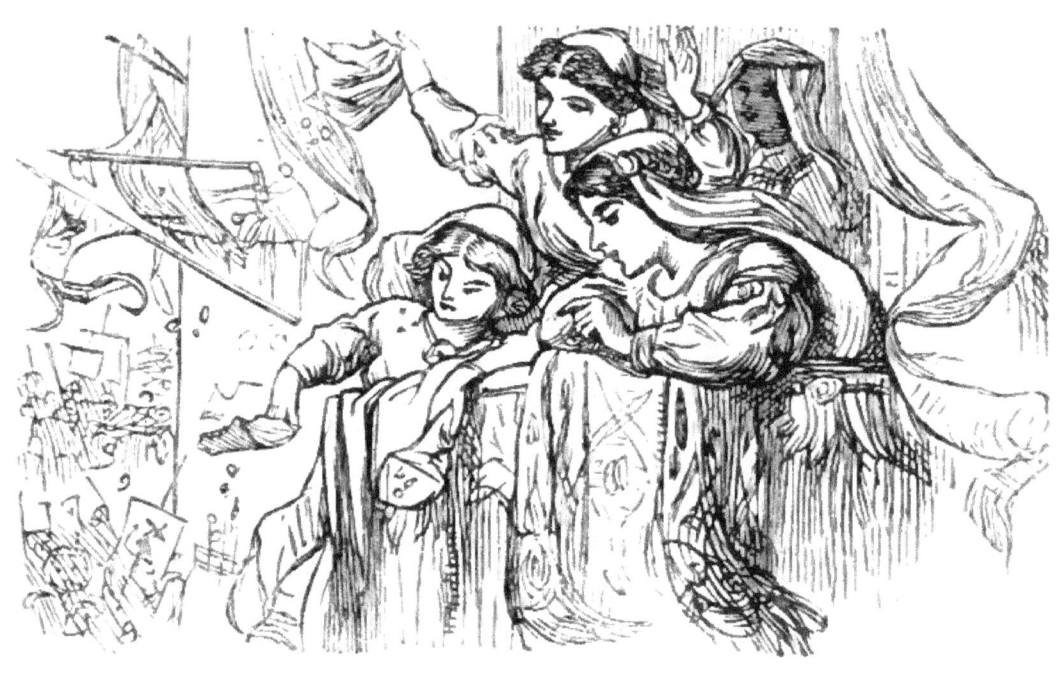

AT THE BALCONIES.

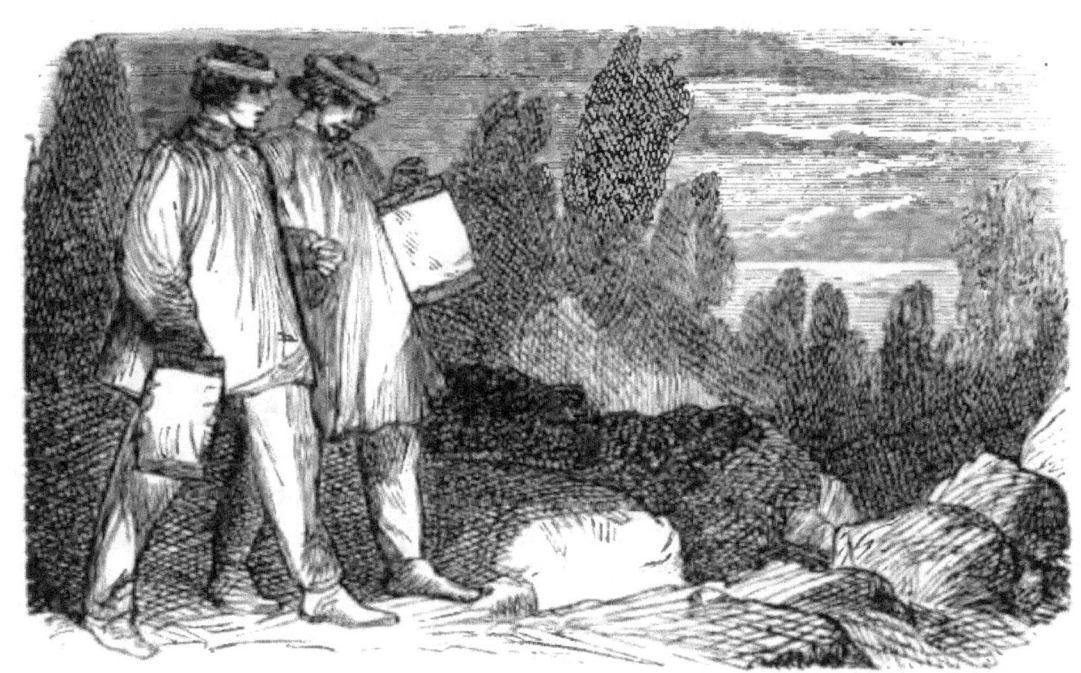

AT PERA.

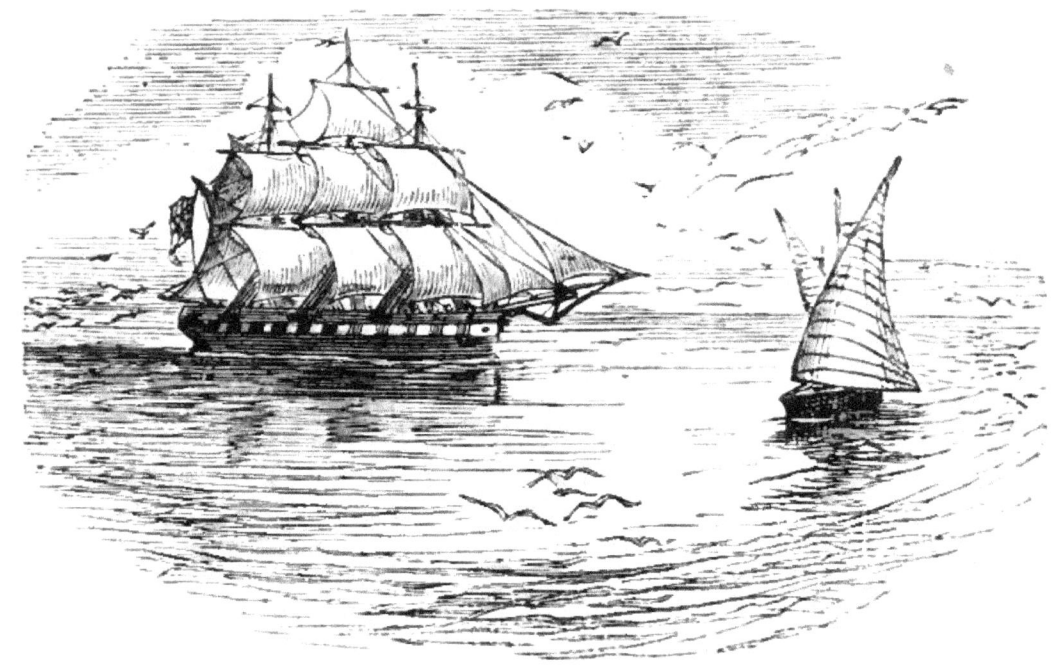

THE BOSPHORUS.

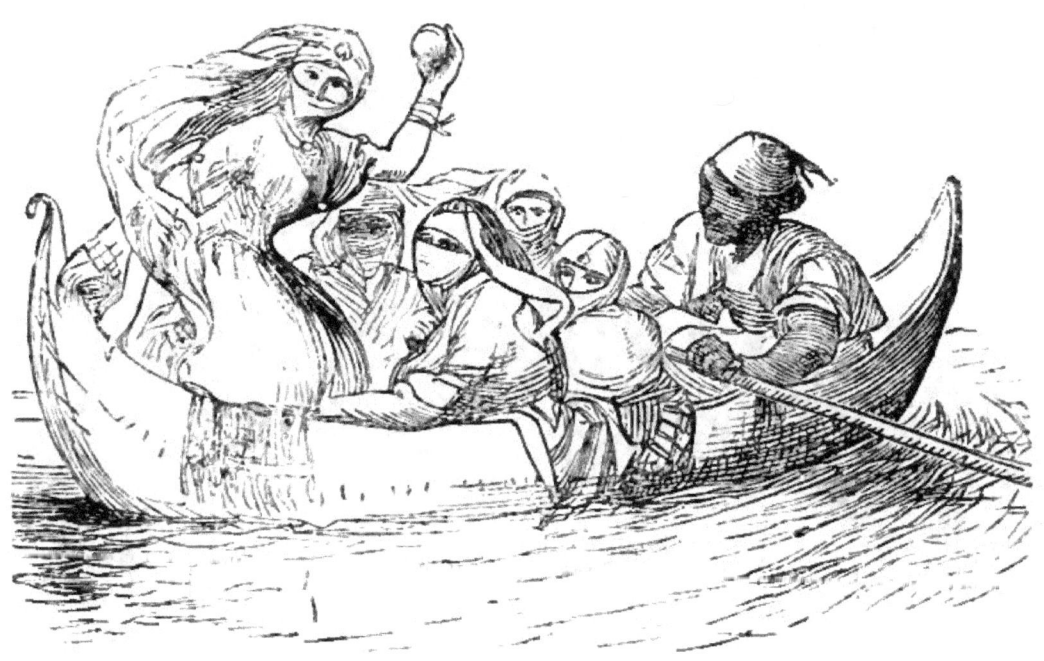

THE TURKISH LADIES IN THE BOAT.

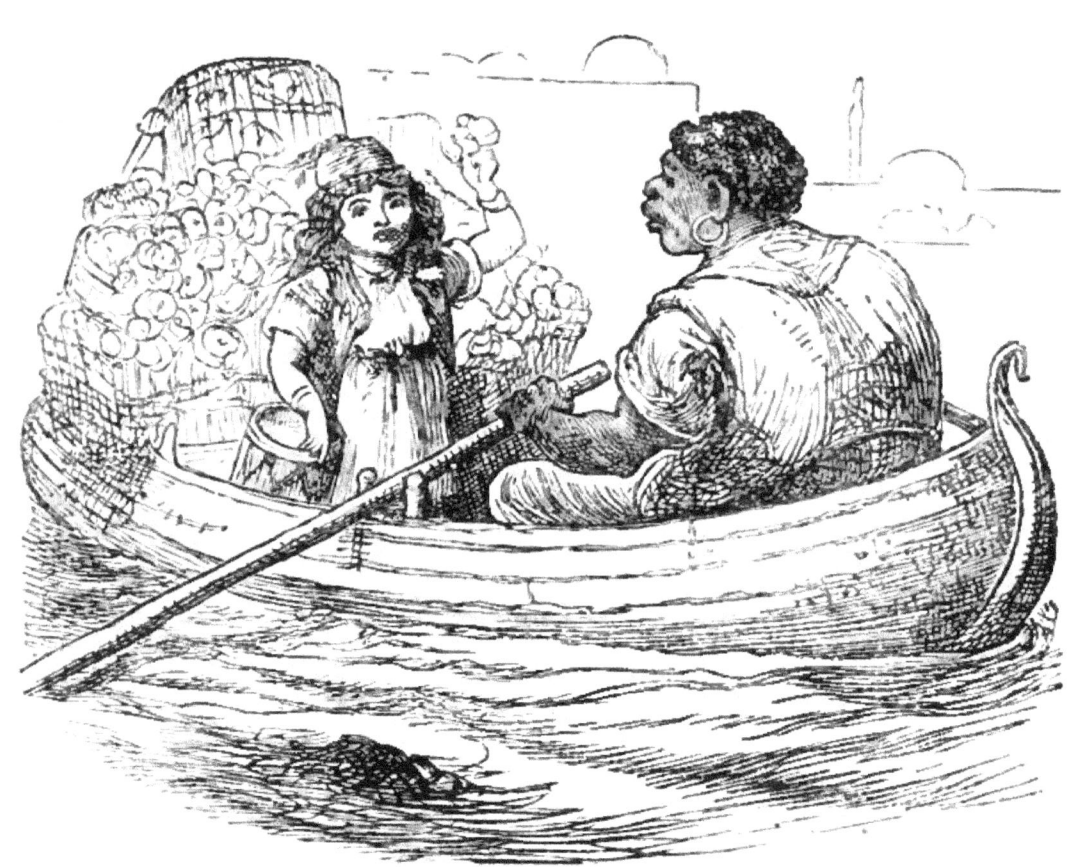

THE LITTLE GREEK MAIDEN.

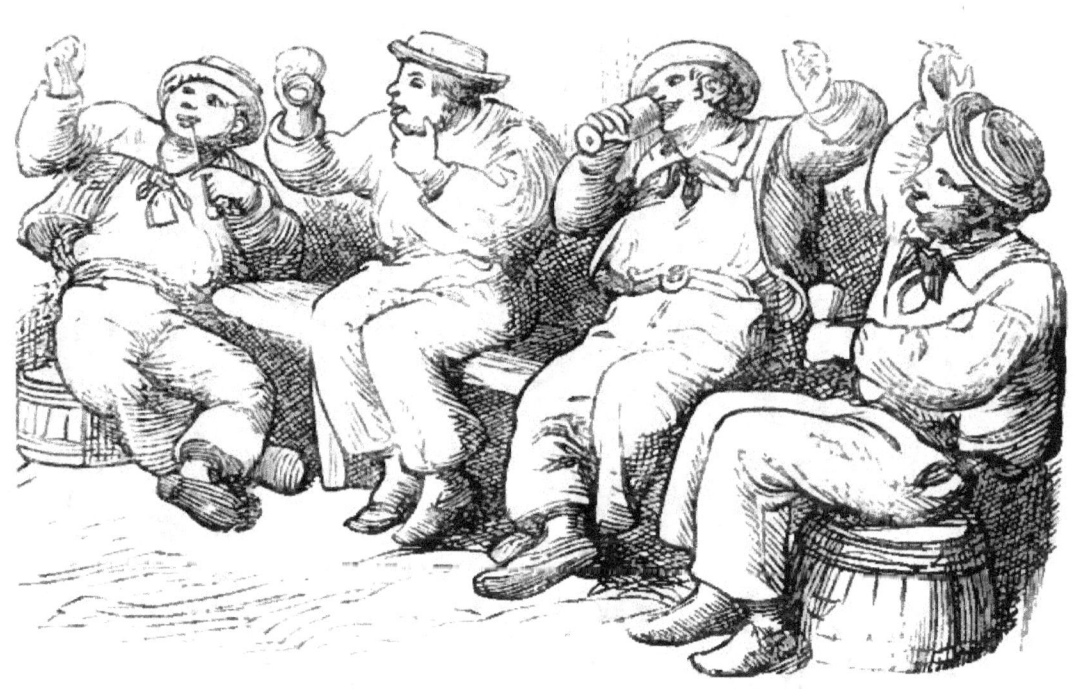

SAILORS CHEERING THE CARRIAGE.

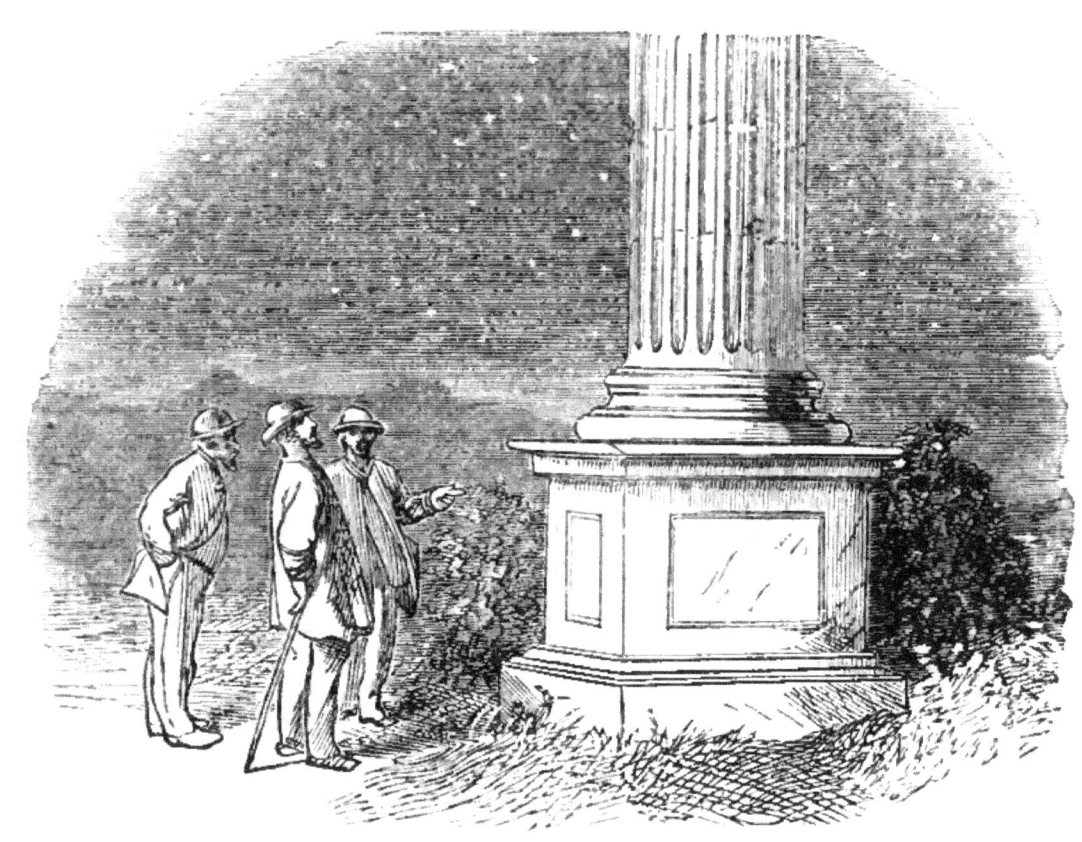

THE SOLITARY COLUMN.

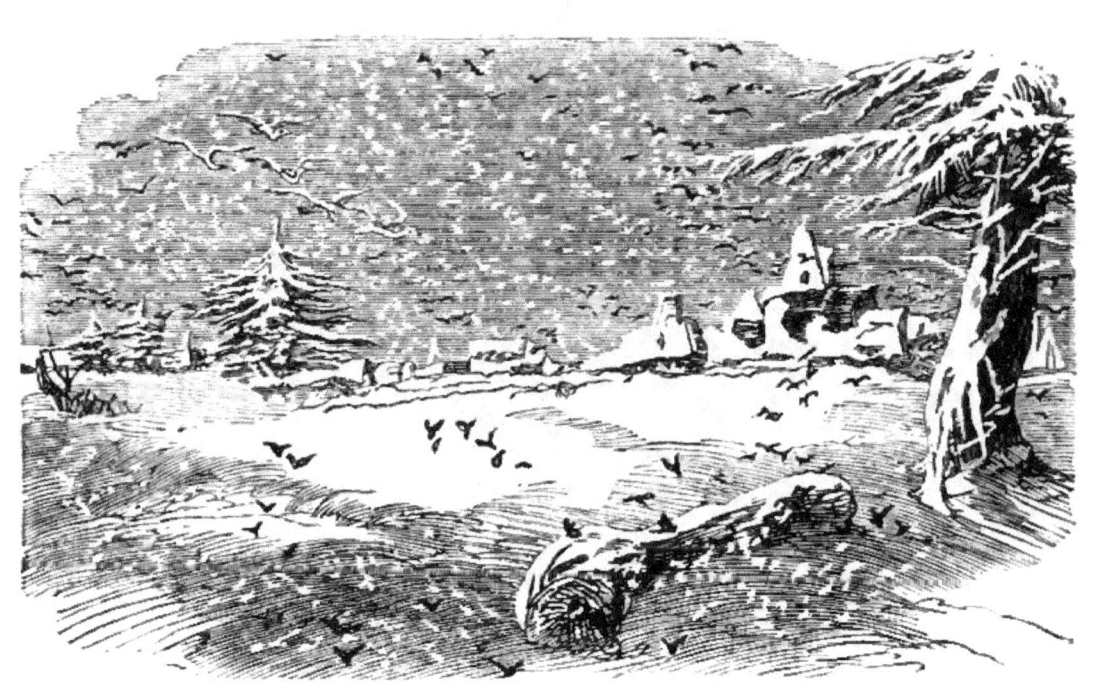

THE SNOW-STORM.

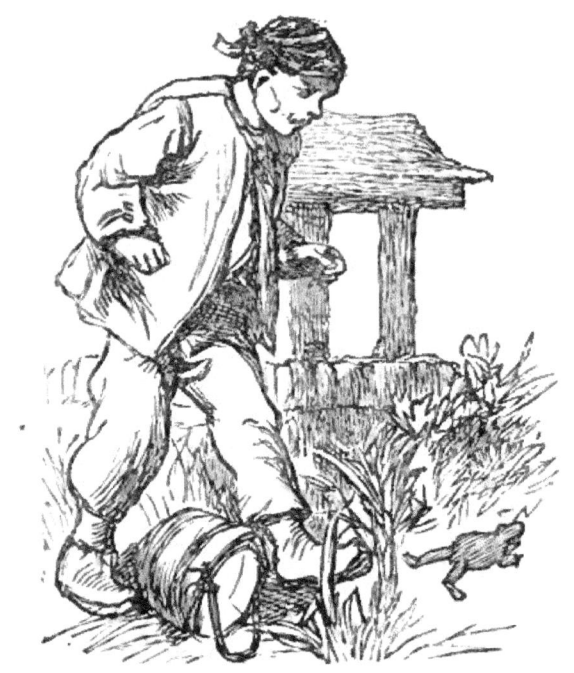

THE TOAD'S RECEPTION IN THE WORLD.

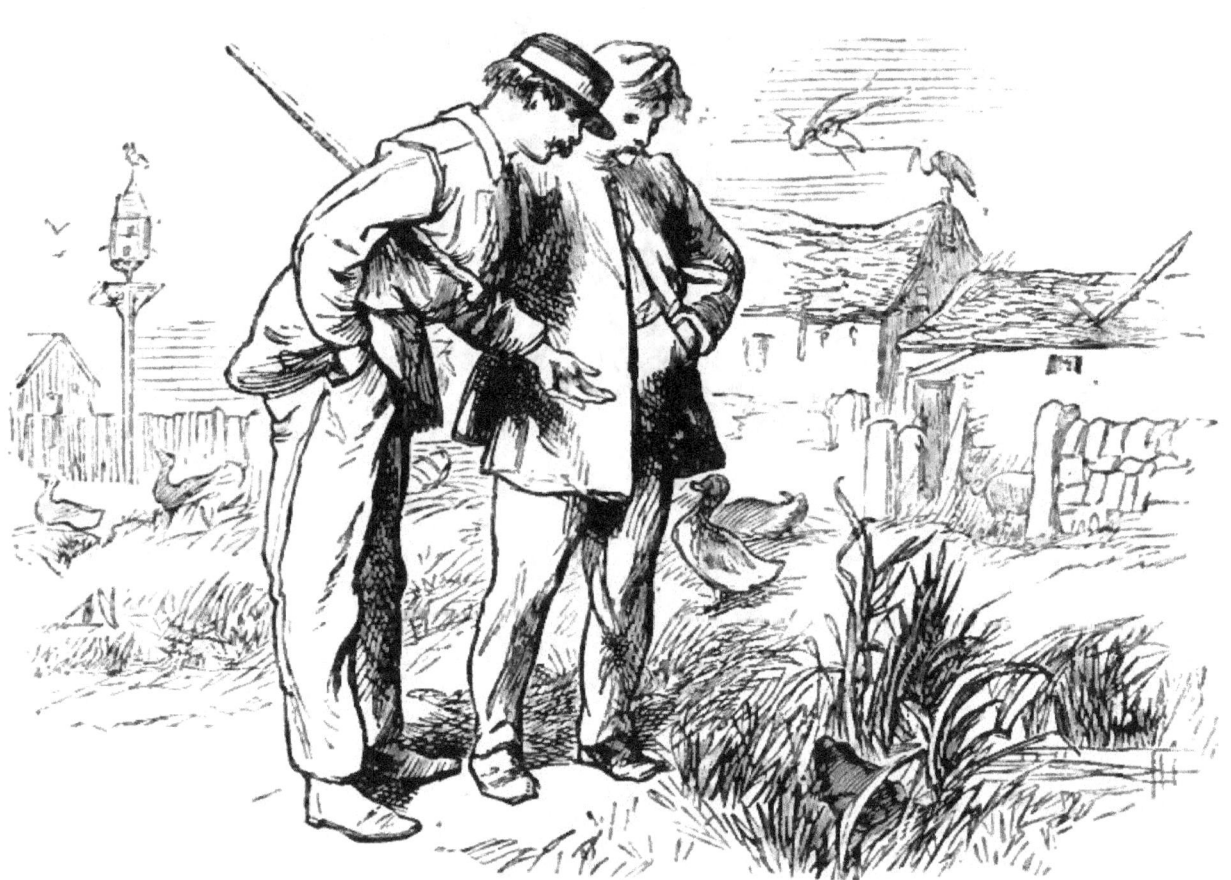

THE STUDENTS.

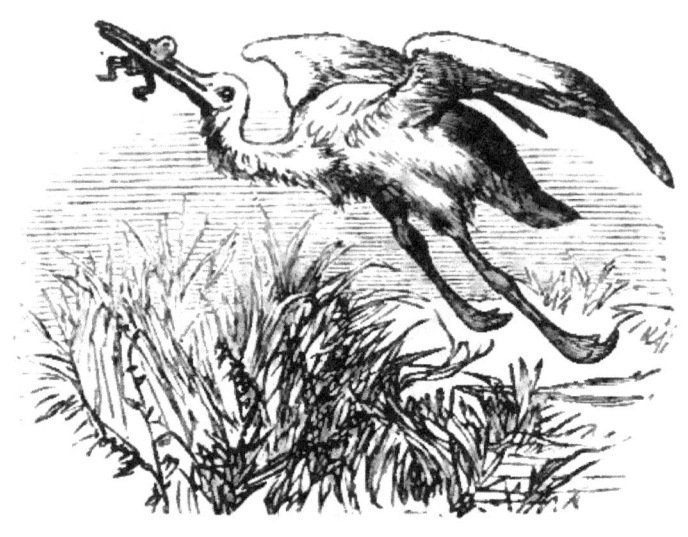

UPWARD!

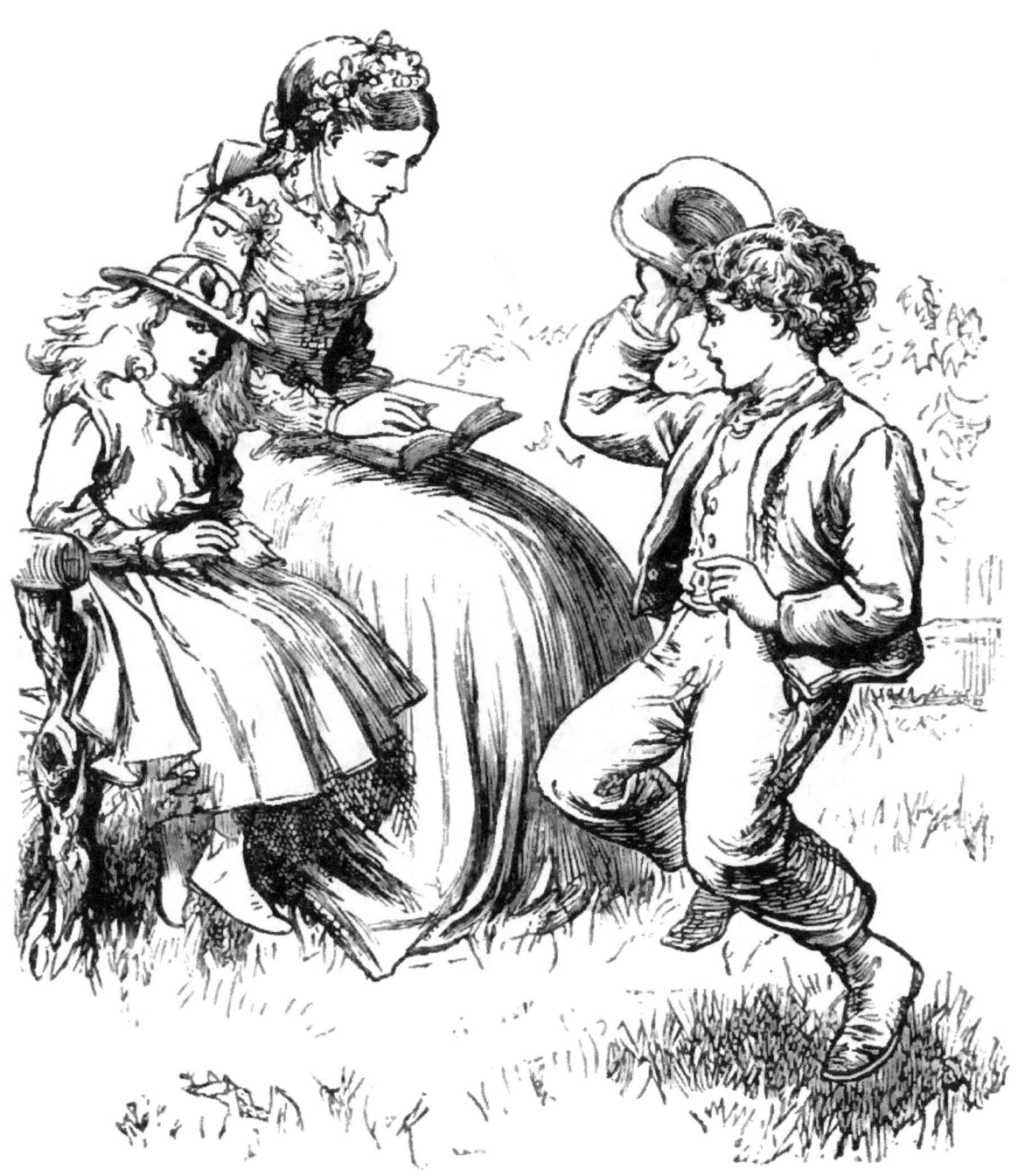

GEORGE AMUSING THE GENERAL'S DAUGHTER.

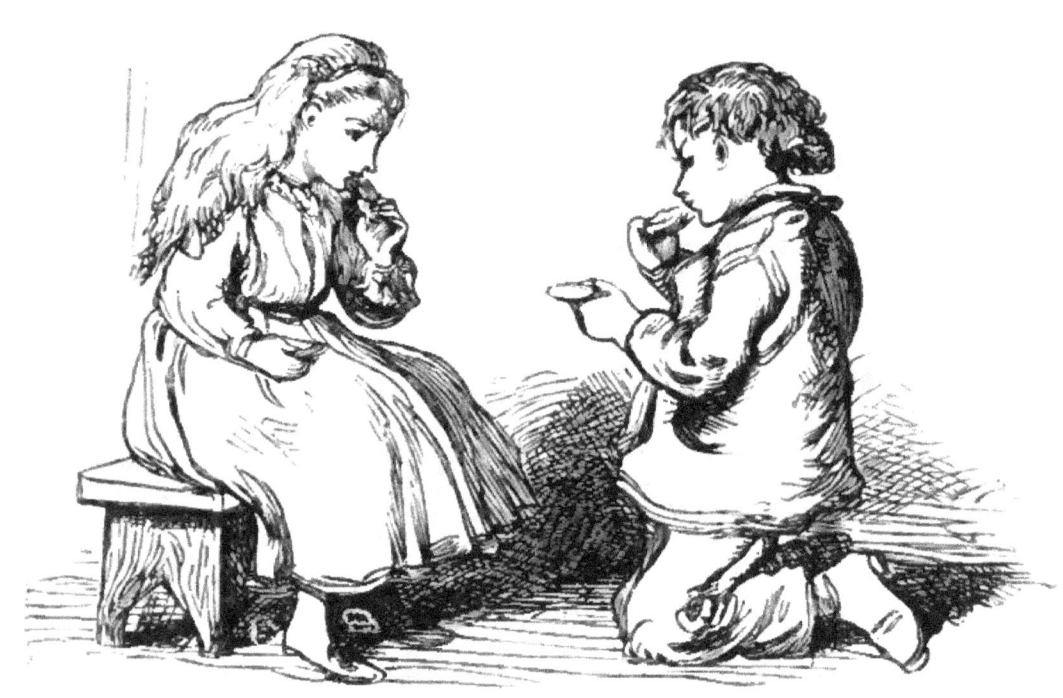

GEORGE AND EMILY'S FEAST.

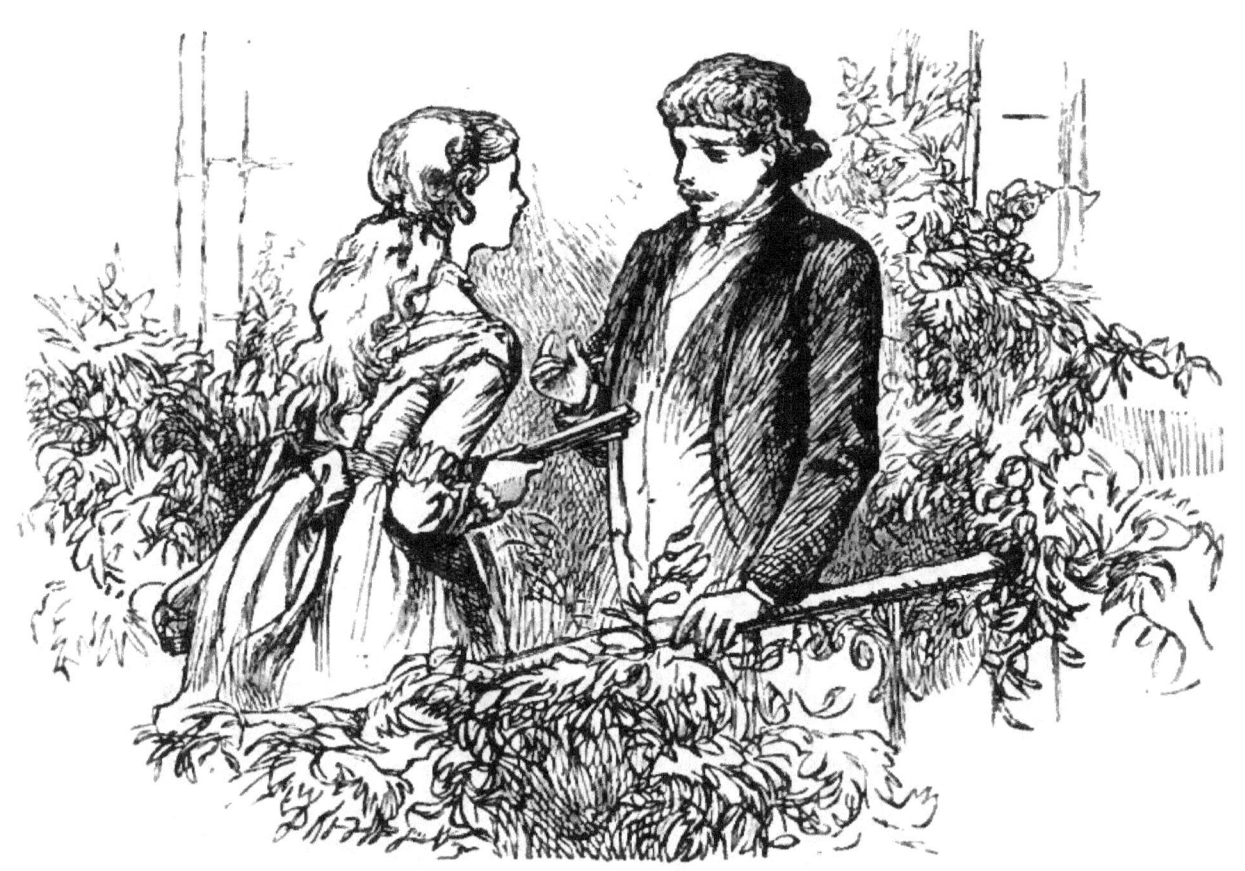

IN THE VERANDAH.

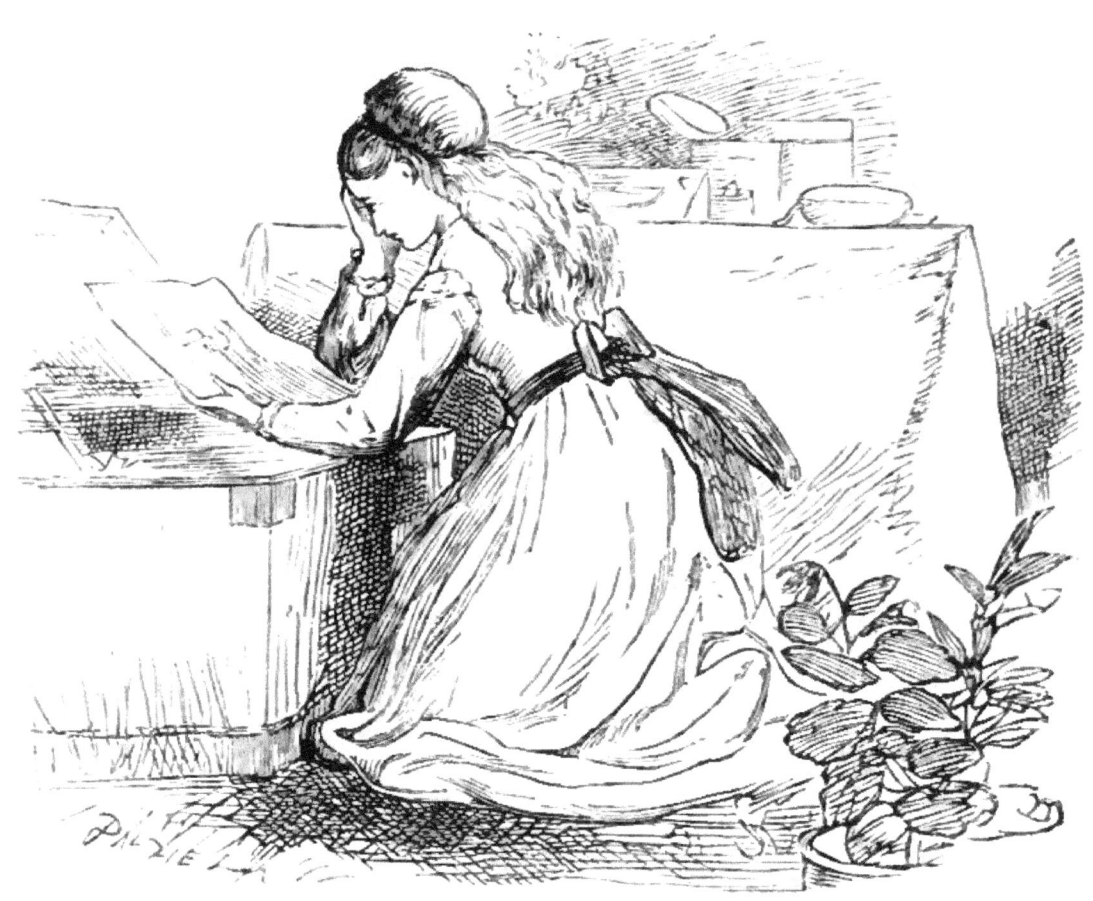

REMEMBRANCES OF GEORGE.

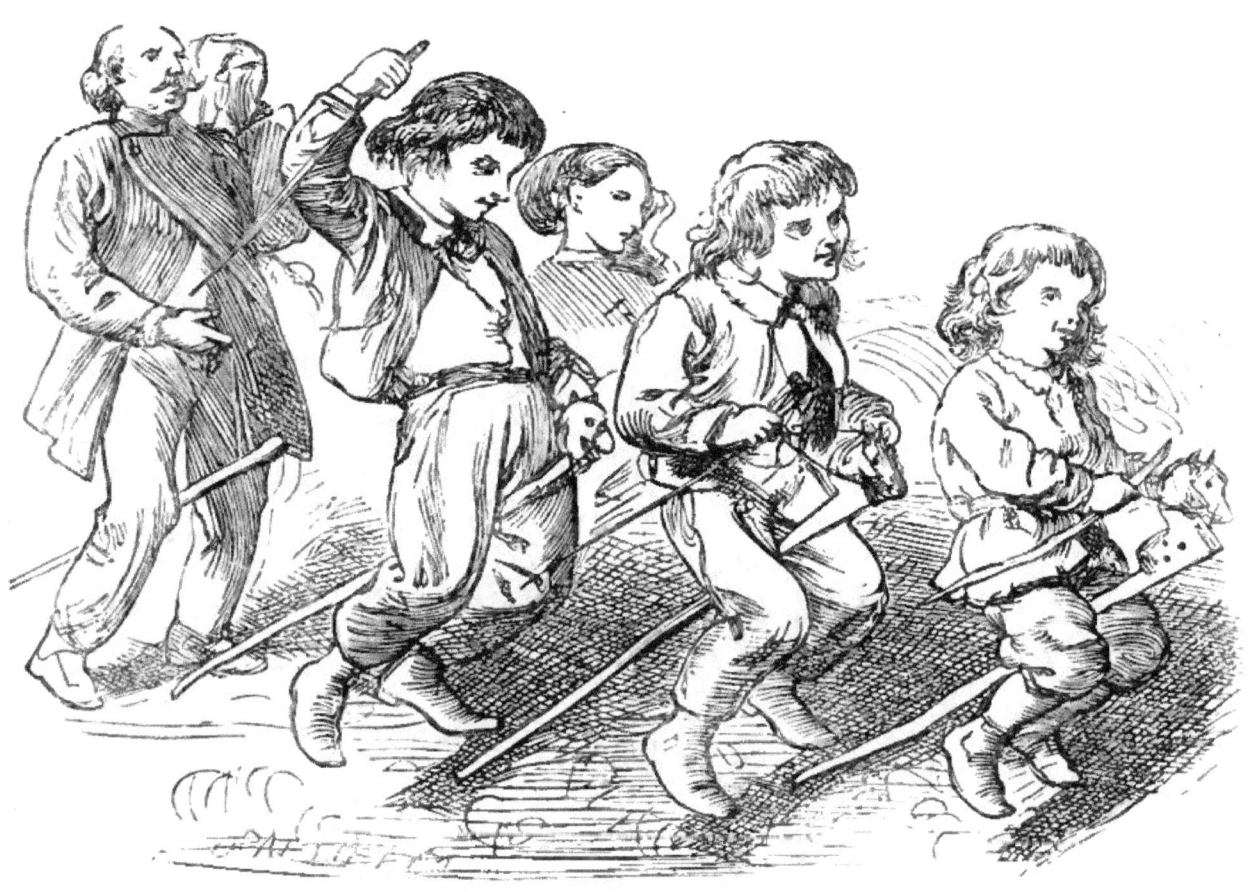

AT THE GENERAL'S.

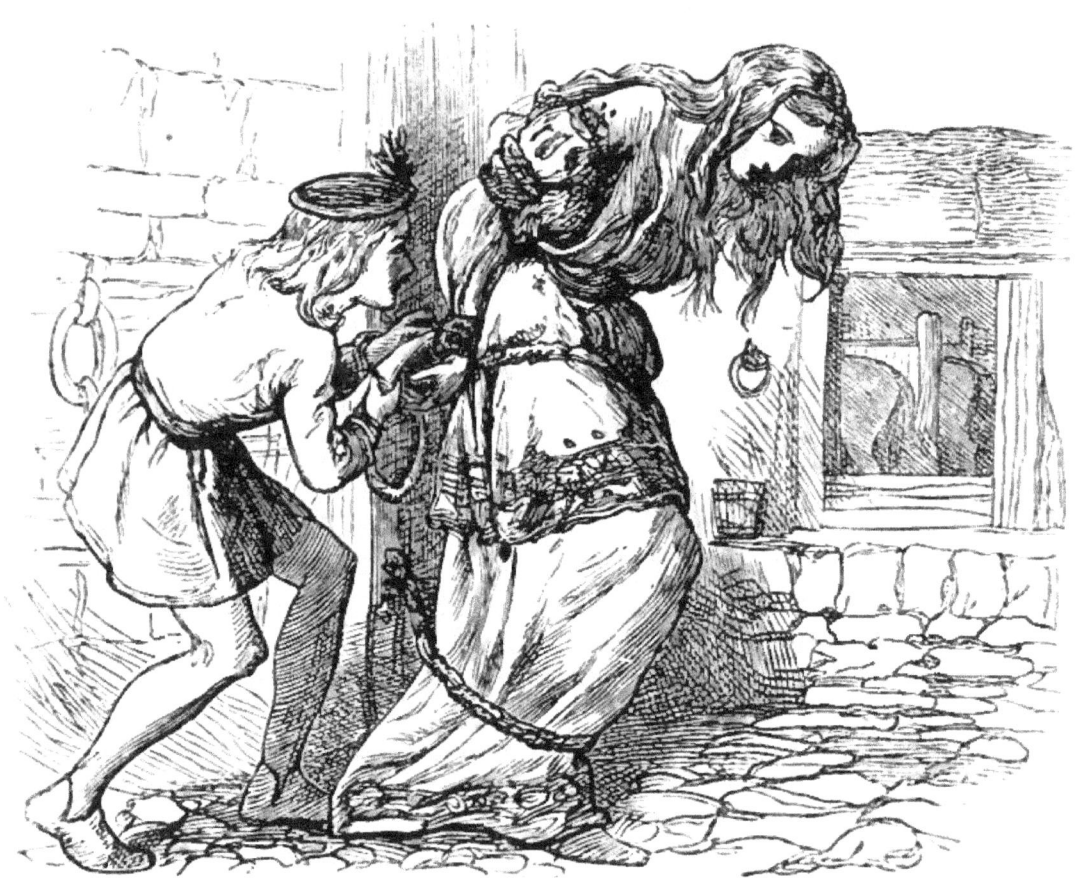

THE BOY'S GRATITUDE.

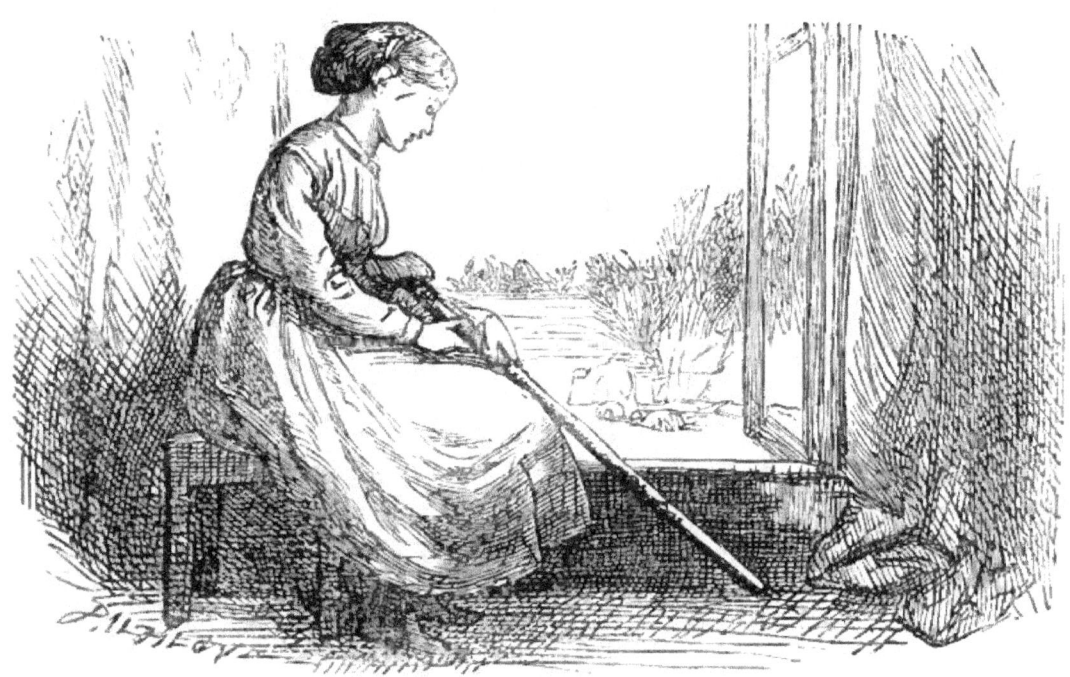

HER WORLD ENLARGED.

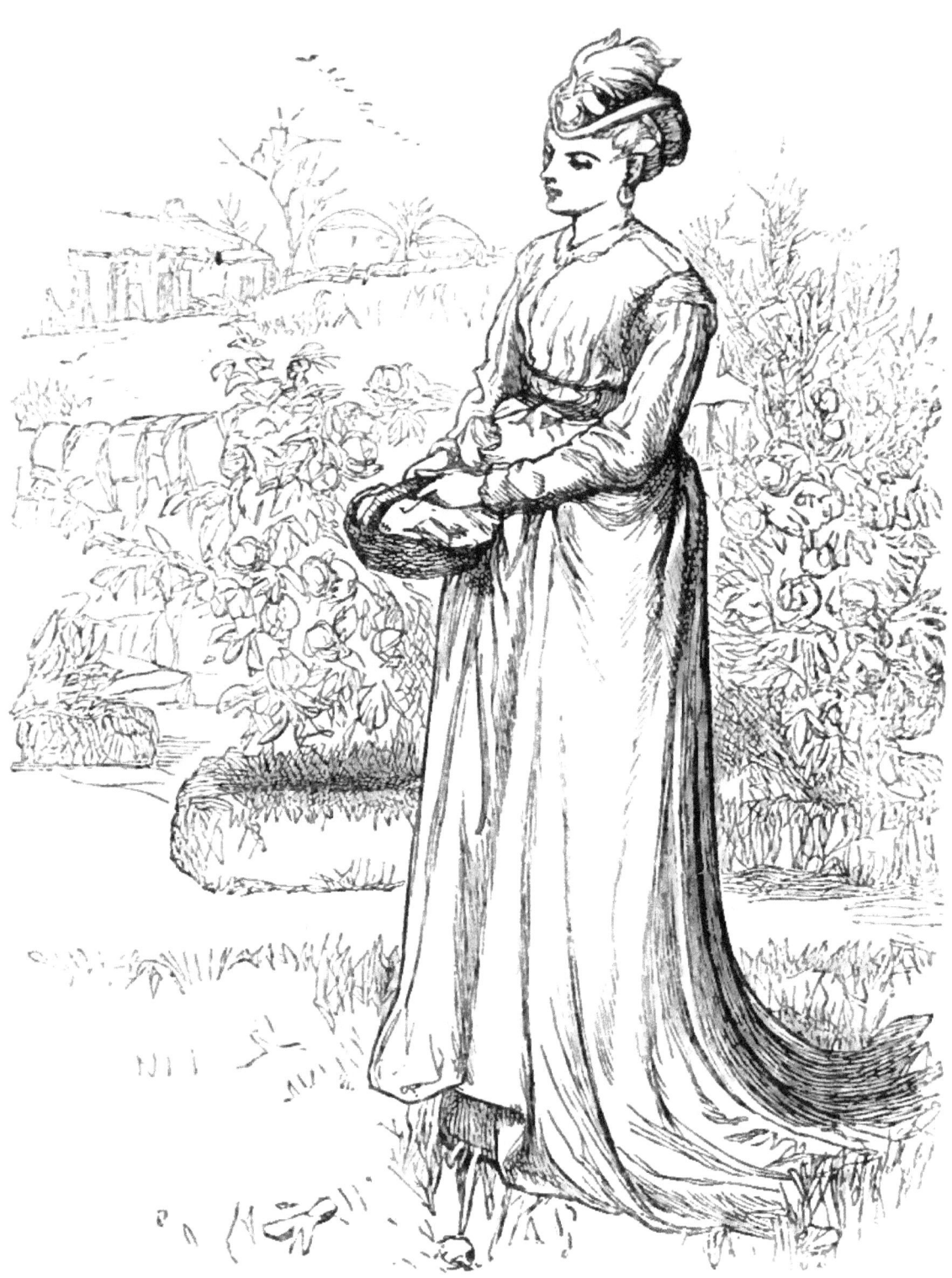

THE JOY OF GOOD DEEDS.

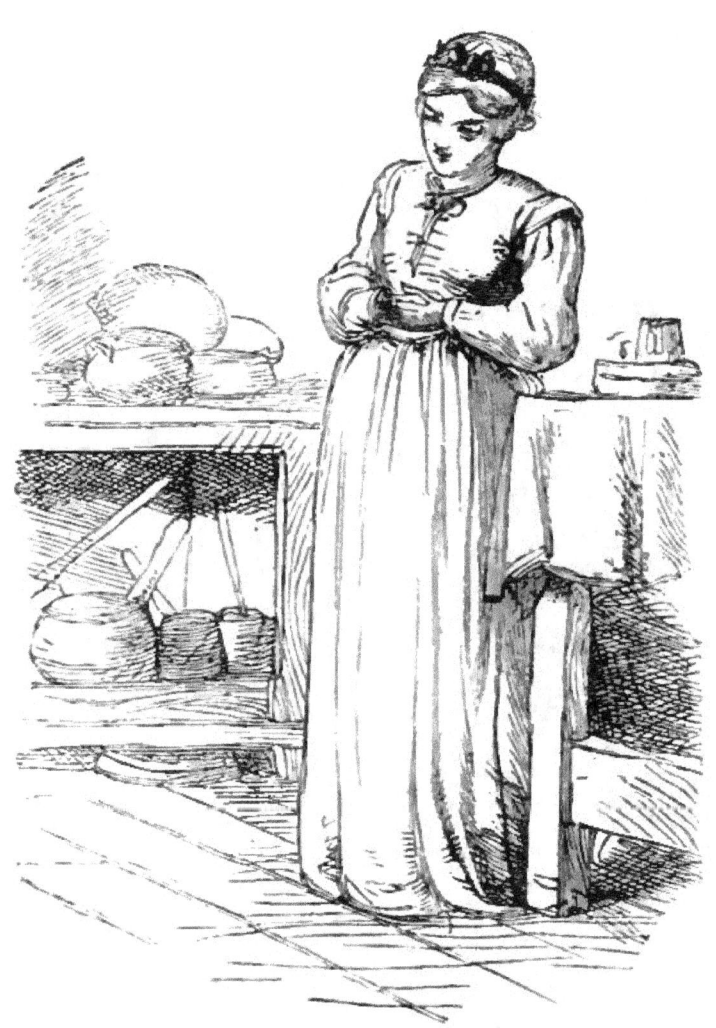

THE MOURNING BOW.

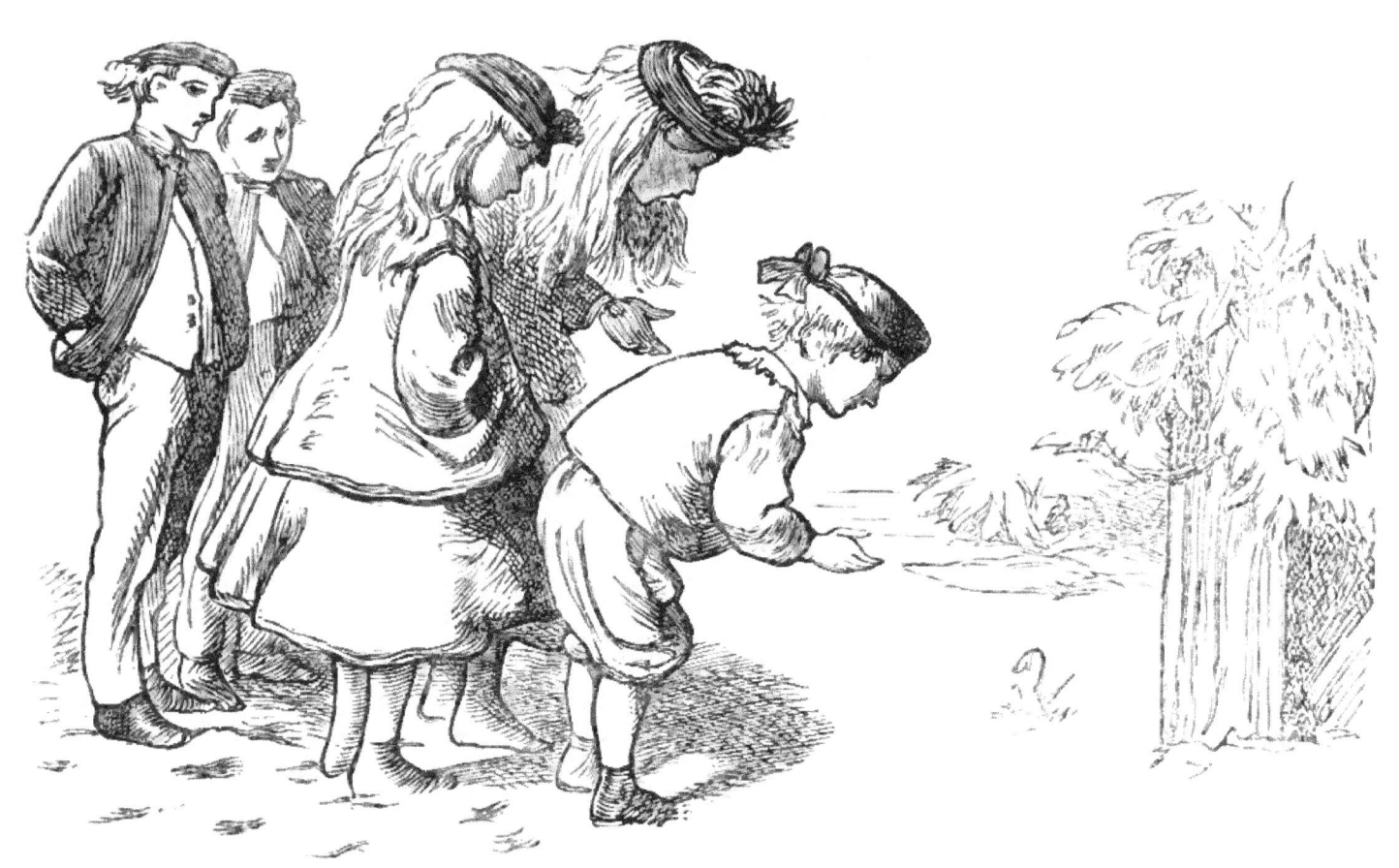

SPRING'S FLOWER.

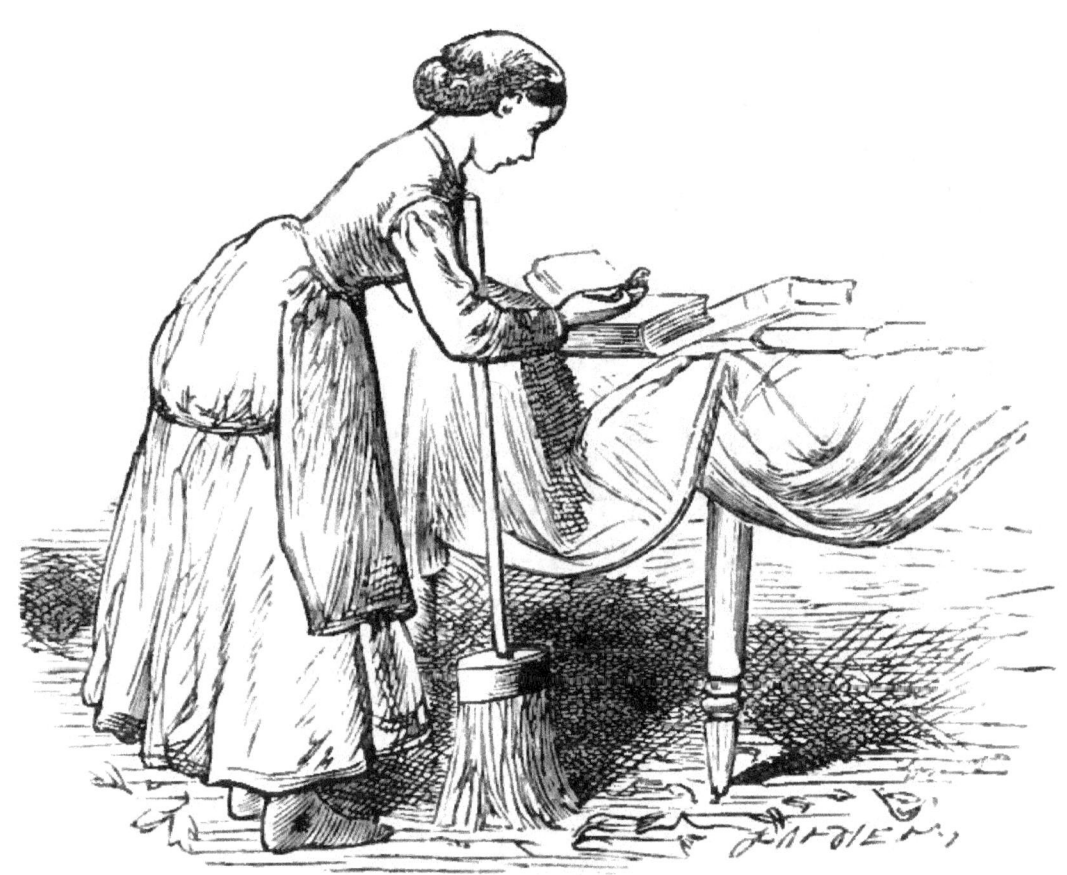

RESTORED TO THE POETS.

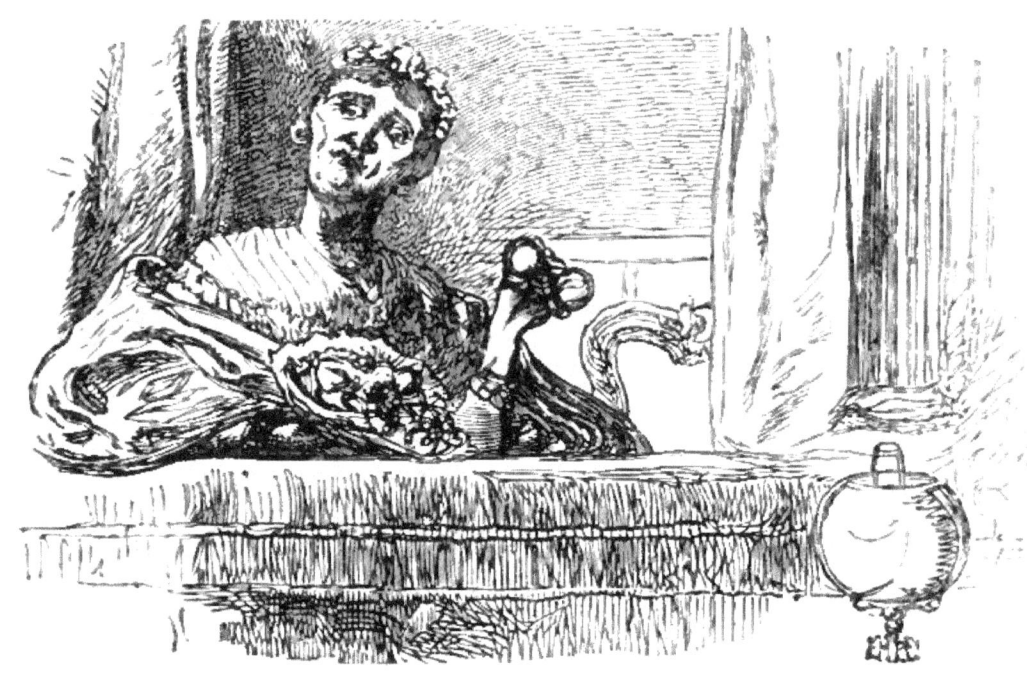

OUR AUNT IN HER GLORY.

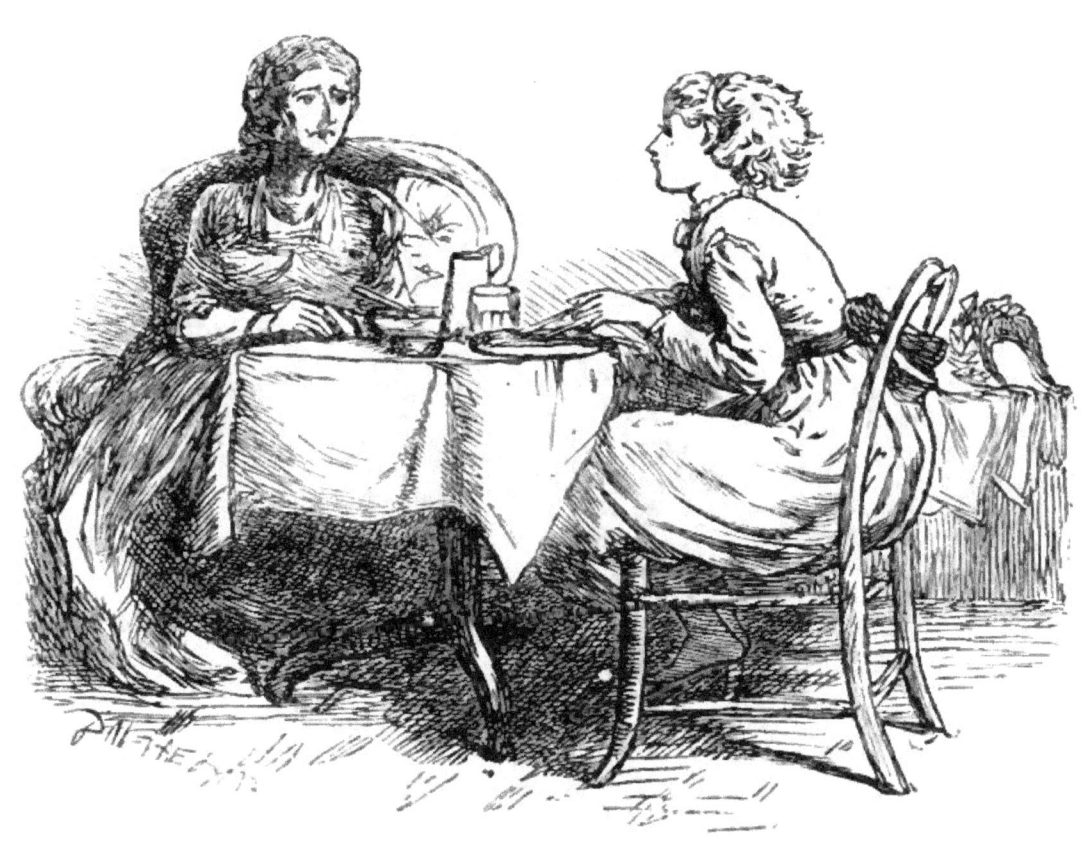

THE BALLET GIRL.

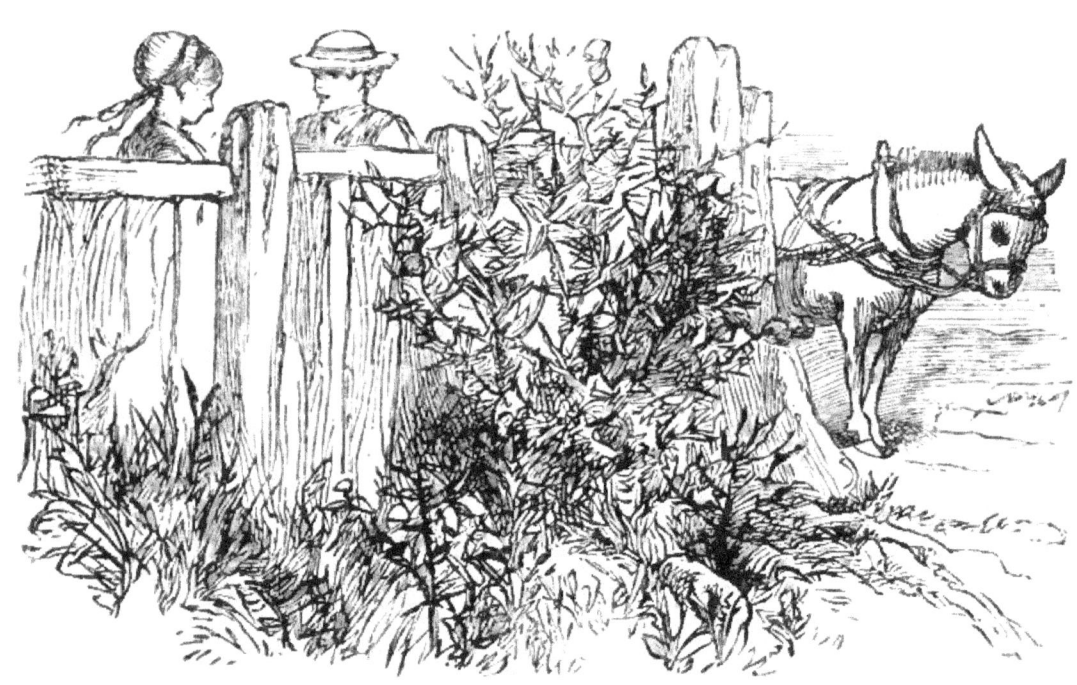

THE ASS AND THE THISTLE.

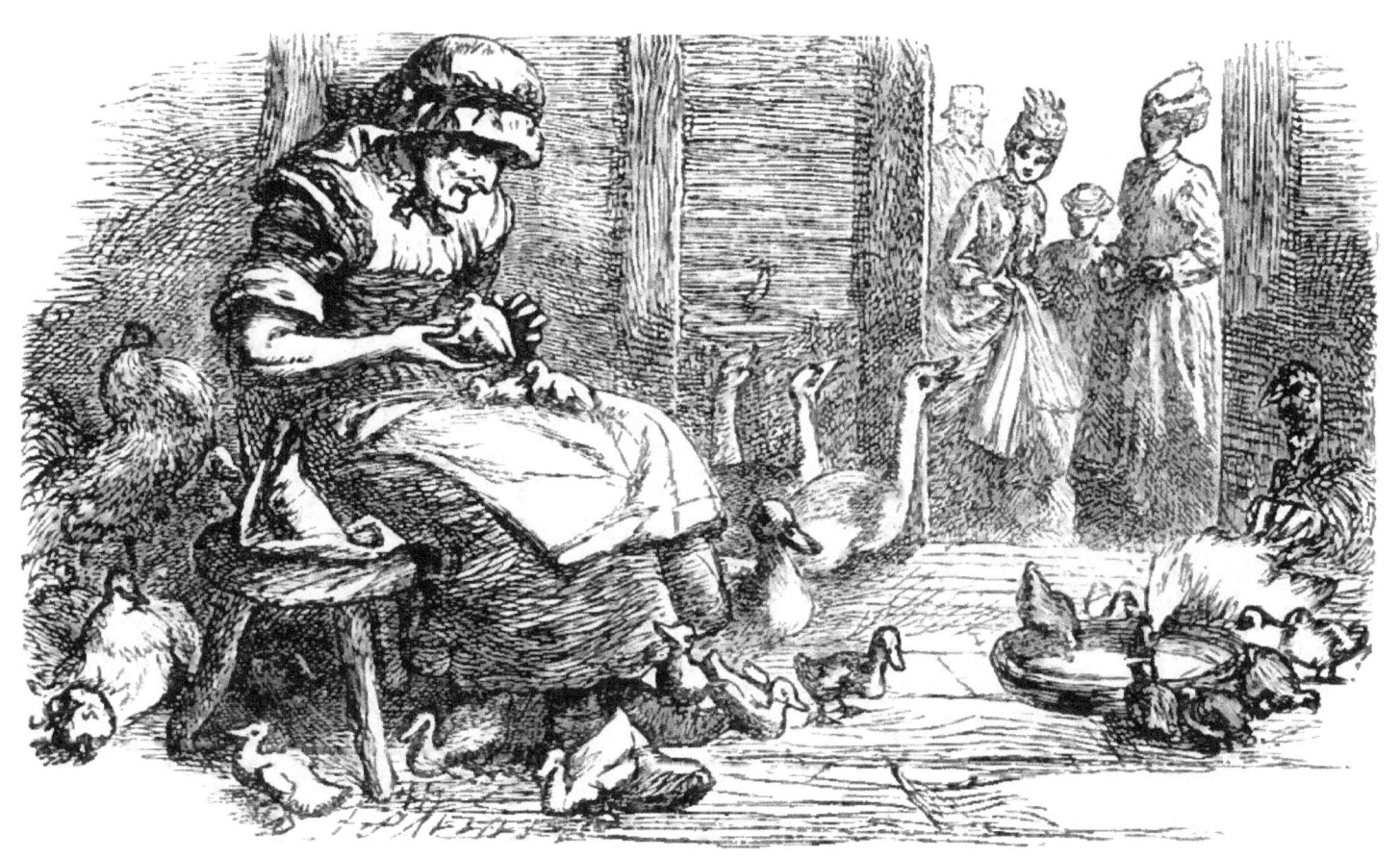

MEG AT HOME.

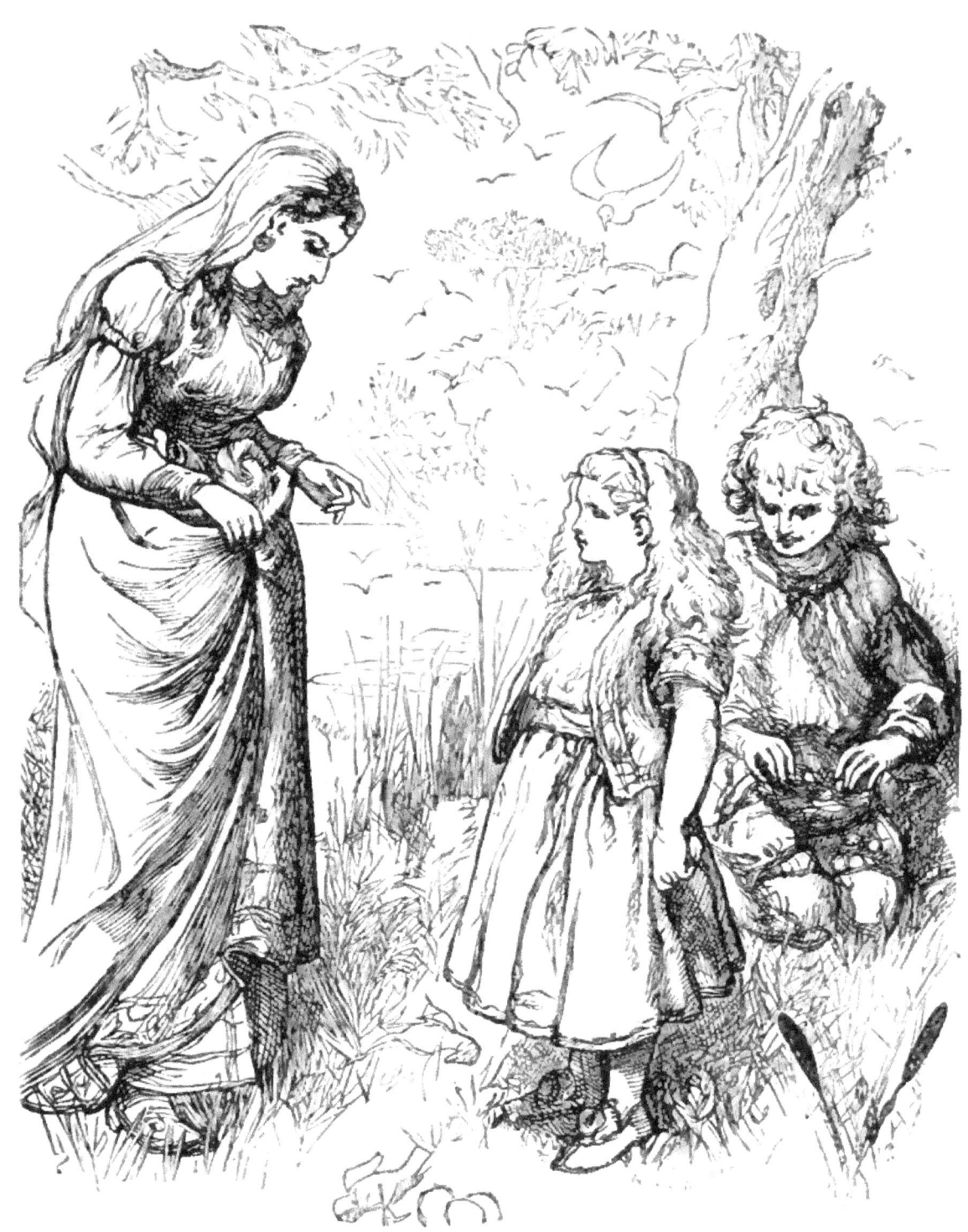

LADY GRUBBE'S REPROOF.

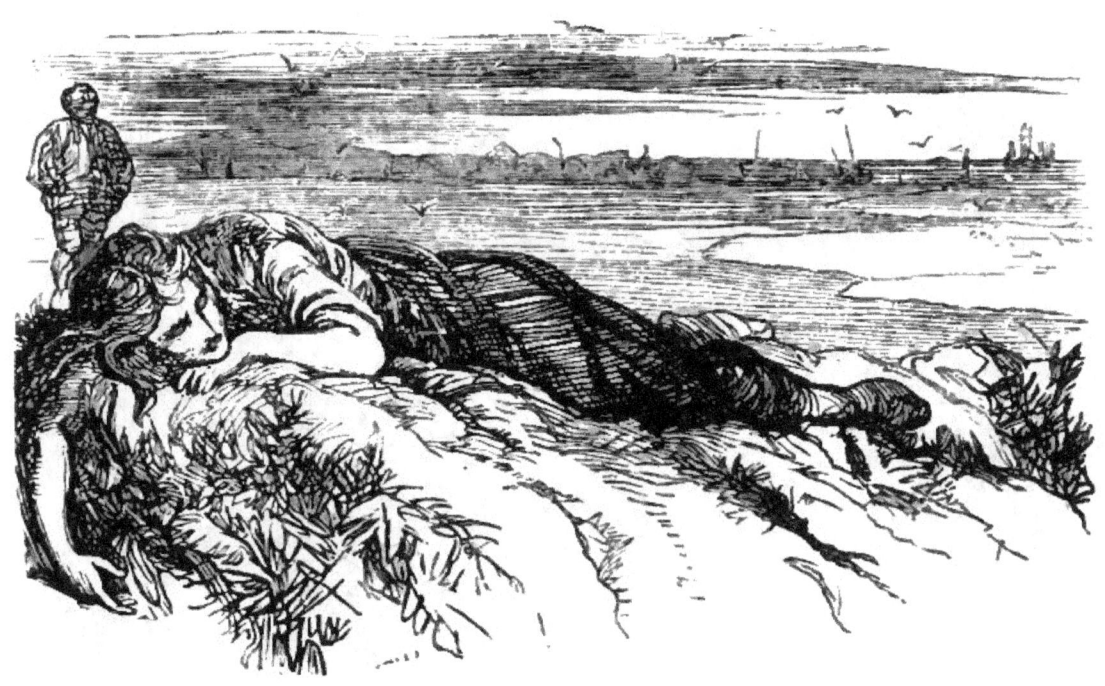

EXHAUSTED.

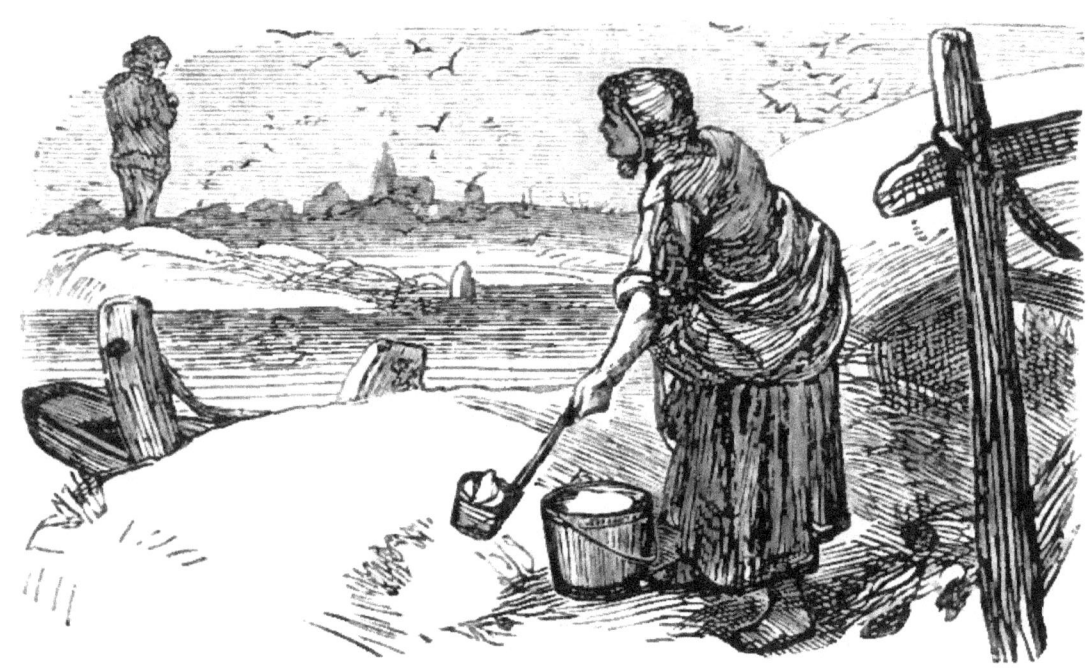

MOTHER SOREN.